Expert Service-Oriented Architecture in C# 2005

Second Edition

Jeffrey Hasan with Mauricio Duran

Apress®

Expert Service-Oriented Architecture in C# 2005, Second Edition

Copyright © 2006 by Jeffrey Hasan, Mauricio Duran

ISBN-13 (pbk): 978-1-59059-701-9

ISBN-10 (pbk): 1-59059-701-X

Printed and bound in the United States of America 9 8 7 6 5 4 3 2 1

Lead Editor: Jonathan Hassell
Technical Reviewers: Mathew Upchurch, Omar Del Rio
Editorial Board: Steve Anglin, Dan Appleman, Ewan Buckingham, Gary Cornell, Jason Gilmore,
    Jonathan Hassell, James Huddleston, Chris Mills, Matthew Moodie, Dominic Shakeshaft,
    Jim Sumser, Matt Wade
Project Manager: Richard Dal Porto
Copy Edit Manager: Nicole LeClerc
Copy Editors: Jennifer Whipple, Ami Knox
Assistant Production Director: Kari Brooks-Copony
Production Editor: Ellie Fountain
Compositor: Dina Quan
Proofreader: Liz Welch
Indexer: Michael Brinkman
Artist: Kinetic Publishing Services, LLC
Cover Designer: Kurt Krames
Manufacturing Director: Tom Debolski

Distributed to the book trade worldwide by Springer-Verlag New York, Inc., 233 Spring Street, 6th Floor, New York, NY 10013. Phone 1-800-SPRINGER, fax 201-348-4505, e-mail orders-ny@springer-sbm.com, or visit http://www.springeronline.com.

For information on translations, please contact Apress directly at 2560 Ninth Street, Suite 219, Berkeley, CA 94710. Phone 510-549-5930, fax 510-549-5939, e-mail info@apress.com, or visit http://www.apress.com.

The source code for this book is available to readers at http://www.apress.com in the Source Code section.

Contents at a Glance

Contents

About the Authors

**JEFFREY HASAN** is the president of Bluestone Partners Inc., a software development and consulting company based in Orange County, California (http://www.bluestonepartners.com). His company provides architectural design and software development services to businesses that implement advanced Microsoft technologies. Jeff is an experienced architect and .NET developer, and is the coauthor of several books and articles on .NET technology, including *Performance Tuning and Optimizing ASP.NET Applications* (Apress, 2003). Jeff has a master's degree from Duke University and is a Microsoft Certified Solution Developer (MCSD). When he is not working, Jeff likes to play guitar, mountain bike, and travel to far-flung corners of the world. His most recent travels have taken him from southern Spain to Monterrey, Mexico, and on to Québec with a few stops in between. Contact Jeff at jeffh@bluestonepartners.com.

MAURICIO DURAN is the vice president of nearshore development of the Venice Consulting Group (http://www.veniceconsulting.com), a consulting firm specializing in time-sensitive and mission-critical system development. He is president of Sieena Software, a software development company that implements solutions using state-of-the-art technology (http://www.sieena.com). He is also a software architect specializing in Microsoft technologies with more than eight years of experience in software development. He has worked as a consultant for companies such as General Electric, Hewlett-Packard, Merrill Lynch, and Boeing. Mauricio holds a bachelor of science degree in computer systems from the Instituto Tecnológico de Monterrey.

About the Technical Reviewers

MATHEW UPCHURCH is a technical consultant with numerous years in the IT industry. He can be seen in Southern California banging his head against the latest beta APIs from Microsoft and wondering when exactly we will reach code nirvana. In between having a loving family— his beautiful wife and three gorgeous daughters—and slaving away at code, he enjoys turning his guitar amplifier to 11 and seeing if the neighbors mind (distortion is good). He would also like to thank God above all else that he is able to do what he loves for a living (and, amazingly, getting paid for it).

OMAR DEL RIO is director of nearshore operations of the Venice Consulting Group, one of the nation's fastest growing and most innovative technology development firms using the hybrid nearshore development model. Omar has more than nine years of experience in software development and its associated processes; he is certified in Microsoft technologies and also holds a Six Sigma certification.

Omar holds a master of business administration degree from the Illinois Institute of Technology, and a computer systems engineering degree from Tec de Monterrey.

Acknowledgments

The book you hold in your hands is the culmination of months of hard work and a passionate desire to create a high-quality, informative text on service-oriented architecture using Web Services Enhancements 3.0. Like all major projects, it would not have been possible without the hard work and dedication of a great many people. The authors wish to thank the superb staff at Apress, and, of course, this book could not have been completed without the support of our friends and families.

Introduction

We software architects and developers live in a fascinating time. With the release of the .NET Framework in 2000, Web services technology has swept into our programming toolset and into our collective consciousness. Web services are the killer application for XML. Web services are the "new way" to call distributed objects remotely. Web services will take all of our integration headaches away and allow formerly incompatible systems to communicate again. What Microsoft developer has not recently thought to himself, "should I be building my application with Web services?"

What .NET developer has not recently thought to himself, "I'm confused"?

Every tidal wave has a genesis, and a momentum, and a final destination where it typically crashes head-on into a stable landmass and causes havoc and confusion. Web services technology is a tidal wave.

The genesis is Microsoft's strategic decision to simplify SOAP-based Web services development using a seamless set of integrated classes in the .NET Framework. The momentum is provided by a relentless marketing machine that promotes Web services as the solution for many of our worst IT problems. One destination is us, the architects and the developers who must understand this technology and learn how to implement it. Another destination is the manager, who must make strategic decisions on how to put this technology to its best use.

The Web services technology tidal wave has created confusion for .NET developers because, quite simply, we do not know the best way to use it. We are wrapped up in misconceptions about what the technology is for, and this affects our judgment in using it properly. We will spend the first chapter clarifying these misconceptions, but let me reveal one:

Misconception: Web services are for making remote procedure calls to distributed objects.

Reality: Web services are not optimized for RPCs. This is not what they are best at. Web services work best when they respond to messages, not to instructions.

Until now, we could safely give developers time to absorb the new Web services technology. We needed time to play around with the .NET Framework and to get used to a new development approach. Web services development using the .NET Framework is stunning in its simplicity. It is equally stunning in its oversimplification of a deep and sophisticated technology. Play time is over; now it's time we grow up.

Web services play a key role in a greater whole known as service-oriented architecture (SOA). Quite simply, SOA is an architecture based on loosely coupled components that exchange messages. These components include the clients that make message-based service requests, and the distributed components that respond to them. In an SOA, Web services are critically important because they consume and deliver messages.

It is difficult to tackle topics such as SOA and Web services without invoking the ire of developers working on other platforms such as J2EE and IBM WebSphere. We have full respect for these platforms and for the efforts of the developers and the architects who use them. These guys and girls "get it," and they have been doing it for longer than we Microsoft-oriented developers have. Let's give credit where credit is due, but then move on. Because if you are reading this book, it is a safe assumption that you are interested in SOA the Microsoft way. If this describes you, then please buy this book and read on!

So why don't we Microsoft/.NET developers "get it"? It is not for lack of intelligence, nor is it for lack of an ability to understand sophisticated architectures. We don't get it because we have been misled as to why Web services are important. Let us roughly restate our original assertion:

Web services work best with messages. They are not optimized to handle specific instructions (in the form of direct, remote procedure calls).

Most of us have been "trained" to this point to use Web services for implementing SOAP-based remote procedure calls. This is where we have been misled, because SOAP is about the worst protocol you could use for this purpose. It is verbose to the point where the response and request envelopes will likely exceed in size the actual input parameters and output response parameters that you are exchanging!

At this point, we hope we have left you with more questions than answers. We have stated things here that you can only take our word on, but why should you believe us?

This is exactly what we are trying to get at. We want to shake you out of your Web services comfort zone and to help you rethink the technology and think of the bigger picture that is SOA. We devote the first part of this book to clearing up the misconceptions. And we devote the second part of this book to showing you how to implement Web services in an SOA.

Free your mind.

Who This Book Is For

This book is a practical reference written for intermediate to advanced .NET solution developers and architects who are interested in SOA and Web services development. The book focuses on two key areas:

- How to build message-oriented and service-oriented Web services

- Understanding WSE 3.0

Solution developers and architects alike will find a lot in this book to hold their interest. The material in the book provides detailed conceptual discussions on SOA combined with in-depth C# code samples. The book avoids rehashing familiar concepts and focuses instead on how to rethink your approach to Web services development using today's best tools and industry-standard specifications. The book was written using the production version of WSE 3.0 that was released shortly following Visual Studio 2005, so you have the benefit of the latest and greatest developments with both Visual Studio and WSE.

What This Book Covers

This book covers SOA and cutting-edge Web services development using the WS- specifications and WSE 3.0. The first half of the book shows you how to think in terms of messages rather than procedure calls. It shows you how to design and build message- and service-oriented Web services that provide the security and the functionality that companies and businesses will require before they are ready to widely adopt Web services technology.

The second half of the book focuses on WSE 3.0, which provides infrastructure and developer support for implementing industry-standard Web service specifications, including

WS-Security: Integrates a set of popular security technologies, including digital signing and encryption based on security tokens, including X.509 certificates.

WS-Policy: Allows Web services to document their requirements, preferences, and capabilities for a range of factors, though is mostly focused on security. For example, a Web service policy will include its security requirements, such as encryption and digital signing based on an X.509 certificate.

WS-Addressing: Identifies service endpoints in a message and allows for these endpoints to remain updated as the message is passed along through two or more services. It largely replaces the earlier WS-Routing specification.

WS-Messaging: Provides support for alternate transport channel protocols besides HTTP, including TCP. It simplifies the development of messaging applications, including asynchronous applications that communicate using SOAP over HTTP.

WS-Secure Conversation: Establishes session-oriented trusted communication sessions using security tokens.

The WS- specifications are constantly evolving as new specifications get submitted and existing specifications get refined. They address essential requirements for service-oriented applications. This book aims to get you up to speed with understanding the current WS- specifications and how the WSE 3.0 product works and where Web services technology is headed for the next few years.

If you are interested in taking your Web services development to the next level, you will find this book to be an invaluable reference.

Chapter Summary

This book is broken into nine chapters, progressing from introductory conceptual information to advanced discussions of the WS- specifications and their implementation in WSE 3.0. You will get the most out of this book if you read at least the first five chapters in sequence. These chapters contain reference information and conceptual discussions that are essential to understanding the material in the second half of the book. The remaining chapters of the book cover all of the WS- specifications that are implemented by WSE 3.0. Finally, the book closes with a chapter on the Windows Communication Foundation (WCF), which is the name for a managed communications infrastructure for building service-oriented applications. The purpose of the WCF chapter is to show you the direction that service-oriented application development is headed, and to show you how your work with WSE 3.0 will help you make the transition to WCF very smooth.

The summary of the chapters is as follows:

Chapter 1, Introducing Service-Oriented Architecture: This chapter introduces the concepts behind SOA and the characteristics of a Web service from the perspective of SOA. This chapter reviews the following topics:

- SOA concepts and application architecture.

- The WS-I Basic Profile.

- The WS- specifications.

- WSE 3.0 (an introduction).

Chapter 2, The Web Services Description Language: This chapter reviews the WSDL 1.1 specification and the elements of a WSDL document. This information is essential to understanding what makes up a service. The concepts that are presented here will come up repeatedly throughout the book, so make sure you read this chapter! This chapter includes the following:

- The seven elements of the WSDL document (types, message, operation, portType, binding, port, and service), which together document abstract definitions and concrete implementation details for the Web service.

- How to work with WSDL documents using Visual Studio .NET.

- How to use WSDL documents.

Chapter 3, Design Patterns for Building Message-Oriented Web Services: This chapter shows you how to build message-oriented Web services, as opposed to RPC-style Web services, which most people end up building with ASP.NET even if they do not realize it. The goal of this chapter is to help you rethink your approach to Web services design so that you can start developing the type of message-oriented Web services that fit into an SOA framework. This chapter covers the following:

- Definition of a message-oriented Web service.

- The role of XML and XSD schemas in constructing messages.

- How to build an XSD schema file using the Visual Studio .NET XML Designer.

- Detailed review of a six-step process for building and consuming a message-oriented Web service. This discussion ties into the sample solutions that accompany the chapter.

Chapter 4, Design Patterns for Building Service-Oriented Web Services: This chapter extends the discussion from Chapter 3 and shows you how to build Web services that operate within a service-oriented application. This chapter includes the following:

- A discussion on building separate type definition assemblies that are based on XSD schema files.

- How to build a business assembly for delegating service processing.

- Detailed review of a six-step process for building and consuming a service-oriented Web service. This discussion ties into the sample solutions that accompany the chapter.

- How to build a service agent, which is unique to SOA.

Chapter 5, Web Services Enhancements 3.0: This chapter provides a detailed overview of WSE 3.0. This chapter covers the following:

- Overview of the WS- specifications.

- Introduction to WSE 3.0—what it contains, what it does, how it integrates with ASP.NET, and how to install it.

- Overview of X.509 certificates—the WSE sample digital certificates are used frequently throughout the sample applications. Certificate installation can be difficult, so this section shows you what you need to do.

Chapter 6, Secure Web Services with WS-Security: This is the first of three chapters that provide detailed discussions on the WSE implementations of the WS- specifications. *Security* typically refers to two things: authentication and authorization. This chapter contains the following:

- Overview of the WS-Security specification and implementation, including the enhanced declarative model in WSE 3.0.

- Review of common security scenarios, including an overview on important security objects and concepts such as security tokens, digital signatures, and encryption.

- How to implement WS-Security using WSE 3.0 and the username-ForCertificateSecurity turnkey security assertion.

- Review of declarative vs. imperative authorization.

Chapter 7, Extended Web Services Security with WS-Security and WS-Secure Conversation: This chapter reviews how WSE 3.0 can secure other common Web service deployment scenarios. This chapter covers the following:

- Overview of the direct and brokered authentication models.

- How to implement brokered authentication using Kerberos and mutual certificates.

- How to prevent reply attacks, using time stamps, digital signatures, and message correlation.

- Overview of the WS-Secure Conversation specification, which is enhanced in WSE 3.0.

- How to implement a secure conversation between a Web service and its client, using a security token service provider.

Chapter 8, SOAP Messages: Addressing, Messaging, and Routing: This chapter covers several WS- specifications that work together to provide a new messaging framework for Web services. Traditional Web services are built on the HTTP request/response model. WSE 3.0 provides a messaging framework that expands the supported transport protocols to include TCP and an optimized in-process transport protocol, in addition to HTTP. These protocols are not natively tied to a request/response communications model, so you can implement alternative models, such as asynchronous messaging solutions. This chapter also reviews the WS-Addressing specification, which enables messages to store their own addressing and endpoint reference information. This chapter includes the following:

- Overview of communication models for Web services.

- Overview of the WS-Addressing specification, including a discussion of message information headers vs. endpoint references.

- Overview of how WSE implements the WS-Addressing specification.

- Overview of the WS-Messaging specification and the WSE implementation, which provides support for alternate message transport protocols and communication models.

- How to implement a TCP-based Web service using SOAP sender and receiver components.

- Overview of the WS-Routing and WS-Referral specifications, which allow messages to be redirected between multiple endpoints.

- How to build a SOAP-based router using WSE, WS-Routing, and WS-Referral.

- How to integrate MSMQ with Web services in order to implement one form of reliable messaging.

Chapter 9, Beyond WSE 3.0: Looking Ahead to Windows Communication Foundation (WCF): WCF (formerly code named *Indigo*) provides infrastructure and programming support for service-oriented applications. WCF will be released in late 2006 as part of the upcoming Vista operating system. It focuses on messages, providing support for creating messages, for delivering messages, and for processing messages. With WCF there is less ambiguity in your services: the infrastructure forces you to be message oriented and to work with well-qualified XML-based data types. WSE 3.0 and its future revisions will provide you with excellent preparation for working with WCF in the future. This chapter contains the following:

- Overview of WCF architecture, including the Indigo service layer, the WCF connector, hosting environments, messaging services, and system services.

- Understanding WCF Web services.

- Understanding WCF applications and infrastructure.

- How to get ready for WCF.

- WSE 3.0 and WCF.

Notes on the Second Edition

This book is the second edition release of *Expert Service-Oriented Architecture: Using the Web Services Enhancements 2.0*. Readers of the previous edition will find that about 60 percent of the material has been rewritten to cover breaking changes and new features in WSE 3.0. The five introductory chapters of this book are similar to the first edition, although all code samples and screen captures have been updated to reflect WSE 3.0 and Visual Studio 2005.

The most significant change in WSE 3.0 is in the area of security implementation, with the introduction of the *turnkey security scenarios*, which are natively supported, common security scenarios that can be implemented using straightforward policy declaration files. Policy files were important in WSE 2.0, but in WSE 3.0 they assume an even greater importance, to the point that in most cases you will not need to write custom code with the WSE 3.0 API. Correspondingly, the second edition of this book reduces the amount of .NET code compared to what was presented in the first edition, and instead focuses more on how to achieve your goals using declarative policy files. The exception is in the area of SOAP messaging, which allows you to build custom SOAP senders and receivers that operate over alternate protocols instead of HTTP. This area is still code-intensive compared to other functional areas that are supported by WSE 3.0.

It is important to note that the WSE 3.0 product is not a full upgrade to WSE 2.0; rather it is a complementary product that improves on certain areas (such as security implementation) while leaving other areas essentially untouched (such as SOAP messaging). The full WSE 2.0 functionality has been subsumed into the WSE 3.0 product, so you will not need to use both products. However, what this means is that you can leverage many aspects of your WSE 2.0 experience into WSE 3.0, which will prevent productivity disruption and will allow you more time to focus on important enhancements in WSE 3.0.

If you have already purchased the first edition of this book you will still find a lot of value in this second edition, particularly in Chapters 6 and 7 on security implementations, which are significantly enhanced in WSE 3.0. These chapters have been completely rewritten for this edition. If you are new to this book you will find it to be a comprehensive resource for building service-oriented Web services using the WSE 3.0 product.

Code Samples and Updates

This book is accompanied by a rich and varied set of example solutions. The sample solutions were built using the production version of WSE 3.0 that was released on November 7, 2005. The code examples are chosen to illustrate complicated concepts clearly. Although Web Services Enhancements are conceptually complicated, this does not mean that they translate into complex code. In fact, the situation is quite the opposite. You will be surprised at how clear and straightforward the code examples are, plus you will find that most WSE-supported functionality can be accessed and administered via declarative policy files that do not require you to write a single line of .NET code.

Note The sample solutions are available for download at http://www.apress.com.

Visit `http://www.bluestonepartners.com/soa.aspx` for updates to the book and sample solutions, and for errata corrections. Check there often, because WSE is expected to undergo several revisions between now and the release of the WCF. In addition, the topic of SOA continues to evolve rapidly, and every month brings new, interesting developments.

And now, once more into the breach, dear friends, once more . . .

■ ■ ■

CHAPTER 1

Introducing Service-Oriented Architecture

Service-oriented architecture (SOA) represents a new and evolving model for building distributed applications. *Services* are distributed components that provide well-defined interfaces that process and deliver XML messages. A service-based approach makes sense for building solutions that cross organizational, departmental, and corporate domain boundaries. A business with multiple systems and applications on different platforms can use SOA to build a loosely coupled integration solution that implements unified workflows.

Overview of Service-Oriented Architecture

The concept of services is familiar to anyone who shops online at an e-commerce web site. Once you place your order, you have to supply your credit card information, which is typically authorized and charged by an outside service vendor. Once the order has been committed, the e-commerce company coordinates with a shipping service vendor to deliver your purchase. E-commerce applications provide a perfect illustration of the need for an SOA. If the credit card billing component is offline or unresponsive, you do not want the sales order process to fail. Instead, you want the order to be collected and the billing operation to proceed at a later time. Figure 1-1 provides a conceptual workflow for an e-commerce business that uses multiple services to process orders.

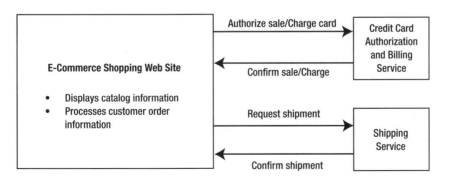

Figure 1-1. *Service-based workflow for an e-commerce business*

SOA is like other distributed architectures in that it enables you to build applications that use components across separate domain boundaries. SOA uses Web services as application entry points, which are conceptually equivalent to the proxy and stub components of traditional component-based distributed systems, except that the interactions between the Web service provider and the consumer are more loosely coupled.

SOA is also unique in that it incorporates those factors that are critically important to business: service reliability, message integrity, transactional integrity, and message security. In the real world, businesses cannot take a chance on services that may not successfully process a request. It is a given that disparate systems may be up or down at various times, or that systems may differ in their responsiveness due to varying loads, but none of this is an excuse for allowing service request messages to simply drop away into the void. Furthermore, there can be no ambiguity as to how a service must be called. If a system publishes its capabilities as a web-enabled service, it needs to clearly document how the service must be called.

SOA addresses many of the availability and scalability issues in today's applications. Most applications implement a rigid synchronous communication model with a linear workflow that is highly susceptible to failures at any point. SOA assumes that errors can and will occur, so it implements strategies for handling them. For example, if a service fails to accept a message request the first time, the architecture is designed to retry the delivery. And if the service is entirely unavailable (which should never occur in a robust SOA), the architecture is designed to avoid possible catastrophic failures that may disrupt the entire service request. SOA improves reliability because temporary failure in one part of the workflow will not bring down the entire business process.

In a broader sense, SOA represents a maturing process, that is, the "growing up" of Web services and integration technologies. SOA recognizes that mission-critical systems built on distributed technology must provide certain guarantees. They must ensure that service requests will be routed correctly, that they will be answered in a timely fashion, and that they will clearly publish their communication policies and interfaces.

In an SOA solution, the distributed application uses service components that reside in separate domains. Service components operate inside their own trust boundary and encapsulate their own data. They are maintained and updated independently of, though loosely coupled with, the applications that use them.

Figure 1-2 shows a conceptual SOA that summarizes the three main entities in a typical SOA solution:

- Service providers

- Service consumers

- Service directories

The consumer can use the Universal Discovery, Description, and Integration (UDDI) registry to discover or reference the description of a service provider. Interestingly, in Figure 1-2, Service Provider #1 references a service provider (Service Provider #2). In this role, Service Provider #1 is equivalent to a service consumer and can reference the UDDI registry for information about Service Provider #2.

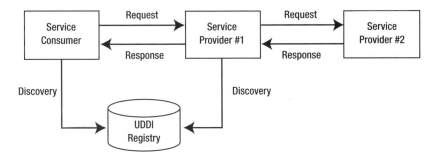

Figure 1-2. *Conceptual SOA solution*

The communication between the services and the consumer is in the form of XML messages that are qualified according to defined XSD schemas. XML messages are discrete entities that may be transported, rerouted, and referenced at any point along the business workflow. Messages promote higher levels of reliability and scalability because they can be stored, and the services that process the messages can append additional information, which provides for a clear and unambiguous chain of custody across the business workflow. In addition, messages can be queued in the event that a service is temporarily unavailable or backlogged.

XML messages are unlike traditional remote procedure calls (RPCs), which do not provide a discrete structure for encapsulating a method "request." Traditional RPCs cannot typically be cached or held in a queue to wait for a better time to service the request. Instead, traditional RPCs typically time out if the receiving component does not respond within the expected length of time. In addition, RPCs are not qualified to a reference schema (although they must conform to type libraries for custom data types). Here lies the first important lesson for developing SOA solutions: the Web services in the solution must be designed to be message-oriented rather than RPC-oriented. This topic is the exclusive focus of Chapter 3.

What Are Web Services, Really?

Many of us are so familiar with current Web services technology that we often do not stop to think about what services really are. However, you will need to if you are going to fully understand what makes SOA so significant. Let's pull out four definitions that collectively describe what services are:

- Services are autonomous components that process well-defined XML messages.

- Services provide a well-defined interface that is described by an XML-based document called the Web Services Description Language (WSDL) document, otherwise known as the *WSDL contract*. This documents the operations (methods) that the service supports, including data type information and binding information for locating and communicating with the Web service operations.

- Services provide endpoints that consumers and other services can bind to, based on the service's port address (typically a URL).

- Services are analogous to traditional object-oriented (OO), type-based components in that they provide a defined interface and they execute one or more operations. However, a key difference is that service consumers can flexibly bind to a service, whereas OO component consumers must set more rigid references. Service consumers can respond flexibly to changes in a service provider interface because it is easy to regenerate the proxy class using the updated WSDL document. However, if a traditional component changes its interface, the consumer itself must be recompiled in order to avoid type mismatch errors. Components are tightly integrated to their consumers and can break them. Service consumers, however, do not have to recompile if their service changes. Instead, they simply have to rebind to the updated WSDL document. This is what is known as *loose coupling*, or *loosely coupled services*.

Of course, if the service drastically changes its method signatures, problems may result in the consumer. For example, the consumer may not have the ability to supply new and modified input parameters for the updated methods. But as with any kind of interface-based programming, it is understood that you cannot make significant changes to an existing method signature, especially in terms of dropping existing input parameters, or changing the type definitions for existing input or output parameters. In Web services terms, this extends to the XML schema–based input and output messages that are exchanged by the service, as well as to its supported operations. Just as with traditional components, services should ideally remain backward-compatible as their interfaces evolve, although this is not a requirement as it is for classic OO programming. Web services technically only need to honor their current contract as documented by their WSDL document, which allows potential clients to dynamically bind to the service using the latest contract interface. Still, it is a significant advantage that service consumers are autonomous from the services that they consume. This promotes better stability in the SOA solution as the member services evolve.

There are five important properties of services in contrast to traditional type-based components:

Services are described by a WSDL contract, not by type libraries: The WSDL contract fully describes every aspect of the service, including its operations, its types, and its binding information. WSDL is fully described in Chapter 2. In this sense it is much more complete than traditional type libraries.

Service descriptions can be easily extended: The WSDL contract is based on an extensible document structure that readily incorporates additional information beyond the core service description. For example, security and policy information may be stored within the WSDL document as custom SOAP elements. In fact, all of the Web services enhancements that implement SOA infrastructure support can be documented as custom SOAP elements. At its most basic level, SOAP is a stateless, one-way messaging protocol. But it is also highly extensible, which makes it an excellent medium for storing and transporting Web service enhancement information.

Services provide a service guarantee: Traditional type definitions provide no guarantees. They are what they are, and you simply use them. But what happens if the type definition gets out of sync with the component it is supposed to describe? This happens all the time in the COM+ world, which relies on the Windows registry to store associated references between registered components and their type libraries. Every developer has experienced so-called DLL Hell, in which successive installations and removals of upgraded components cause incorrect type information to be retained in the registry. Technically, this is a versioning problem. But in more general terms this example points to the fact that there is no service guarantee in the world of type libraries. You just have to hope that the component is registered with the correct type library.

Services, on the other hand, can implement a service guarantee in the form of a policy description that is contained within the WSDL contract. So-called policy assertions are published with the contract to describe what level of service the consumer can expect, and how the service operations can be expected to respond. There are many advantages to policy assertions, not the least of which is that you could implement code in your consumer so that it will only work with a service that enforces a minimum policy guarantee. Should this policy ever change, then your consumer is designed not to use the service any longer. In a very sophisticated application, you could design your consumer to autodiscover an alternate service using the UDDI registry.

Services allow for things to go wrong: When you call a method on a traditional type-based component, you are making a leap of faith that the call will execute successfully. The reality is that the vast majority of calls do go through, creating a sense of complacency that this is always the case. But in the service-oriented world, where the supporting infrastructure is vastly more intricate and decoupled, you cannot have such a high level of faith that calls will always go through. Recall that XML messages are the gold currency of service requests. Messages can experience trouble at many steps along the way. Trouble in the transport channel can prevent them from being delivered. Trouble in the service's server or firewall can prevent the service from ever responding to a received message. Furthermore, messages may be tampered with, so that they are malformed or suspect when they do reach their intended target.

SOA accommodates all of these many potential problems using a set of technologies that maintain the integrity of a service request even if things go wrong along the way. These include reliable messaging, transaction support, and authentication mechanisms to ensure that only trusted parties are involved in the service request (including certificate-based mechanisms).

Services provide flexible binding: Services fully describe themselves using the WSDL contract. This information includes documentation of the service operations as well as data type information, referenced by well-defined XML schemas. This enables clear and unambiguous qualified references. The best part is that a consumer does not have to have any prior knowledge of a data type, as long as its XML namespace is documented by or referenced by the WSDL contract. For example, consider a consumer that calls a stock quote service. This service provides a RequestQuote method that returns a custom complex data type called Quote, which includes current and previous share price information, as well as 52-week high and low values. The consumer has no advanced knowledge of how the Quote data type is structured, but it does not need to as long as it can reference the qualified associated XSD schema.

Services can also be registered in a UDDI registry, which enables them to be searched for by consumers and other services. The UDDI registry is very thorough and includes a reference to the WSDL contract information, as well as a summary of supported messages in a search-efficient format. This is useful for many reasons. For example, a consumer may only wish to call services that utilize a specific set of XSD schemas (such as industry-specific standard schemas). The UDDI registry enables that consumer to search for services that conform to this requirement.

Components of Web Service Architecture

Experienced developers are comfortable with *n*-tier application architecture, in which the components of an application are broken out across separate layers, or tiers. At a minimum, this includes the three classic layers: user interface (front end), business layer (middle tier), and data layer (back end).

Now let's consider how an SOA solution is broken out in terms of layers and constituent components. Figure 1-3 illustrates a basic SOA solution.

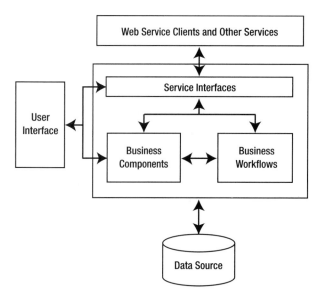

Figure 1-3. *Basic SOA solution*

The box around *service interfaces, business components,* and *business workflows* represents the conceptual business layer (middle tier). This layer encapsulates the service interfaces, which in .NET terms are the .asmx Web service files and the code-behind that directly relates to verifying and relaying incoming messages (but excludes actual business logic). The .asmx files should delegate the business processing to dedicated business components and/or a business workflow process (essentially a sequenced chain of components in a workflow). This may be a different approach to Web services coding than you are used to, because, typically, all processing code is placed directly in the code-behind file of the .asmx Web service. In an SOA, it is important to design the Web service components themselves so that they truly act as gateways to dedicated business components or workflows.

The service interface has the following properties:

- It supports the communication requirements that the service specifies in its WSDL contract (specifically, in its binding information). This includes the format and transport protocols that the service responds to (e.g., SOAP over HTTP).

- It supports the security requirements that the service specifies. In .NET terms, the .asmx code-behind can implement code that verifies incoming XML messages to ensure that they contain the required security tokens or headers.

- It supports the methods (operations) that the service specifies in its WSDL contract. In .NET terms, the .asmx file provides methods that correspond to the service operations, but the actual business processing should be handed off to dedicated components and workflow.

Figure 1-3 also shows that there are two categories of service consumers that have entry points into the business layer. The first is a traditional *user interface*, shown on the left of the diagram, such as a Windows form or an ASP.NET web page. This type of user interface is part of the same domain where the service components reside. The second category of front-end consumers is the external *Web service clients and other services*, shown at the top of the diagram. These two categories are well-known to developers. If you develop a Web service for external use, you can just as easily call it internally within its application domain. Of course, it is more efficient to call the Web service's delegated business components, because when you are internal to the domain, you do not need to route requests through the .asmx gateway using special transport and messaging protocols (e.g., HTTP and SOAP). This is yet another reason all Web services logic should be abstracted out to dedicated business components.

The architecture in Figure 1-3 is a good start, but it quickly breaks down under the demand of more sophisticated SOA applications. Figure 1-4 provides one example of a more complex SOA solution.

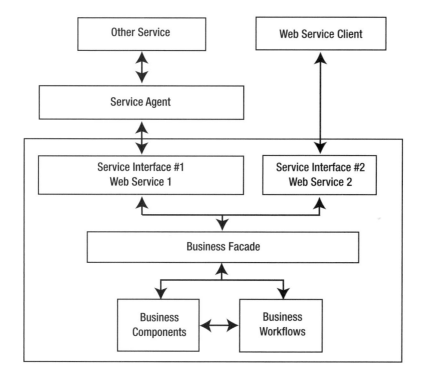

Figure 1-4. *Complex SOA solution*

Figure 1-4 illustrates an architecture in which two separate Web services access the same back-end business components. Each Web service provides a distinct service interface, each of which is suitable for a different type of client. For example, Web Service 1 may provide access to a public, unsecured subset of functions, whereas Web Service 2 provides access to a restricted, secured subset of functions. In addition, Figure 1-4 introduces two new entities that play an important role in complex SOA solutions:

Service agent: The service agent manages communications between one service and another, or between a business object and an external service. In doing so, it simplifies those interactions by shielding translation quirks between the consumer and the provider.

Business facade: The business facade acts as a trust boundary between incoming service requests (from a client, another service, or a service agent) and the middle-tier business components that service those requests.

Let's consider each of these in turn.

Service Agent

Business components are the engines of applications because they contain the logic to make the application work. In addition, business components know where to find information, whether it comes from a back-end database or from an external data source. In classic Windows-based *n*-tier architecture, we are used to thinking of business components as self-sufficient. But sometimes business components need to retrieve information from external sources in order to do their work. In SOA terms, sometimes business components need to call external services.

The service agent is responsible for managing communication between a business object and an external service. Service agents are extremely important because they simplify the amount of work that a business object has to do when it needs to use an external service. A service agent is a locally installed assembly that provides a well-known interface to the business object. Service agents do the manual legwork of communicating with external services and implementing whatever infrastructure is required to do so. This is useful for two important reasons:

- Business objects do not have to implement the infrastructure that is required to communicate with an external service. Instead, they communicate their requests to a local assembly (the service agent) using a mutually understood interface.

- Business objects avoid the maintenance work that is required to keep service interactions up-to-date. For example, if an external Web services interface changes, the service agent takes care of updating its proxy class and reworking the code implementation as needed. The business object can continue to communicate with the service agent in the same manner, even as the underlying communication details change.

We cannot resist using a travel analogy to describe the role that service agents play. Let's say you and a friend are traveling in Madrid. Your friend is fluent in both English and Spanish, but is too lazy to read the guidebook and has no idea what to see in the city. You only speak English, but you read the guidebook cover to cover, and you know that the Prado Museum cannot be missed—if only you knew how to get there from your hotel. So you need to ask directions, but cannot communicate with the locals. Your friend can ask for directions, but needs to know from you where you are trying to go. The analogy is hopefully clear! You are the business component, your friend is the service agent, and the friendly locals act as the external service.

Business Facade

The business facade is not as intuitive as the service agent because it has no analogy in traditional component-based development. Essentially, the business facade is a trust boundary that sits between middle-tier business components and the service interfaces that call them. The business facade plays the roles of both a service agent and a service interface, and it only applies in situations where there are two or more service interfaces associated with the middle tier. It provides a common interface for multiple service interfaces to interact with. In addition, the business facade may provide additional security, authentication, or screening on incoming service requests.

Figure 1-5 provides another SOA solution that illustrates the usefulness of the business facade.

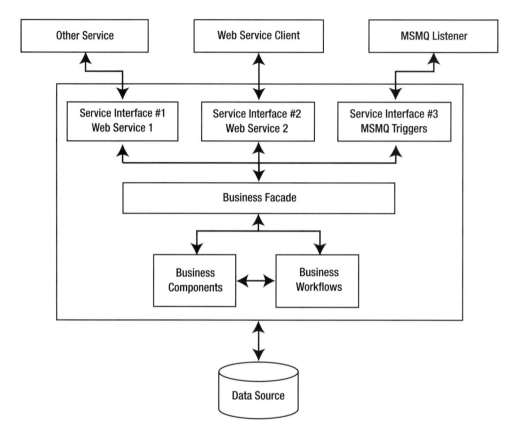

Figure 1-5. *SOA illustrating the business facade*

In this example, the service layer must handle requests from a wide variety of services, and it must support three separate service interfaces. A business facade is necessary to manage requests from several incoming service interfaces and to ensure that the requests get communicated to the business components in a consistent fashion.

■**Note** The concept of a business facade follows the well-known session facade design pattern. For an overview of this design pattern, please consult the article "Java Modeling: A UML Workbook" at `http://www-106.ibm.com/developerworks/java/library/j-jmod0604/`.

WS-I Basic Profile, WS- Specifications, and Web Services Enhancements

The difference between Web services technology today vs. SOA is in the level of available infrastructure support. Infrastructure in this context refers to the helper technologies and assemblies that support the implementation of an SOA solution. Stand-alone Web services require very little additional infrastructure support beyond what they already get from the .NET Web services assemblies and the built-in HTTP handlers. However, as you have seen in the conceptual overview, SOA requires a lot of infrastructure support, including multiple transport options, security infrastructure, and support for reliable messaging, to name a few. Different companies, including Microsoft and IBM, are working together to establish standard specifications that cover the full range of supporting technologies for SOA infrastructure.

It is an unfortunate reality that Web services specifications are developed and advanced in a politically charged environment where companies are often rivals rather than partners. Corporate animosity causes companies to disagree on the right specifications. Sometimes different groups of companies pursue separate specifications that apply to the same purpose. Nonprofit organizations such as OASIS provide a forum for companies to cooperate in the advancement and development of Web services specifications. Read more about OASIS at `http://www.oasis-open.org`.

Introducing the WS-I Basic Profile

The Web Services Interoperability Organization (WS-I) has one primary goal: to establish standard specifications so that Web services can be interoperable across different platforms. In other words, the organization wants Web services to be able to work together no matter which platform they reside on or which development tool they were created with. The specifications cover a wide range of areas, from transport protocols to security, and are collectively grouped together as the WS-I Basic Profile.

■**Note** The WS-I Basic Profile is the first in what is expected to be several future and evolving profiles. The Basic Profile specifies exact version numbers for its compliant specifications. For example, it includes SOAP 1.1, WSDL 1.1, and XML 1.0. Future profiles will use updated versions, but it takes a long time to establish new specifications, so do not expect new profiles very frequently. View the WS-I Basic Profile Version 1.1 at `http://www.ws-i.org/Profiles/BasicProfile-1.1-2004-08-24.html`.

Figure 1-6 illustrates the high-level grouping of interoperable Web services specifications that have been published jointly by Microsoft, IBM, and others. The WS-I Basic Profile covers most of the specifications in the bottom three layers of the diagram, namely the specifications for Transport, Messaging, and Description. The additional layers are covered by the various WS- specifications including WS-Security, WS-Reliable Messaging, and WS-Transactions, to name just a few. Some of the WS- specifications fall within the lower three layers as well, including WS-Addressing for the Messaging layer, and WS-Policy for the Description layer.

Note that this figure is adapted directly from a joint Microsoft-IBM white paper titled "Secure, Reliable, Transacted Web Services: Architecture and Composition" (September 2003). Please see the "References" section in the Appendix of this book for more information.

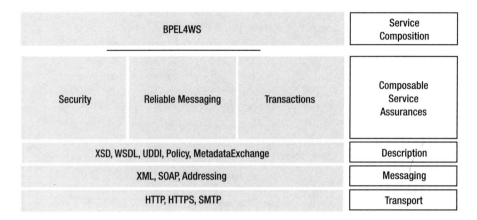

Figure 1-6. *Interoperable Web services specifications, including the WS-I Basic Profile*

The high-level groupings of Web services specifications fall into these categories:

Transport: This group defines the communication protocols for moving raw data between Web services. It includes HTTP, HTTPS, and SMTP.

Messaging: This group defines how to format the XML messages that Web services exchange. It includes the SOAP specification for encoding messages, and the XML and XSD specifications for the message vocabulary. The specifications are independent of a particular transport protocol. The Messaging group also includes the WS-Addressing specification, which decouples destination information for the request from the underlying transport protocol. WS-Addressing can, for example, be used to define multiple destinations for an XML message.

Description: This group defines specifications that allow a Web service to describe itself. The core specifications are WSDL (for the service contract), and XSD (for defining data type schemas). It also includes the WS-Policy specification, which describes the policy that a Web service enforces when it communicates with a client. For example, a Web service may have specific requirements for how its interface operations are called. The WS-Policy specification allows the Web service to tell prospective clients what rules to follow in order to execute a successful service request. Finally, this group includes the UDDI specification for discovering and describing Web services.

Service Assurances: Web services cannot simply exchange XML messages. They must also provide the client with some assurance that the messages will be transmitted in a secure way and that the client can expect some kind of response, even if something goes wrong at some point in the workflow. This group of specifications includes WS-Security (which provides authentication mechanisms), WS-Reliable Messaging (to ensure the delivery of messages over unreliable networks), and several transaction-related specifications.

Service Composition: The wide array of specifications in the WS-I Basic Profile cannot be implemented in every Web service. Developers must pick and choose which specifications are important for a particular Web service. To enable this, Web services supports service composition, which allows developers to selectively pick specifications and to aggregate them and record them in the WSDL document.

Introducing the WS- Specifications

We introduce you to the WS- specifications again in Chapter 5, and then cover them in detail in the remaining chapters of this book. Briefly, here is a summary of the most important WS- specifications and their purposes:

WS-Security: Integrates a set of popular security technologies, including digital signing and encryption based on security tokens, including X.509 certificates.

WS-Policy: Allows Web services to document their requirements, preferences, and capabilities for a range of factors, though it is mostly focused on security. For example, a Web service policy will include its security requirements, such as encryption and digital signing based on an X.509 certificate.

WS-Addressing: Identifies service endpoints in a message and allows for these endpoints to remain updated as the message is passed along through two or more services. It largely replaces the earlier WS-Routing specification.

WS-Messaging: Provides support for alternate transport channel protocols besides HTTP, including TCP. It simplifies the development of messaging applications, including asynchronous applications that communicate using SOAP over HTTP.

WS-Secure Conversation: Establishes session-oriented, trusted communication sessions using security tokens.

WS-Reliable Messaging: Provides mechanisms to help ensure the reliable delivery of messages, even when one or more services in the chain are unavailable. This specification includes message delivery notifications so that a sender knows whether a receiver has successfully obtained a sent message. Note that WS-Reliable Messaging will be supported in the upcoming Windows Communication Foundation (WCF) release, formerly code named Indigo.

The WS- specifications are constantly evolving as new specifications get submitted and existing specifications get refined. However, the core set of specifications presented here will likely continue to form the cornerstone of specifications for some time to come, since they address essential requirements for SOA applications.

Introducing Web Services Enhancements

Web Services Enhancements (WSE) provides developers with .NET managed assemblies for implementing the WS- specifications in conformance with the WS-I Basic Profile. WSE is an evolving product and does not currently support all of the Web services specifications, but it does support many important ones, such as WS-Security and WS-Secure Conversation. Keep in mind, though, that even currently supported specifications will continue to evolve in future releases of WSE. In some cases, this is because the specification is currently only partially implemented in WSE.

At a more conceptual level, WSE currently exists to provide additional infrastructure support for SOA solutions, beyond what is already provided by the .NET Framework. Microsoft chose to put WSE on a different release cycle than its .NET Framework releases, so that it would have the flexibility to vary the release schedule. Recall that SOA is governed by a number of technology standards and specifications that are themselves going through changes. WSE has to be on a flexible release cycle in order to keep up with the newer versions of these technology standards.

WSE is introduced again in Chapter 5 and is also the focus of the second half of this book, where we will cover the various WS- specifications in detail. WSE is what allows you to code several of the WS- specifications in message-oriented, service-oriented .NET applications.

■**Note** WSE 3.0 is now a fully supported product that is wire-level compatible with the upcoming WCF, and is scheduled for release at the end of 2006. This means that you can confidently build your Web services with WSE 3.0 without being concerned about needing future expensive and disruptive migration efforts to make your Web services WCF-compatible.

Summary

This chapter introduced the main concepts behind SOA, which refers to distributed applications based on Web services technology. We defined what Web services actually are, within the context of SOA, and reviewed the main aspects of SOA. We briefly introduced the WS-I Basic Profile, the WS- specifications, and WSE, all of which are covered in detail in the second half of this book starting with Chapter 5.

■ ■ ■

CHAPTER 2

The Web Services Description Language

Web services are formally and fully described using an XML-based document called the Web Services Description Language (WSDL) document. The WSDL document communicates metadata information about the Web service to potential clients and shows them what operations (methods) the Web service supports and how to bind to them.

Visual Studio .NET automatically generates WSDL documents for your XML Web services and uses them behind the scenes, although it conveniently allows you to avoid opening the actual WSDL documents. WSDL documents are, for example, used by Visual Studio .NET when you select the Add Web Reference menu option to allow your project to use the methods of an outside Web service.

In this chapter, we will describe the elements of a WSDL document so that you can understand how it fully describes a Web service. We will also show you those aspects of the WSDL document that you may wish to edit manually.

Elements of the WSDL Document

In an SOA, the WSDL document is a critically important document, and one that you will need to understand in detail so that you can exert tighter control over the Web services that you develop. This is because development tools such as Visual Studio .NET create the most generic WSDL documents with bindings only for the SOAP protocol.

Web services can exchange messages over several different protocols in addition to SOAP, including HTTP POST, HTTP GET, and SMTP. However, keep in mind that SOAP is the most suitable protocol for exchanging complex XML-based messages. If you have built a true service-oriented Web service, then these messages cannot, for example, be represented using simple URL arguments as are used by the HTTP GET protocol. You can use the HTTP POST protocol to exchange XML messages, but XML is not qualified with namespaces, nor does it provide the organized SOAP structure that is so critical to technologies such as WSE 2.0. You can see a comparison between the messages exchanged over SOAP vs. HTTP POST by browsing a Web service directly. Visual Studio .NET generates a generic input page for each Web method that shows you how the exchanged input and output messages will be generated.

WSDL documents fully describe a Web service, including the operations that it supports, the messages that it exchanges, and the data types that these messages use (both intrinsic and custom). The best way to approach a WSDL document is to understand that different XML elements take responsibility for describing different levels of detail. For example, the <message> element is a detailed listing of the types that factor into a given message. On the other hand, the <operation> element simply lists the messages that factor into a given operation without going into any detail as to what these messages look like. This additional information would be unnecessary because the <message> element already does an excellent job of documenting the types that factor into a given message. This division of responsibility makes the WSDL document very efficient but at the same time hard to read, because you have to look in several places to assemble the full details of the documented Web service. But if you keep in mind that this is the approach that the WSDL document is following, you will find the document much easier to understand.

■Note All chapter code samples installed on a Windows 2003 server will try to install their web sites under IIS (Internet Information Services) if IIS is installed and configured. If IIS 6 is installed, make sure to configure .NET 2.0 to be the default version for IIS to use. Visual Studio will prompt you to convert the project to .NET 2.0 if this is not done.

The WSDL document is itself an XML document, so it obeys the rules that you expect for any well-formed XML document. This begins with schema namespace definitions, which are included as a root element in the WSDL document that's using the <definitions> element. A typical WSDL document includes several schema definitions, but the most important one is the following:

```
<definitions xmlns="http://schemas.xmlsoap.org/wsdl/">
```

The <definitions> root element encloses the contents of the WSDL document entirely. All of the elements presented next are child elements of the <definitions> root element.

The WSDL document contains seven primary XML elements (in addition to the <definitions> root element), all of which belong to the schema listed previously. The seven XML elements fall into two main groups:

- *Abstract description*: XML elements that document the Web service interface, including the methods that it supports, the input parameters, and the return types

- *Concrete implementation*: XML elements that show the client how to physically bind to the Web service and to use its supported operations

There are four XML elements for abstract description:

<types>: This element lists all of the data types that are exchanged by the XML messages as input parameters or return types. The <types> element is equivalent to an embedded XSD schema definition file.

<message>: This element describes a SOAP message, which may be an input, an output, or a fault message for a Web service operation. A SOAP message is subdivided into parts that are represented by <part> child elements and that document the types that are included in the SOAP message.

<operation>: This element is analogous to a method definition; however, it only allows you to define input, output, and fault messages that are associated with the operation. You can then consult the individual message details to determine what input parameters and return types are involved.

<portType>: This element lists all of the operations that a Web service supports. The <port> element corresponds to a single Web service, while the <portType> element describes the available operations. The previous three elements (<types>, <message>, and <operation>) all describe granular, individual pieces of the Web service operations and its message types. The <portType> element avoids many of these lower-level details and instead provides a high-level summary of the operations (and associated input, output, and fault messages) that the Web service provides. The <portType> element provides a single location for a client to browse the offerings of a particular Web service.

There are three XML elements for concrete implementation:

<binding>: This element links the abstract and concrete elements together within a WSDL document. The <binding> element is associated with a specific <portType> element, and it also lists the address of the Web service that is associated with the <portType> element. Finally, the <binding> element lists the protocol that is used to communicate with the Web service.

<port>: This element defines the Uniform Resource Identifier (URI) where the Web service is located, and it also implements a <binding> element.

<service>: This element encloses one or more <port> elements.

Figure 2-1 shows the high-level structure of a WSDL document and how the various XML elements relate to each other within the document. The following sections examine each of the seven elements in further detail.

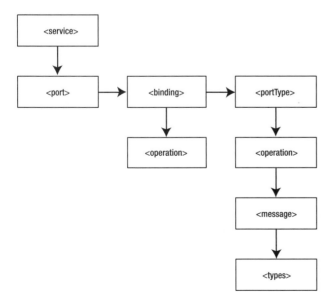

Figure 2-1. *WSDL document structure*

The <types> Element

The <types> element lists all of the data types that are exchanged by the XML messages as input parameters or return types. The <types> element is equivalent to an embedded XSD schema definition file. For design purposes, it is useful to separate your XSD schema definitions into another file. This allows you to reference type information independently of the WSDL document, which is important because it provides a central reference point for validating XML documents against a single source. You can then import the XSD schema file into the WSDL document using a separate <import> root element as follows:

```
<import namespace="http://www.bluestonepartners.com/schemas/StockTrader/"
    location="http://www.bluestonepartners.com/schemas/StockTrader.xsd" />
```

With this approach the <types> element is no longer needed, so you can just include it as an empty element as follows:

```
<types/>
```

Having shown you this approach, we need to immediately point out that it does not conform to the WS-I Basic Profile, which states that the <import> element may only be used to import another WSDL document, not an external XSD schema file. You will still need to design and build XSD schema files separately from the WSDL document; however, once this task is complete, you will need to embed the XSD elements directly within the WSDL document's <types> section. The <import> element must not appear within a WSDL document for XSD schema information. This rule holds true for WSDL documents that are generated by either WSE 2.0 or by WSE 3.0.

You cannot omit the <types> element, even if it is unused, because this will generate parsing errors in the WSDL document.

XSD schema definition files are described in detail in Chapter 3. They are essential documents for describing the data types of XML messages in an SOA. The discussion in Chapter 3 shows you how to build XSD schema files manually and then incorporate them into a WSDL document. You will also use XSD schema files to autogenerate code-based type definitions.

The <message> Element

The <message> element describes a SOAP message, which may be an input, an output, or a fault message for a Web service operation. A SOAP message is subdivided into parts that are represented by <part> child elements and that document the types that are included in the SOAP message.

For example, consider a Web method called RequestQuote. It accepts a stock ticker symbol and returns a complex XML Quote message, which contains multiple levels of detail, including the opening and closing prices of the stock, as well as long-term statistics such as 52-week high and low values. A client that expects to use the RequestQuote method does not care how this Web method is implemented. However, the client does need to know the structure of the messages for communicating with the Web method (or *operation*, as it is referred to in WSDL).

The RequestQuote operation uses a request (input) message and a response (output) message. The input message looks like this:

```
<message name="RequestQuoteSoapIn">
  <part name="Symbol" element="s1:Symbol" />
</message>
```

The output message looks like this:

```
<message name="RequestQuoteSoapOut">
  <part name="RequestQuoteResult" element="s1:Quote" />
</message>
```

Both messages use types from a namespace called StockTrader, which is referenced in the <definitions> element of the WSDL document. The <message> element does not need to document what these types look like; it simply needs to reference them. Notice that the operation's parameters are documented within the <message> root element using <part> child elements. If the RequestQuote operation required five input parameters, the corresponding input <message> element would include five corresponding <part> child elements.

The <operation> Element

The <operation> element is analogous to a method definition; however, it only allows you to define input, output, and fault messages that are associated with the operation. You can then consult the individual message details to determine what input parameters and return types are involved.

In the previous section, we described the <message> element using an example operation called RequestQuote. We presented the input and output messages, but observant readers will notice that we did not formally associate these messages to the same operation beyond verbally stating that they were associated. This is what the <operation> element is for. It is responsible for formally associating messages with a given operation. The <message> element is a root element; so, in theory, you can define a message within the WSDL document and then use it across multiple operations. This is perfectly legal within the WSDL document.

Here is what the <operation> element looks like for the RequestQuote operation:

```
<operation name="RequestQuote">
  <input message="tns:RequestQuoteSoapIn" />
  <output message="tns:RequestQuoteSoapOut" />
  <fault message="tns:ExceptionMessage" />
</operation>
```

Notice that no additional description is provided for the messages beyond their names. For more details, you must reference the corresponding <message> elements.

Operations can be defined in one of four modes:

- *Request/Response*: The client sends a request message to the Web service, and the Web service returns a response message.

- *One Way*: The client sends a request message to the Web service but receives no response message in return.

- *Solicit/Response*: This is the reverse of Request/Response. The Web service sends a message to the client, and then the client sends a response message to the Web service.

- *Notification*: This is the reverse of One Way. The Web service sends a message to the client but receives no response message in return.

The WSDL document does not contain special attributes for describing how an operation is called. Instead, you must infer this information by the arrangement and inclusion (or exclusion) of input and output messages. Although we have used the concept of request and response messages to describe the interaction between Web service and client, this model does not really apply in a WSDL document. Instead, we refer to input and output messages. The difference may be semantic, but in a WSDL document, Web services never make requests or send input messages to a client. Any message that originates from a Web service is referred to as an *output message*, even in Solicit/Response or Notification mode. Accordingly, here is how you define each of the four modes in WSDL:

- *Request/Response*: The client sends a request message to the Web service, and the Web service returns a response message.

```
<operation name="MyOperation">
  <input message="MyInputMessage" />
  <output message=" MyOutputMessage" />
</operation>
```

- *One Way*: The client sends a request message to the Web service but receives no response message in return.

```
<operation name="MyOperation">
  <input message="MyInputMessage" />
</operation>
```

- *Solicit/Response*: This is the reverse of Request/Response. The Web service sends a message to the client, and then the client sends a response message to the Web service. The <operation> element lists the output and input messages in reverse order.

```
<operation name="MyOperation">
  <output message=" MyOutputMessage" />
  <input message="MyInputMessage" />
</operation>
```

- *Notification*: This is the reverse of One Way. The Web service sends a message to the client but receives no response message in return.

```
<operation name="MyOperation">
  <output message=" MyOutputMessage" />
</operation>
```

The <portType> Element

The <portType> element lists all of the operations that a Web service supports. The <port> element (described later in this chapter) corresponds to a single Web service, while the <portType> element describes the available operations. The previous three elements (<types>, <message>, and <operation>) all describe granular, individual pieces of the Web service operations and its message types. The <portType> element avoids many of these lower-level details and instead provides a high-level summary of the operations (and associated input, output, and fault messages) that the Web service provides. The <portType> element provides a single location for a client to browse the offerings of a particular Web service.

The four elements that we have discussed so far are presented in order of decreasing granularity. Whereas an <operation> element lists a collection of <message> elements (which in turn list a collection of <types> elements), a <portType> element lists a collection of <operation> elements.

For example, here is the <portType> element (named StockTraderServiceSoap) for a Web service that supports two operations, RequestQuote and PlaceTrade:

```
<portType name="StockTraderServiceSoap">
  <operation name="RequestQuote">
    <input message="tns:RequestQuoteSoapIn" />
    <output message="tns:RequestQuoteSoapOut" />
    <fault message=" tns:ExceptionMessage" />
  </operation>
  <operation name="PlaceTrade">
    <input message="tns:PlaceTradeSoapIn" />
    <output message="tns:PlaceTradeSoapOut" />
  </operation>
</portType>
```

You may be surprised to see the <portType> listing like this. We have pointed out on several occasions how the WSDL document is designed for efficiency. If this were entirely the case, then you would expect the <portType> element to look more like this:

```
<portType name="StockTraderServiceSoap">>
  <operation name="RequestQuote" />
  <operation name="PlaceTrade" />
</portType>
```

There is no easy explanation as to why the WSDL document takes a less efficient approach with the <portType> element other than to speculate that it is designed to be a one-stop location for a client to retrieve a summary of the operations that the Web service supports.

The <binding> Element

The <binding> element links the abstract and concrete elements together within a WSDL document. The <binding> element is associated with a specific <portType> element, and it also lists the address of the Web service that is associated with the <portType> element. Finally, the <binding> element lists the protocol that is used to communicate with the Web service.

Keep in mind that the <portType> element is nothing more than an abstract definition for a Web service, which is a concrete entity that implements a set of operations. The <binding> element simply formalizes the association between a <portType> and a Web service.

Here is what the <binding> element looks like for a Web service that supports a single operation called RequestQuote, and which communicates using the SOAP protocol:

```
<binding name="StockTraderServiceSoap" type="tns:StockTraderServiceSoap">
  <soap:binding transport="http://schemas.xmlsoap.org/soap/http"
      style="document" />
  <operation name="RequestQuote">
   <soap:operation
   soapAction="http://www.bluestonepartners.com/schemas/StockTrader/RequestQuote"
      style="document" />
   <input>
    <soap:body use="literal" />
   </input>
   <output>
    <soap:body use="literal" />
   </output>
  </operation>
</binding>
```

There is no new abstract information here that you do not already know from the discussion so far. For example, you already know the name of the <portType>, which is StockTraderServiceSoap. And you already know that it includes an <operation> element named RequestQuote. But the concrete information is new. The <binding> element informs you that the Web service uses the SOAP transport protocol. The <soap:operation> element tells you the name of the Web method that is associated with the RequestQuote operation, but it does not reveal the physical location of the Web service. (The soapAction attribute includes the namespace for the RequestQuote schema element, which appears to resemble a physical URL path.) Finally, you learned that the Web method uses literal encoding and a document style, which are both required settings for exchanging SOAP messages.

The <port> Element

The <port> element defines the URL where the Web service is located, and it also implements a <binding> element. As you know, we have already defined the <binding> element for the Web service, but it does not indicate the physical location of the Web service. This is what the <port> element is for.

Here is what the <port> element looks like for the StockTraderServiceSoap <binding> element:

```
<port name="StockTraderServiceSoap" binding="tns:StockTraderServiceSoap">
  <soap:address location="http://localhost/StockTrader/StockTrader.asmx" />
</port>
```

Finally, you learn the physical location of the Web service, via the <soap:address> element.

The <service> Element

The <service> element encloses one or more <port> elements. It is essentially a collection of one or more Web service bindings. In most cases, your WSDL document will describe one Web service only, so the <service> element itself will provide no additional value. However, the WSDL specification requires that all <port> elements be contained within the <service> element. The listing in the previous section actually appears within a <service> element called StockTraderService as follows:

```
<service name="StockTraderService">
  <port name="StockTraderServiceSoap" binding="tns:StockTraderServiceSoap">
    <soap:address location="http://localhost/StockTrader/StockTrader.asmx" />
  </port>
</service>
```

The WSDL 1.1 Specification

The WSDL 1.1 specification that describes the complete document structure can be found at http://www.w3.org/TR/wsdl. It is worth looking at the original specification because you will find useful elements that you can use even though they are not widely known or even generated using GUI tools such as Visual Studio .NET. For example, the <operation> element contains a child element called <documentation> that allows you to insert an English language description of what the operation does. Here is an example:

```
<operation name="RequestQuote">
  <documentation>
        Returns a delayed 30-minute quote for a given stock ticker symbol.
        This operation returns a Quote XML type as defined in the XSD schema at:
        http://www.bluestonepartners.com/schemas/StockTrader.xsd
  </documentation>
  <input message="s1:RequestQuoteSoapIn" />
  <output message="s1:RequestQuoteSoapOut" />
</operation>
```

The <documentation> element adds a welcome level of readability to the WSDL document, which is challenging at best to read with human eyes.

If you were to distill a WSDL document down to its most basic set of associated elements, it would look like this:

```
<definitions>
    <types />
    <message />
    <operation>
        <message />
    </operation>
    <portType>
        <operation />
    </portType>
```

```
    <binding>
        <operation />
    </binding>
    <service>
        <port>
            <binding />
        </port>
    </service>
</definitions>
```

Listing 2-1 shows the actual WSDL document for the StockTrader Web service that we will be working with in detail in the following chapters. You do not need to read the document line-by-line; but try scanning it and notice how much information you can get about the Web service without having seen any other documentation about it.

Listing 2-1. *The WSDL Document for the StockTrader Web Service*

```
<?xml version="1.0" encoding="utf-8" ?>
<definitions xmlns:http="http://schemas.xmlsoap.org/wsdl/http/"
    xmlns:soap="http://schemas.xmlsoap.org/wsdl/soap/"
    xmlns:s="http://www.w3.org/2001/XMLSchema"
    xmlns:s0="http://www.bluestonepartners.com/schemas/StockTrader/"
    xmlns:soapenc="http://schemas.xmlsoap.org/soap/encoding/"
    xmlns:tns="http://www.bluestonepartners.com/schemas/StockTrader"
    xmlns:tm="http://microsoft.com/wsdl/mime/textMatching/"
    xmlns:mime="http://schemas.xmlsoap.org/wsdl/mime/"
    targetNamespace="http://www.bluestonepartners.com/schemas/StockTrader"
    xmlns="http://schemas.xmlsoap.org/wsdl/">
<import namespace="http://www.bluestonepartners.com/schemas/StockTrader/"
    location="http://www.bluestonepartners.com/schemas/StockTrader.xsd" />
<types/>
<message name="RequestAllTradesSummarySoapIn">
    <part name="Account" element="s1:Account" />
</message>
<message name="RequestAllTradesSummarySoapOut">
    <part name="RequestAllTradesSummaryResult" element="s1:Trades" />
</message>
<message name="RequestTradeDetailsSoapIn">
    <part name="Account" element="s1:Account" />
    <part name="TradeID" element="s1:TradeID" />
</message>
<message name="RequestTradeDetailsSoapOut">
    <part name="RequestTradeDetailsResult" element="s1:Trade" />
</message>
<message name="PlaceTradeSoapIn">
    <part name="Account" element="s1:Account" />
    <part name="Symbol" element="s1:Symbol" />
    <part name="Shares" element="s1:Shares" />
```

```
        <part name="Price" element="s1:Price" />
        <part name="tradeType" element="s1:tradeType" />
    </message>
    <message name="PlaceTradeSoapOut">
        <part name="PlaceTradeResult" element="s1:Trade" />
    </message>
    <message name="RequestQuoteSoapIn">
        <part name="Symbol" element="s1:Symbol" />
    </message>
    <message name="RequestQuoteSoapOut">
        <part name="RequestQuoteResult" element="s1:Quote" />
    </message>
    <portType name="StockTraderServiceSoap">
        <operation name="RequestAllTradesSummary">
            <input message="tns:RequestAllTradesSummarySoapIn" />
            <output message="tns:RequestAllTradesSummarySoapOut" />
        </operation>
        <operation name="RequestTradeDetails">
            <input message="tns:RequestTradeDetailsSoapIn" />
            <output message="tns:RequestTradeDetailsSoapOut" />
        </operation>
        <operation name="PlaceTrade">
            <input message="tns:PlaceTradeSoapIn" />
            <output message="tns:PlaceTradeSoapOut" />
        </operation>
        <operation name="RequestQuote">
            <input message="tns:RequestQuoteSoapIn" />
            <output message="tns:RequestQuoteSoapOut" />
        </operation>
    </portType>
    <binding name="StockTraderServiceSoap" type="tns:StockTraderServiceSoap">
        <soap:binding transport="http://schemas.xmlsoap.org/soap/http"
            style="document" />
        <operation name="RequestAllTradesSummary">
            <soap:operation
                soapAction="http://www.bluestonepartners.com/schemas/StockTrader/ ➡
                    RequestAllTradesSummary" style="document" />
            <input>
                <soap:body use="literal" />
            </input>
            <output>
                <soap:body use="literal" />
            </output>
        </operation>
        <operation name="RequestTradeDetails">
            <soap:operation
                soapAction="http://www.bluestonepartners.com/schemas/StockTrader/ ➡
```

```
                      RequestTradeDetails" style="document" />
        <input>
            <soap:body use="literal" />
        </input>
        <output>
            <soap:body use="literal" />
        </output>
    </operation>
    <operation name="PlaceTrade">
        <soap:operation soapAction="http://www.bluestonepartners.com/schemas/ ➥
            /StockTrader/PlaceTrade" style="document" />
    <input>
    <soap:body use="literal" />
    </input>
    <output>
    <soap:body use="literal" />
    </output>
    </operation>
    <operation name="RequestQuote">
        <soap:operation
            soapAction="http://www.bluestonepartners.com/schemas/StockTrader/ ➥
                RequestQuote" style="document" />
        <input>
            <soap:body use="literal" />
        </input>
        <output>
            <soap:body use="literal" />
        </output>
    </operation>
</binding>
<service name="StockTraderService">
   <port name="StockTraderServiceSoap" binding="tns:StockTraderServiceSoap">
     <soap:address location="http:// www.bluestonepartners.com/StockTrader.asmx" />
   </port>
</service>
</definitions>
```

This concludes the overview of the elements that make up a WSDL document. You can reference the complete WSDL document for this Web service in the sample code (available from the Source Code/Download section of the Apress web site at http://www.apress.com), under Chapter 2\WSDL Documents\. You may find the file easier to read if you open it in Visual Studio .NET or from within XML document editing software.

Working with WSDL Documents

Now that you understand the structure of a WSDL document, the next questions are how do you actually generate one, and what do you do with it once you have it generated? These are not trivial questions, because the WSDL document is complex, and you will want to keep your manual alterations of the document to a minimum. Parsing errors are very easy to generate in a WSDL document from even the smallest of misapplied edits.

How to Generate a WSDL Document

The easiest way to generate a WSDL document is to use a tool such as Visual Studio .NET. There is very much a chicken-and-the-egg relationship between a WSDL document and the Web service implementation that it describes. That is, you can write the code first and generate the WSDL document later. Or you can manually write the WSDL document first, and then use it to autogenerate the code definition. Because it is very difficult to generate a WSDL document by hand, you are better off writing the code implementation first and then using Visual Studio .NET to generate the WSDL document for you.

Web services must be message-oriented if they are to be of any use in an SOA. Chapters 3 and 4 provide a detailed discussion of how to build message-oriented Web services. It is essential that you follow good design patterns and practices when building Web services for an SOA.

Assuming that you have built a message-oriented Web service according to the best patterns and practices (as discussed in the following chapters), you can generate a WSDL document by browsing the .asmx file of your Web service and clicking the Service Description link in the default client page. This link simply appends ?WSDL to the URL of the .asmx file. Figure 2-2 shows the default client page for the StockTraderService Web service and the corresponding Service Description link.

Figure 2-2. *The default client page for the StockTraderService Web service*

The Service Description link will display the WSDL document in a tree view–like format, wherein you can collapse and expand individual elements. This format is very useful for working your way through the document and learning how it is structured. Alternatively, you can copy the WSDL document from the browser window and then view it in an XML document editing application.

What to Do with the WSDL Document

Once you have autogenerated the WSDL document, there are three main things that you will want to do with it. First, you will need to abstract out the data type information from the embedded <types> element into a separate XSD schema file. This is essential in an SOA so that other Web services and clients can have access to the same centralized schema definition file of the custom data types.

Second, you can use a command-line tool called wsdl.exe to autogenerate proxy classes that clients can use to interact with the Web service. You can replicate the same feature in Visual Studio .NET by adding a Web reference from a client project to a Web service.

Third, you can use the same utility with alternate switches to generate server-side code implementations of the Web service contract. You may either generate abstract classes, or you can generate service interface code methods that can be directly implemented rather than overridden. These code-generation capabilities are useful for creating a server-side "back-end" implementation based on an established Web service contract. You will see examples of this in Chapters 3 and 4, where we use the utility to generate stub classes for the sample Web service implementation.

As you become a more sophisticated Web services developer, you will end up spending more time developing outside of the comfortable environment of Visual Studio .NET. This is because you will grow to need a higher level of control over your Web services development than Visual Studio .NET can currently provide.

Summary

In this chapter, you studied the structure of a WSDL document and found that it contains seven XML elements in addition to a root element called <definitions>. The seven additional elements are divided into two groups: one set provides an abstract description of the Web service, while the other set provides concrete implementation details that associate the abstract descriptions with the physical Web service.

The XML elements for abstract description are:

<types>: This element lists all of the data types that are exchanged by the XML messages as input parameters or return types.

<message>: This element describes a SOAP message, which may be an input, output, or fault message for a Web service operation.

<operation>: This element is analogous to a method definition; however, it only allows you to define input, output, and fault messages that are associated with the operation.

<portType>: This element lists all of the operations that a Web service supports.

The XML elements for concrete implementation are:

<binding>: This element links the abstract and concrete elements together within a WSDL document.

<port>: This element defines the URL where the Web service is located, and it also implements a <binding> element.

<service>: This element encloses one or more <port> elements.

This chapter concluded with a brief look at how to generate and work with WSDL documents. In the following two chapters, we will give you a detailed look at how to build message-oriented Web services and how to work with WSDL documents and XSD schema definition files.

■ ■ ■

CHAPTER 3

Design Patterns for Building Message-Oriented Web Services

In an SOA, the purpose of Web services is to exchange and process XML messages, not simply to act as hosts for remote procedure call (RPC) style methods. The difference is that messages are bound to rich and complex operations, whereas RPC-style methods simply return a discrete result that is directly correlated to a specific set of input parameters. For example, a message-oriented Web method will accept a stock ticker symbol and return a detailed stock quote in response. In contrast, an RPC-style Web method will return a simple output value.

Unfortunately, development tools such as Visual Studio place a method-centric focus on Web services that causes you to lose sight of the bigger design picture and to take the underlying infrastructure for granted. It is very easy to build a Web service by creating an .asmx file and then throwing together several loosely related RPC-style Web method implementations. However, this is the wrong design approach because such a Web service fails to provide an integrated set of message endpoints. In simpler terms, the Web service fails to provide a service. The right design approach is always to think in terms of operations and XML messages and to consider how the Web service methods work together to provide a service.

This chapter begins with a challenge for you to set aside what you have learned about Web services development until now and to open your mind to a different design approach—one that is based on integrated XML messages, not on RPC-style methods.

How to Build a Message-Oriented Web Service

There are six steps involved in building a message-oriented Web service, which is simply a Web service that exchanges XML schema–based input and output messages rather than simple parameter-oriented values. The steps are described in the following sections.

Step 1: Design the Messages and the Data Types

Conceptually design what the messages and data types will look like. UML class diagrams are the best way to capture this information, and there is the added benefit that many of today's UML tools support XML schema generation directly from UML class diagrams.

Step 2: Build the XSD Schema File for the Data Types

Use an XML designer tool to build the XSD schema file for all of the data types that are exchanged by the Web service methods. Visual Studio 2005's XML Designer is a good tool, but you can use any XML designer tool that you are comfortable working with.

Step 3: Create a Class File of Interface Definitions for the Messages and Data Types

The interface definition class (IDC) file provides the abstract definitions of the Web service methods and its data types. This class file derives from the System.Web.Services.WebService class, so it can be readily implemented in a Web services code-behind file. The .NET Framework provides a command-line tool called xsd.exe for generating an IDC file based on an XSD schema file. This will manually generate class definitions for the data types. You can add this class file to your Web service project and then manually insert abstract definitions for the Web methods.

Optional Step 3A: Generate the WSDL Document Manually

If you are brave enough, you can generate the WSDL document manually once you have built the XSD schema file. However, the only real benefit you gain from this step is that you are then able to fully generate the IDC file using the wsdl.exe command-line tool. It is easier to follow step 3 (explained previously), using xsd.exe combined with manual coding of the abstract method definitions. The syntax of WSDL documents is very difficult to build correctly by hand. (Chapter 2 of this book, which reviews the structure of WSDL documents, is essential reading, so that you can understand how the WSDL document is structured and how it relays Web service metadata to Web service clients.)

Step 4: Implement the Interface in the Web Service Code-Behind File

Your hard work in steps 1 through 3 pays off, and you are now ready to implement code for the Web methods. The Web service .asmx code-behind class derives from the System.Web.Services.WebService class by default, as does the IDC file from step 3, so you can derive the .asmx code-behind class directly from the interface definition class instead of directly from System.Web.Services.WebService. You can then implement code for each of the methods.

Step 5: Generate a Proxy Class File for Clients Based on the WSDL Document

Web services have no reason to exist unless they are being used by clients. In this step, you generate a proxy class file based on the Web service WSDL document so that clients know how to call your Web service, and know what messages and data types will be exchanged. The wsdl.exe command-line tool will automatically generate this proxy class for you based on the WSDL document. And Visual Studio 2005 will automatically generate the WSDL document for you, so no manual work is required.

You can actually skip this step if you are developing with Visual Studio 2005, because it will dynamically generate the proxy class file for you when you add a Web reference (for your Web service) to a client project. However, we prefer to manually generate the proxy class file so that we can either alter it or have it ready for clients who are using a development tool without code-generating wizards.

Step 6: Implement a Web Service Client Using a Proxy Class File

This final step hooks a client to your Web service. If you are using Visual Studio 2005, simply add a (dynamic) Web reference to the Web service in your client project, and this will automatically generate the proxy class file for you. This wizard will also make the necessary adjustments to your application configuration file to record the location of the Web service. Alternatively, you can manually add the proxy class file from step 5 to your project, update the configuration file, and begin coding. The client essentially does nothing more than delegate method calls to the Web service. Valid clients include Web applications, Windows Forms applications, console applications, or even other Web services.

Next Steps

This process is obviously more involved than simply creating a new .asmx file and immediately implementing code. But it is the right way to do things because it abstracts out the Web service definitions and the code implementations. Visual Studio and the .NET Framework provide all of the tools that you need to autogenerate the XML-based files and the code, so the amount of manual work is kept to a minimum.

The rest of this chapter dissects the various moving parts that make up a message-oriented Web service. You will gain a precise understanding of how multiple files and tools work together to define and implement a message-oriented Web service. We will also provide selective implementation examples that collectively show you how to build this type of Web service from scratch.

WHAT ARE DESIGN PATTERNS?

Design patterns are loosely described as time-tested, established solutions to recurring design problems. Formal design patterns are highly structured and follow strict templates. The design patterns that are presented in this book do not follow this rigorous format, but they are in keeping with the spirit of design patterns because they factor in industry-accepted practices for approaching recurring design problems.

Design and Build a Message-Oriented Web Service

This section provides the information that you need in order to build a message-oriented Web service. It is organized along the same six steps presented earlier and provides both conceptual information and implementation information.

The Role of XML Messages and XSD Schemas

The starting point in designing a Web service is to determine what XML messages it will exchange—specifically, what messages it will respond to, and what messages it will return. Figure 3-1 shows the standard architecture for a client that interacts with a Web service via a proxy class. This architecture is based on the principle that the client and the Web service both have a common understanding of the messages and data types that are exchanged between them. This understanding can only be achieved if the Web service publishes a clear document of the operations that it supports, the messages it exchanges, and the types that it uses. This document is the WSDL document (described in Chapter 2). The WSDL document is the main reference for describing a Web service, and it includes embedded type definitions and message definitions, among other things.

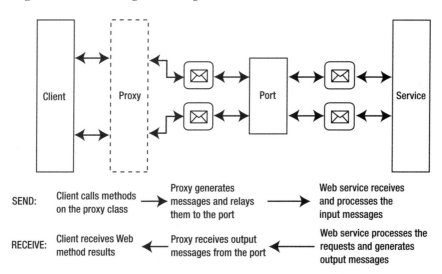

Figure 3-1. *Web services architecture showing communication between the client and service*

Consider the example Web service, StockTrader, from Chapter 2 that provides methods for retrieving stock quotes and placing trades. Listing 3-1 presents one of the Web methods called RequestQuote that accepts a stock ticker symbol and returns a detailed stock quote.

Listing 3-1. *Pseudocode for the RequestQuote Web Method*

```
[WebMethod]
public Quote RequestQuote(string Symbol)
{
    // implementation code
}

public class Quote
    {
        public string Symbol;
        public string Company;
        public string DateTime;
        public System.Double High;
        public System.Double Low;
        public System.Double Open;
        public System.Double Last;
        public System.Double Change;
        public System.Double PercentChange;
        public System.Double Previous_Close;
        public string High_52_Week;
        public string Low_52_Week;
    }
```

This code listing represents a Quote type object and a method called RequestQuote that returns a Quote object. The RequestQuote method actually represents two messages: an input (or request) message that includes a stock ticker symbol; and an output (or response) message that provides a detailed stock quote. A client can only use the RequestQuote method if it can also understand the response. In other words, the client has to fully understand the definition of the Quote type in order to make use of the RequestQuote method. This is exactly the kind of information that WSDL documents and XSD schema files document.

Listing 3-2 shows what the RequestQuote input and output messages look like in WSDL.

Listing 3-2. *WSDL for the RequestQuote Input and Output Messages, Including Associated Types*

```
<wsdl:message name="RequestQuoteSoapIn">
    <wsdl:part name="parameters" element="tns:RequestQuote" />
</wsdl:message>
<wsdl:message name="RequestQuoteSoapOut">
    <wsdl:part name="parameters" element="tns:RequestQuoteResponse" />
</wsdl:message>

<wsdl:portType name="StockTraderSoap">
    <wsdl:operation name="RequestQuote">
        <wsdl:input message="tns:RequestQuoteSoapIn" />
        <wsdl:output message="tns:RequestQuoteSoapOut" />
    </wsdl:operation>
</wsdl:portType>
```

```
<wsdl:types>
    <s:schema elementFormDefault="qualified"
        targetNamespace="http://www.bluestonepartners.com/schemas/StockTrader/">
    <s:import namespace="http://www.bluestonepartners.com/Schemas/StockTrader/" />
    <s:element name="RequestQuote">
        <s:complexType>
            <s:sequence>
                <s:element minOccurs="0" maxOccurs="1"
                    name="Symbol" type="s:string" />
            </s:sequence>
        </s:complexType>
    </s:element>
    <s:element name="RequestQuoteResponse">
        <s:complexType>
            <s:sequence>
                <s:element minOccurs="0" maxOccurs="1"
                    name="Quote" type="s1:Quote" />
            </s:sequence>
        </s:complexType>
        </s:element>
    </s:schema>
</wsdl:types>
```

Listing 3-3 shows what the Quote type and Symbol type look like in an XSD schema file.

Listing 3-3. *XSD Schema for the Quote and Symbol Types*

```
<?xml version="1.0" encoding="utf-8" ?>
<xs:schema id="StockTrader"
    targetNamespace="http://www.bluestonepartners.com/Schemas/StockTrader/"
    elementFormDefault="qualified"
    xmlns="http://www.bluestonepartners.com/Schemas/StockTrader/"
    xmlns:mstns="http://www.bluestonepartners.com/Schemas/StockTrader/"
    xmlns:xs="http://www.w3.org/2001/XMLSchema" version="1.0">
    <xs:complexType name="Quote">
        <xs:sequence>
            <xs:element name="Symbol" type="xs:string" />
            <xs:element name="Company" type="xs:string" />
            <xs:element name="DateTime" type="xs:string" />
            <xs:element name="High" type="xs:double" />
            <xs:element name="Low" type="xs:double" />
            <xs:element name="Open" type="xs:double" />
            <xs:element name="Last" type="xs:double" />
            <xs:element name="Change" type="xs:double" />
            <xs:element name="PercentChange" type="xs:double" />
            <xs:element name="High_52_Week" type="xs:double" />
            <xs:element name="Low_52_Week" type="xs:double" />
        </xs:sequence>
```

```
  </xs:complexType>
  <xs:element name="Symbol" type="xs:string"></xs:element>
</xs:schema>
```

This schema representation of the Quote type is significant because it qualifies the type definition based on a specific target namespace, in this case `http://www.bluestonepartners.com/schemas/StockTrader/`. Although there may be many variations of the Quote type in the world, this specific qualified definition is unique. The Symbol type is nothing more than a standard string type element, but it is qualified to a specific namespace and therefore becomes more than just a standard element. Schema files are essential to ensure that a Web service and its clients are absolutely clear on the messages and type definitions that are being exchanged between them. Schema files are how you define messages.

■Note XSD schema files should always define types using nested elements rather than attributes. This makes the file easier to read and reduces the possibility of errors during processing.

The Quote and Symbol types look very similar if they are embedded directly in the WSDL document within the <types> section; and you should always assign qualified namespace information to embedded types. In addition, you should always abstract type definitions out to a separate XSD schema file for reference purposes, even though it is redundant to the embedded type information contained within the WSDL document. Separate XSD schema files are useful for a lot of reasons. Most importantly, they allow different Web services to use the same qualified types and to reference them based on a single XSD schema file in a single physical location. Life would get very confusing if you had multiple embedded definitions of the same qualified data type floating around in cyberspace. In addition, dedicated XSD schema files help you validate XML messages. In .NET you can load an XSD file into an Xml-ValidatingReader object and use it to validate XML messages. You can also use schema files with the xsd.exe command-line utility to generate class file definitions for types.

■Note The target namespace is typically expressed as a Uniform Resource Identifier (URI), but it is not required to resolve to an actual location. The schema definitions that are presented in this book happen to be stored as XSD files at `http://www.bluestonepartners.com/soa.aspx`. For your convenience, they are also included in the sample code downloads (available in the Source Code/Download section on the Apress web site at `http://www.apress.com`).

Design the XML Messages and XSD Schemas (Step 1)

XML messages represent the operations that your Web service supports, and they correlate to implemented Web methods. XML messages do not contain implementation logic. Instead, they simply document the name of an operation and its input and output types. XML messages must be designed in conjunction with XSD schema files. The best starting point is to construct a UML diagram for the operation. Figure 3-2 shows a UML class diagram for the RequestQuote operation and its associated input and output data types.

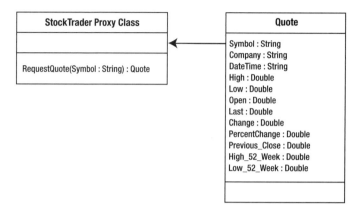

Figure 3-2. *UML class diagram for the RequestQuote operation*

The UML class diagrams will map conceptually to XSD schemas, so you do not have to sketch out any XML during the design phase unless it helps you to better visualize the XML messages and types. For example, here is what the Quote type will look like within a SOAP response (with the embedded namespaces omitted for clarity):

```
<Quote>
    <Symbol>MSFT</Symbol>
    <Company>Microsoft Corporation</Company>
    <DateTime>11/17/2003 16:00:00</DateTime>
    <High>26.12</High>
    <Low>24.68</Low>
    <Open>25.49</Open>
    <Last>25.15</Last>
    <Change>-0.36</Change>
    <PercentChange>-0.0137</PercentChange>
    <Previous_Close>25.49</Previous_Close>
    <High_52_Week>35</High_52_Week>
    <Low_52_Week>22</Low_52_Week>
</Quote>
```

For design purposes, you can simplify the XML down to this:

```
<Quote>
    <Symbol />
    <Company />
    <DateTime />
    <High />
    <Low />
    <Open />
    <Last />
```

```
        <Change />
        <PercentChange />
        <Previous_Close />
        <High_52_Week />
        <Low_52_Week />
    </Quote>
```

Clearly, it is a lot of work to sketch out even this simplified XML by hand, and it does not provide any additional value beyond what the UML diagram provides. In fact, it provides less because this sketched out XML provides no type information. So the message here is that for efficiency you should design your XML messages using UML or any appropriate shorthand notation. This is the extent of the design work that is minimally required, and you should never shortcut this step.

Build the XSD Schema File (Step 2)

Once you have established what your XML messages and data types will look like, it is time to start building them. XSD schema files are the building blocks for XML messages, so you need to design the schema files first. XSD schema files may be coded by hand, but it is easier to use a visual designer tool, such as Visual Studio 2005's XML Designer. To access the designer, simply add a new XSD schema file to a project. Visual Studio provides both a visual design view and an XML design view. Figure 3-3 illustrates the visual design view for StockTrader.xsd, which defines all of the data types for this chapter's StockTrader sample application.

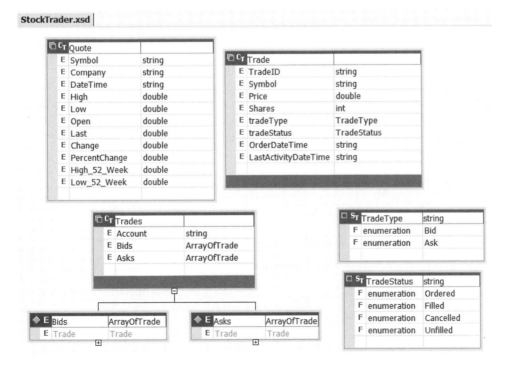

Figure 3-3. *The Visual Studio 2005 XML Designer, showing the StockTrader.xsd schema*

The XML Designer includes toolbox elements that you can drag onto the surface of the designer and then fill in, as shown in Figure 3-4. For example, it provides a toolbox element for XML complex types. Simply drag this element onto the designer and provide a name for the complex type. Then start specifying the included types by their name and type. Once you are finished defining all of the types, switch to the XML view to view the resulting XML. You can then copy and paste the XML into a Notepad file and save it with an .xsd extension.

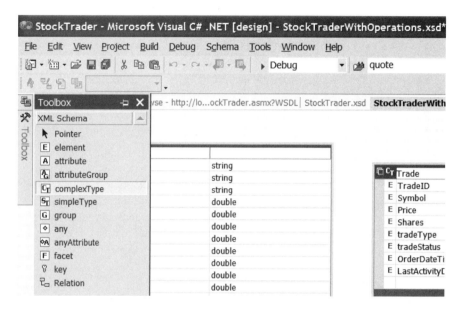

Figure 3-4. *The Visual Studio 2005 XML Designer toolbox*

You do not need to build the XML message documents by hand because they are created as part of the WSDL document, which Visual Studio 2005 will automatically generate. But you will need to code the abstract method definitions in an IDC file so that the WSDL generator knows what XML messages to create. The IDC file contains type definitions and abstract method definitions.

The Role of the Interface Definition Class File

The IDC file contains two important sets of information:

- Class definitions for all custom types that are exchanged by the Web service

- Abstract class definitions for each operation that the Web service supports

Listing 3-4 provides the code for an IDC file for the RequestQuote operation and its associated types.

Listing 3-4. *The IDC File for the RequestQuote Operation and Its Associated Types*

```
using System;
using System.Web.Services;
using System.Web.Services.Description;
using System.Web.Services.Protocols;
using System.Xml.Serialization;

namespace StockTrader
{

    public abstract class StockTraderStub : System.Web.Services.WebService
    {
        public abstract Quote RequestQuote(string Symbol);
    }

    [XmlTypeAttribute(Namespace=
      "http://www.bluestonepartners.com/schemas/StockTrader/")]
    public class Quote
    {
        public string Symbol;
        public string Company;
        public string DateTime;
        public System.Double High;
        public System.Double Low;
        public System.Double Open;
        public System.Double Last;
        public System.Double Change;
        public System.Double PercentChange;
        public System.Double Previous_Close;
        public System.Double High_52_Week;
        public System.Double Low_52_Week;
        }

}
```

Notice the following important points:

- The definition file includes one stub class that encapsulates all operations and then any number of additional classes for the data types.

- The interface definitions for the operations are enclosed within an abstract class called StockTraderStub. The stub class derives from the System.Web.Services.WebService class, so it can be implemented in a Web service. In this listing it contains a single abstract function definition for the RequestQuote operation.

- The definition file contains a separate class definition for the Quote type. This is how you are able to reference the Quote type from code-behind.

- The definition file only contains class definitions for custom types (such as Quote), not for simple elements such as Symbol, which is a standard string (as qualified in the http://www.w3.org/2001/XMLSchema namespace). We make special mention of this because it may appear inconsistent with our earlier XSD schema file that includes an element definition for Symbol. But it is not inconsistent, because the xsd.exe compiler resolves the Symbol element to a standard string, which therefore requires no special entry in the IDC file.

Note You may be confused by the difference between abstract classes vs. interfaces. An *interface* is a completely abstract set of members with no implementation logic. An *abstract class* supports implementations in its methods (although it is not required). Abstract classes are useful because they provide the benefits of interfaces combined with the convenience of reusable code. (Notice, however, that abstract classes may limit extensibility in C#, which does not permit multiple inheritance.)

XML Serialization Attributes

The interface definition classes are decorated with XML serialization attributes that bind the classes to specific namespaces, attributes, and elements in the XSD schema file. Consider, for example, the following:

```
[return: XmlElement("Quote",
    Namespace = "http://www.bluestonepartners.com/schemas/StockTrader/")]
public abstract Quote RequestQuote(string Symbol);
```

This unambiguously states that the RequestQuote operation returns an object of type Quote, as qualified in the http://www.bluestonepartners.com/schemas/StockTrader/ namespace. In fact, this namespace is documented liberally throughout the IDC file. It can never appear too often because XML messages must be as unambiguous as possible.

XML and SOAP serialization attributes give you direct control over the way in which the XML messages get serialized within the request and response SOAP messages. You should always set the SoapDocumentMethod reflection attribute to use bare encoding for parameters. This ensures that complex types (such as Quote) remain serialized as elements within the SOAP message:

```
[WebMethod()]
[SoapDocumentMethod(Use=SoapBindingUse.Literal,
    ParameterStyle=SoapParameterStyle.Bare)]
public abstract Quote RequestQuote(string Symbol);
```

If you do not use bare encoding, complex types may end up serialized as attributes, which may interfere with schema validation. This is known as *wrapped encoding*. Bare encoding looks like this

```
<Quote>
    <Symbol>MSFT</Symbol>
</Quote>
```

while wrapped encoding looks like this

```
<Quote Symbol="MSFT" />
```

Wrapped encoding will generate fewer XML characters and a smaller SOAP payload, but it may create big problems if custom types cannot be validated against their XSD schema files.

Table 3-1 summarizes important properties of the serialization attribute, including how certain property values influence the processing behavior of a Web service.

REFLECTION ATTRIBUTES

Reflection attributes allow you to add additional metadata to a wide variety of code elements, including classes and methods. Attributes modify the way that the element is processed. For example, the [WebMethod] attribute designates a standard method or function as capable of accepting serialized XML messages. Of course, reflection attributes must have meaning to the processing code in order to be applied. Reflection attributes may include properties that provide additional metadata information. For more on reflection attributes, consult the MSDN online article on attributes, located at MSDN Home ➤ MSDN Library ➤ .NET Development ➤ Visual Studio .NET ➤ Visual Basic and Visual C# ➤ Reference ➤ Visual C# Language ➤ C# Language Specification.

Table 3-1. *The SoapDocumentMethod Serialization Attribute and Selected Properties*

Attribute Property	Description
Use	Specifies the encoding style of the messages. The options are *Literal* and *Encoded*. (The options are specified in code using the System.Web.Services.Description.SoapBindingUse enumeration.)
ParameterStyle	Specifies whether the parameters are wrapped in a single element within the body of the SOAP message, or whether they are unwrapped. (The options are specified in code using the System.Web.Services.Protocols.SoapParameterStyle enumeration.)
OneWay	Specifies whether the Web service client will receive a response to its request, or whether the request will be one-way only (without a response).
Binding	Associates a Web method with a specific operation within the binding that is specified for the Web service. The Web service binding is set at the Web service level using the WebServiceBinding serialization attribute—for example, [System.Web.Services. WebServiceBindingAttribute(Name="StockTraderServiceSoap", Namespace="http://www.bluestonepartners.com/schemas/ StockTrader")]public class StockTraderProxy : System.Web.Services.Protocols.SoapHttpClientProtocol {}.
RequestNamespace	Specifies the namespace URI that defines the request elements.
RequestElementName	Specifies the name of the request element as it is defined in the applicable XSD schema file.
ResponseNamespace	Specifies the namespace URI that defines the response elements.
ResponseElementName	Specifies the name of the response element as it is defined in the applicable XSD schema file.

Generate an IDC File (Step 3)

IDC files can be generated in three ways:

- *wsdl.exe*: This command-line tool generates a full IDC file (including abstract classes and types) based on a WSDL document. The tool generates code for XML Web service clients and XML Web services using ASP.NET from WSDL contract files, XSD schemas, and .discomap discovery documents. The general usage of the wsdl.exe utility is wsdl.exe <url or path> <options>. The <options> placeholder is occupied by one or more switches. Table 3-2 summarizes selected command-line switches for the wsdl.exe utility.

Table 3-2. *Selected Command-Line Switches for the wsdl.exe Utility*

Switch	Description
<url or path>	A URL or path to a WSDL contract, an XSD schema, or a .discomap document.
/server	A switch that generates an abstract class for an XML Web service implementation using ASP.NET based on the contracts. The default is to generate client proxy classes.
/out:<filename>	The file name for the generated proxy code. The default name is derived from the service name. The short form is /o:.
/sharetypes	A switch that generates a single type definition for types that are shared between multiple Web service WSDL bindings. This feature is new to .NET Framework 2.0 and avoids creating multiple type definitions (in code) for the same service types. This in turn releases the developer from getting stuck with type definition versioning issues.
/protocol	Overrides the default protocol from HTTP POST to SOAP, SOAP12, or HTTP GET.

- *xsd.exe*: This command-line tool generates the type section only for the IDC file based on an XSD schema file. You can use this autogenerated file as a starting point and then manually insert the abstract class definitions for each of the Web service operations. The general usage of the utility is xsd.exe <schema>.xsd /classes: dataset [/o:]. Table 3-3 summarizes selected command-line switches for the xsd.exe utility.

Table 3-3. *xsd.exe Selected Command-Line Switches*

Switch	Description
<schema>.xsd	The name of a schema containing the elements to import.
/classes	A switch that generates classes for this schema. The short form is /c.
/dataset	A switch that generates subclassed DataSet for this schema. The short form is /d.
/out:<directoryName>	The output directory to create files in. The default is the current directory. The short form is /o.

- *WseWsdl3.exe*: This command-line tool generates code for WSE 3.0 Web service clients based on either a WSDL document or an XSD schema file. You can use this tool to generate a proxy class and a full IDC file (including abstract classes and types), all based on the specified WSDL document. The general usage of the utility is WseWsdl3.exe <schema>.xsd /classes. Table 3-4 summarizes selected command-line switches for the WseWsdl3.exe utility. Note that WseWsdl3.exe supports the same set of switches as the previous WSE 2.0 version of the utility WseWsdl.exe.

Table 3-4. *WseWsdl3.exe Selected Command-Line Switches*

Switch	Description
/type	The switch that overrides the proxy type from SoapClient (default) to WebClient, which derives the generated proxy class from WebServicesClientProtocol, as opposed to the default SoapClient class.
/protocol	The switch that overrides the default protocol from HTTP POST to SOAP, SOAP12, or HTTP GET.
/out:<directoryName>	The output directory to create files in. The default is the current directory. The short form is /o.

Here is how you generate an IDC file using wsdl.exe:

```
C:\> wsdl /server /o:StockTraderStub.cs StockTrader.wsdl StockTrader.xsd
```

Here is how you generate an IDC file using xsd.exe:

```
C:\> xsd StockTrader.xsd /c
```

■**Note** In order to use the wsdl.exe and xsd.exe command-line tools from any directory location on your computer, you will probably need to set an environment variable that points to the directory location of the utilities. On our computer we created a user environment variable called PATH with a value of c:\Program Files\Microsoft Visual Studio 8\SDK\v2.0\BIN. Alternatively, if you are using Visual Studio 2005, from the Programs menu group you can select Visual Studio 2005 Tools ➤ Visual Studio 2005 Command Prompt.

If you are following the steps in this chapter, your only option for generating an IDC file at this point is to partially generate it using xsd.exe and the XSD schema file. You have not yet defined the operations anywhere other than by design in the initial UML diagram in step 1. So your next step is to use the UML diagram to manually add abstract class definitions to the autogenerated IDC file. This is the approach we always take because it is far easier than the alternative, which is to generate WSDL by hand. Generating WSDL manually is prone to errors and takes far longer than it will take you to update a few lines in code, as is the case with the partially generated IDC file.

Implement the Interface Definition in the Web Service (Step 4)

Once the interface definitions are in place, the last remaining step is to implement them in the Web service code-behind. The first step is to derive the Web service class file from the interface definition; and the second step is to override the abstract methods, as shown in Listing 3-5.

Listing 3-5. *Deriving the Web Service .asmx Code-Behind Class from the Generated Interface Definition Class (StockTraderStub)*

```
// Step 1 (Before View): Implement the StockTraderStub class
[WebService(Namespace = "http://www.bluestonepartners.com/schemas/StockTrader")]
[WebServiceBinding(ConformsTo = WsiProfiles.BasicProfile1_1)]
public class StockTraderService : StockTraderStub
{
    // Contains abstract methods (not shown)
}

// Step 2 (After View): Override and implement each of the abstract class methods
[WebService(Namespace = "http://www.bluestonepartners.com/schemas/StockTrader")]
public class StockTraderService : StockTraderStub
{
    [WebMethod]
    [return: XmlElement(ElementName = "Quote",
        Namespace = "http://www.bluestonepartners.com/schemas/StockTrader/")]
    public override Quote RequestQuote(string Symbol)
    {
        // Implementation code goes here
    }
}
```

You need to set namespace names for both the Web service class and the interface definition classes. We usually include all classes within the same namespace, but there is no rule about this. If you do use different namespaces, then in the Web service class file you will need to import the namespace for the interface definition classes.

At this point everything is in place to complete the implementation of the Web service methods. All operations and types are fully described and ready to be referenced from the Web service class file. Listing 3-6 shows an example implementation of the PlaceTrade Web method, which places a trade order and returns the trade details in a custom object type called Trade.

Listing 3-6. *The PlaceTrade Web Method*

```
[WebMethod]
[SoapDocumentMethod(RequestNamespace=
    "http://www.bluestonepartners.com/schemas/StockTrader/",
    ResponseNamespace="http://www.bluestonepartners.com/schemas/StockTrader/",
    Use=SoapBindingUse.Literal, ParameterStyle=SoapParameterStyle.Bare)]
[return: XmlElement("Trade", Namespace=
```

```
    "http://www.bluestonepartners.com/schemas/StockTrader/")]
public override Trade PlaceTrade(string Account, string Symbol, int Shares, ➥
    System.Double Price, TradeType tradeType)
{
    Trade t = new Trade();
    t.TradeID = System.Guid.NewGuid().ToString();
    t.OrderDateTime = DateTime.Now.ToLongDateString();
    t.Symbol = Symbol;
    t.Shares = Shares;
    t.Price = Price;
    t.tradeType = tradeType;
    // Initialize the Trade to Ordered, using the TradeStatus enumeration
    t.tradeStatus = TradeStatus.Ordered;
    // Code Not Shown: Persist trade details to the database by account number
    // and trade ID, or to a message queue for later processing
    // Code goes here
    return t; // Return the Trade object
}
```

Notice that we have reapplied all of the XML and SOAP serialization attributes that were included in the IDC file. You need to do this to ensure that they take effect. Also notice the use of several custom types, including Trade (a complex type that stores the trade details), Trade-Type (an enumeration for the type of trade being executed), and TradeStatus (an enumeration for the current status of the trade).

Assuming that you have followed the steps so far, your Visual Studio 2005 Solution Explorer will look like Figure 3-5.

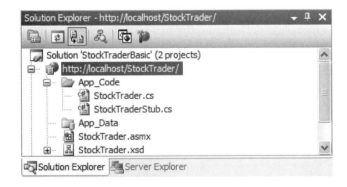

Figure 3-5. *The Visual Studio 2005 Solution Explorer showing the StockTrader Web service*

Messages vs. Types

The discussion so far has drawn a distinction between messages and types. For example, Figure 3-2 outlines a message called RequestQuote that returns a type called Quote. This begs the question as to why they are different. Why can't the IDC file treat the RequestQuote message as just another custom data type? This means you would need to include a custom class to represent RequestQuote, just as you create one to represent Quote.

This is not a trick question. The answer is that you can. There is no reason you cannot add a RequestQuote data type as its own custom class in the proxy stub file. To illustrate the distinction, Listing 3-7 shows you what this would look like. The listing is based on the shell of an autogenerated proxy stub file with different class signatures for RequestQuote and Quote. In addition, we have added a new custom data type for RequestQuote, shown in bold.

Listing 3-7. *A Proxy Stub File That Includes the RequestQuote Message As a Custom Data Type*

```
public abstract class StockTraderService : System.Web.Services.WebService
{
    public abstract Quote RequestQuote(string Symbol);
}

public class Quote
{
    // Quote properties not shown (e.g., Symbol, Open, Last, etc.)
}

public class RequestQuote
{
    public string Symbol;
}
```

Notice that the class signature for the RequestQuote operation contains no mention of the Quote object, which as you know is the output data type of the operation. It is not mentioned because the class signature reflects the input parameters only. Figure 3-6 shows a partial view of the StockTraderWithOperations.xsd schema file, which adds four additional complex types for each of the four supported Web service operations.

Not only is it legal to include separate class signatures for the Web service operations, but you will need to do so if you have to manually retrieve the SOAP message body for a requested operation. Chapter 8 reviews services that use the TCP protocol and a specialized class called the SoapReceiver, which manually deserializes an incoming SOAP request message. The deserialized message body is mapped to an instance of the RequestQuote class, so you need to have a defined class signature. (Otherwise, you will need to write custom XPath queries to extract the operation name and input parameter values.)

Chapter 9 is many pages and concepts away, so until we reach there, it will not be necessary to create separate class signatures for the Web service operations. And, unfortunately, the .NET Framework's WSDL generator will not be able to differentiate a message from a data type, unless you have implemented RequestQuote as a Web method in an .asmx file (to use just one example of a Web service operation). So for no other reason than convenience, you should continue creating .asmx code for each of the supported Web service operations. You can also start adding the operations to the associated XML schema file, so that they are there when you need them in the future. (The sample project for this chapter includes two versions of the StockTrader XML schema file: StockTrader.xsd and StockTraderWithOperations.xsd.)

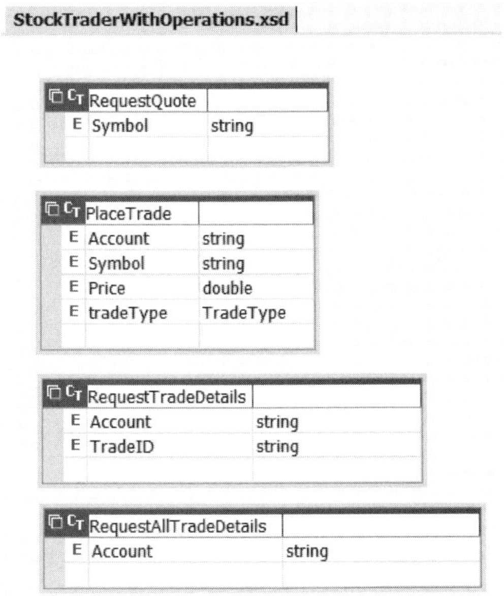

StockTraderWithOperations.xsd

$^{C}_{T}$ RequestQuote	
E Symbol	string

$^{C}_{T}$ PlaceTrade	
E Account	string
E Symbol	string
E Price	double
E tradeType	TradeType

$^{C}_{T}$ RequestTradeDetails	
E Account	string
E TradeID	string

$^{C}_{T}$ RequestAllTradeDetails	
E Account	string

Figure 3-6. *The Visual Studio 2005 XML Designer, showing the StockTraderWithOperations.xsd schema*

Consume the Web Service

The hard part of the development is done, as is much of the value-added material in this chapter. By now you should have a good understanding of how to approach the development process for message-oriented Web services. Visual Studio 2005 allows you to take shortcuts in the development process, but you need to avoid temptation and do the manual work that is required to create well-documented Web services.

Build the Web Service Consumer

The proxy class file provides synchronous and asynchronous invocation mechanisms for each of the Web service operations and derives from System.Web.Services.Protocols.SoapHttp-ClientProtocol. It also provides class definitions for the Web service types, just like the IDC file. The proxy file does not include abstract methods; it only includes implemented methods. So you do not have to implement every method that the proxy class file provides. In addition, the consumer class does not need to derive from the service proxy class. You simply create instances of the proxy class as needed.

Generate the Client Proxy Class File (Step 5)

You have done a lot of manual work to get to this point: You have manually created schema files and interface definitions, and you have implemented the operations as Web service methods. To generate a client proxy file, you can rely on the wsdl.exe utility to do the work for you in generating the proxy stub. The proxy file is similar to the IDC file in that it includes class definitions for types and operations. But it is derived from the System.Web.Services. Protocols.SoapHttpClientProtocol namespace, and its purpose is to provide a programmatic interface between the client and the Web service. The proxy class works with the underlying Web services infrastructure to make requests and receive responses using SOAP.

■**Note** You can ignore the material in this section if you use Visual Studio 2005 and work with the Add Web Reference Wizard. This wizard will automatically generate the proxy file for you, and you will not need to work directly with the WSDL document. Read this section only if you want to know what happens under the hood when you create a client proxy class file.

Assuming that you have completed the previous development steps correctly, your WSDL document will be in good shape, and you can trust that it accurately represents the messages and types that your Web service exchanges. You can use Visual Studio 2005 to generate the WSDL file.

To generate the WSDL document, right-click the StockTrader.asmx file and select the View in Browser menu option. Append ?WSDL to the end of the URI, as in

```
http://localhost/StockTrader.asmx?WSDL
```

The WSDL document will open in a new browser window. You can copy and paste the XML into Notepad and save it with a .wsdl file extension. You will need to edit this file in three ways:

- Remove dash characters from the WSDL browser view.

- Verify that the embedded type information (within the <types> tags) matches the type definitions within the XSD schema file you generated earlier.

- Remove the <service> element, which will bind the proxy to a static Web service location. (Instead, you will add a dynamic location to the client's configuration file.)

Listing 3-8 shows what the processed WSDL document will look like, assuming that RequestQuote is the only operation that the Web service supports.

Listing 3-8. *The WSDL Document for the StockTrader Web Service Filtered to Show All Elements Related to the RequestQuote Web Method*

```
<?xml version="1.0" encoding="utf-8" ?>
<definitions xmlns:http="http://schemas.xmlsoap.org/wsdl/http/"
    xmlns:soap="http://schemas.xmlsoap.org/wsdl/soap/"
    xmlns:s="http://www.w3.org/2001/XMLSchema"
```

```
    xmlns:s0="http://www.bluestonepartners.com/schemas/StockTrader/"
    xmlns:soapenc="http://schemas.xmlsoap.org/soap/encoding/"
    xmlns:tns="http://www.bluestonepartners.com/schemas/StockTrader"
    xmlns:tm="http://microsoft.com/wsdl/mime/textMatching/"
    xmlns:mime="http://schemas.xmlsoap.org/wsdl/mime/"
    targetNamespace="http://www.bluestonepartners.com/schemas/StockTrader"
    xmlns="http://schemas.xmlsoap.org/wsdl/">
<import namespace="http://www.bluestonepartners.com/schemas/StockTrader/"
    location="http://www.bluestonepartners.com/schemas/StockTrader.xsd" />
<types />
<message name="RequestQuoteSoapIn">
    <part name="Symbol" element="s0:Symbol" />
</message>
<message name="RequestQuoteSoapOut">
    <part name="RequestQuoteResult" element="s0:Quote" />
</message>
<portType name="StockTraderServiceSoap">
    <operation name="RequestQuote">
        <input message="tns:RequestQuoteSoapIn" />
        <output message="tns:RequestQuoteSoapOut" />
    </operation>
</portType>
<binding name="StockTraderServiceSoap" type="tns:StockTraderServiceSoap">
    <soap:binding transport="http://schemas.xmlsoap.org/soap/http"
      style="document" />
    <operation name="RequestQuote">
    <soap:operation
      soapAction="http://www.bluestonepartners.com/schemas/StockTrader/RequestQuote"
      style="document" />
        <input>
            <soap:body use="literal" />
        </input>
        <output>
            <soap:body use="literal" />
        </output>
    </operation>
</binding>
</definitions>
```

Notice that we are using the <import> tag to pull in the type definitions from the reference XSD schema file, which is qualified at http://www.bluestonepartners.com/schemas/, and which is physically located at http://www.bluestonepartners.com/schemas/StockTrader.xsd. We are using this tag in order to avoid reprinting the lengthy embedded type information. This approach does not technically invalidate the WSDL file, although it does put the file out of compliance with the WS-I Basic Profile, Rule R2001, which disallows the import of external XSD schema files as a substitute for embedded type information.

Next, run the wsdl.exe command-line utility to generate a client proxy file:

```
C:\> wsdl /o:StockTraderProxy.cs StockTrader.wsdl StockTrader.xsd
```

You can then add the proxy class file to the Web service consumer's project, as we will discuss in the next section.

Implement the Web Service Consumer (Step 6)

Listing 3-9 shows a sample of the autogenerated service proxy class.

Listing 3-9. *The Autogenerated Service Proxy Class*

```
[System.Web.Services.WebServiceBindingAttribute(Name="StockTraderServiceSoap",
    Namespace="http://www.bluestonepartners.com/schemas/StockTrader")]
public class StockTraderProxy : ➥
    System.Web.Services.Protocols.SoapHttpClientProtocol {

    public StockTraderProxy() {}

    [System.Web.Services.Protocols.SoapDocumentMethodAttribute(
        "http://www.bluestonepartners.com/schemas/StockTrader/RequestQuote",
        Use=System.Web.Services.Description.SoapBindingUse.Literal,
        ParameterStyle=System.Web.Services.Protocols.SoapParameterStyle.Bare)]
    [return: System.Xml.Serialization.XmlElementAttribute("Quote",
        Namespace="http://www.bluestonepartners.com/schemas/StockTrader/")]
    public Quote RequestQuote([System.Xml.Serialization.XmlElementAttribute(
      Namespace="http://www.bluestonepartners.com/schemas/StockTrader/")]
      string Symbol)
    {
      object[] results = this.Invoke("RequestQuote", new object[] {Symbol});
      return ((Quote)(results[0]));
    }

    public System.IAsyncResult BeginRequestQuote(string Symbol, ➥
        System.AsyncCallback callback, object asyncState)
    {
        return this.BeginInvoke("RequestQuote", new object[] { ➥
                Symbol}, callback, asyncState);
    }

    public Quote EndRequestQuote(System.IAsyncResult asyncResult)
    {
        object[] results = this.EndInvoke(asyncResult);
        return ((Quote)(results[0]));
    }
}
```

```
[System.Xml.Serialization.XmlTypeAttribute(
    Namespace="http://www.bluestonepartners.com/schemas/StockTrader/")]
public class Quote
{
    string Symbol;
    // Additional type definitions go here (not shown)
}
```

This class was entirely autogenerated by the wsdl.exe utility. The only modification we made was to change the autogenerated name of the proxy class from StockTraderService to our preferred name of StockTraderProxy.

Figure 3-7 shows the Visual Studio 2005 Solution Explorer as it appears when you add a consumer project to the same solution file as the StockTrader Web service. Note that this is done for convenience to make debugging the projects simpler. In reality, the Web service and the consumer projects would be located on separate servers, and likely in different domains.

Note This chapter does not provide specific instructions for how to create the consumer project, so please refer directly to the code samples that accompany this chapter.

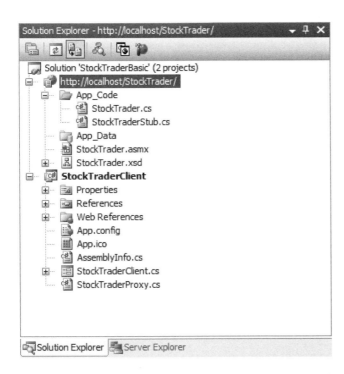

Figure 3-7. *The Visual Studio 2005 Solution Explorer shows the StockTrader Web service and the Web service consumer project.*

Figure 3-8 shows a form-based implementation of the consumer that allows you to receive stock quotes and place trades.

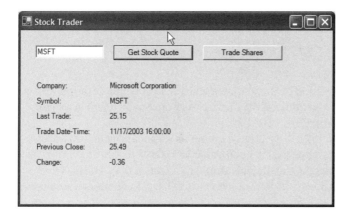

Figure 3-8. *A consumer application for the StockTrader Web service*

Listing 3-10 shows a sample of the implementation code behind the RequestQuote button.

Listing 3-10. *Web Service Consumer Code*

```
private void btnQuote_Click(object sender, System.EventArgs e)
{
    // Create an instance of the Web service proxy
    StockTraderProxy serviceProxy = new StockTraderProxy();

    // Retrieve the Web Service URI from app.config
    serviceProxy.Url = ConfigurationSettings.AppSettings["remoteHost"];

    // Call the Web service to request a quote
    Quote q = serviceProxy.RequestQuote(this.txtSymbol.Text);

    // Display the Quote results in the form
    this.lblCompany.Text = q.Company;
    this.lblSymbol.Text = q.Symbol;
    this.lblTradeDateTime.Text = q.DateTime;
    this.lblLastTrade.Text = q.Last.ToString();
    this.lblPreviousClose.Text = q.Previous_Close.ToString();
    this.lblChange.Text = q.Change.ToString();
}
```

Notice that the client code references a configuration element called <remoteHost> that provides the URI for the StockTrader Web service. It should be entered into the project's .config file as shown in Listing 3-11.

Listing 3-11. *The Web.config File for the Web Service Consumer*

```xml
<?xml version="1.0" encoding="utf-8" ?>
<configuration>
    <appSettings>
      <add key="remoteHost" value="http://localhost/StockTrader/StockTrader.asmx"/>
    </appSettings>
</configuration>
```

This concludes the discussion of how to build a basic message-oriented Web service.

Summary

The purpose of Web services is to exchange and process XML messages, not to act as simple endpoints for remote procedure calls. In this chapter, you learned a six-step process for designing and building a message-oriented Web service from scratch:

Step 1: Design the messages and the data types.

Step 2: Build the XSD schema file for the data types.

Step 3: Create a class file of interface definitions for the messages and data types.

Step 4: Implement the interface in the Web service code-behind file.

Step 5: Generate a proxy class file (for clients) based on the WSDL.

Step 6: Implement a Web service client using a proxy class file.

The goal of this chapter is to help you rethink your approach to Web services design so that you can start developing the type of message-oriented Web services that fit into an SOA framework.

CHAPTER 4

■ ■ ■

Design Patterns for Building Service-Oriented Web Services

Message-oriented Web services are the building blocks for service-oriented applications. In the previous chapter, you learned how message-oriented Web services are constructed, and what sets them apart from traditional RPC-style Web services. The main difference is that messages typically include complex types that are defined using custom XML schema files. Message-oriented Web services are effective at executing operations, whereby the input parameters feed into a process rather than dictating the process.

In contrast, procedure-style method calls are straightforward operations with a strong dependency on the input arguments. For example, the message-oriented StockTrader Web service provides a PlaceTrade operation that accepts the trade specifications, executes a complex trade operation, and then returns the details of the trade encapsulated in a complex data type (the Trade object). The simple input parameters trigger a complex operation and cause a complex type to be returned. There is no direct correlation between the input parameters and the complexity of the operation. In contrast, one example of a procedure-style Web method is a simple arithmetic Add operation that accepts two numeric input parameters. This Web method has nothing complicated happening internally, nor does it require that a complex data type be returned. What you get out of the method is directly correlated to what you send into it.

In this chapter, we need to make another conceptual leap, this time from message-oriented Web services to service-oriented Web services. Messages do not go away in this new architecture; they are just as important as ever. What is different is that Web services are not the central player in the architecture.

How to Build Service-Oriented Web Services

Service-oriented Web services act more as smart gateways for incoming service requests than as destinations in and of themselves. Let's revisit the complex SOA diagram from Chapter 1, reprinted here as Figure 4-1.

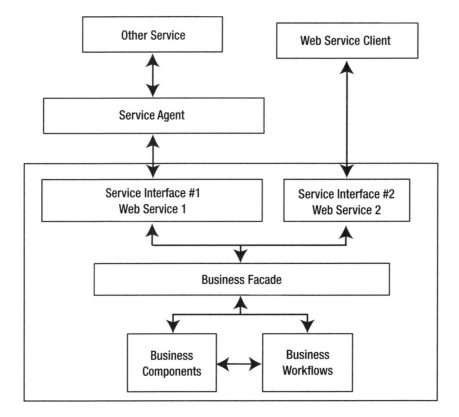

Figure 4-1. *Complex SOA*

Notice that Web services are not the ultimate endpoint destinations in this architecture. Instead, their purpose is to authenticate and authorize incoming service requests, and then to relay the request details to back-end business components and workflows for processing. This fact by no means diminishes the importance of their role; it just switches perspectives. Web services have certain unique properties that make them essential to this architecture:

- Web services process SOAP messages.

- Web services provide accessible (and discoverable) endpoints for service requests.

- Web services (optionally) authenticate and authorize incoming service requests. In this role they selectively filter incoming service requests and keep out unauthorized requests. (This feature is technically optional but it is an important available feature with WSE 3.0, and so is listed here as an essential property).

In contrast, other components in the architecture, such as the business components, do not have any of these properties. They do not expose publicly accessible endpoints. They do not process SOAP requests directly. And they do not have the same ability to filter out incoming service requests based on security tokens. Note that business components can implement custom security checks through mechanisms such as code access security (CAS) and Active Directory checks, but these options are not comparable to the available mechanisms for Web services, which can accept encrypted and signed requests, and which inspect several aspects of the request directly, not just the identity of the caller.

So we have established that Web services play a unique role in SOA, one where they are an important support player rather than the ultimate destination endpoint. But what does this translate to in practical terms, and how is it different from before? The implication is that you need to build Web services differently to maximize the effectiveness of their role in SOA applications. This includes the following:

A renewed emphasis on breaking out Web service code-behind into separate class files and assemblies: This includes abstract IDC files (based on the applicable WSDL document). It also includes generating a dedicated assembly for encapsulating custom data type definitions (so that common data types may be used across multiple services and components using a common reference assembly).

Delegation of all business process logic to back-end business components: The Web service code-behind should be focused exclusively on preprocessing incoming request messages and then relaying the request details to the appropriate back-end business component. The Web service code-behind should not handle any business processing directly.

A focus on new kinds of service-oriented components: SOA architecture creates a need for different kinds of service components that may have no equivalent in other architectures. For example, SOA applications rely heavily on service agent components, which act as the middleman between separate Web services and which relay all communications between them. (You will learn how to build a service agent component in the section "Design and Build a Service Agent" later in this chapter.)

Be forewarned: some of the material in this chapter may strike you as unusual or unorthodox and certainly more complex than you are used to seeing with Web services development. This is not surprising given that SOA applications are still relatively new. Recall that it took several years for the *n*-tier architecture model to become fully formed and to gain wide acceptance as a standard. SOA will also go through an evolution. Some ideas will gain acceptance, while others will fall by the wayside. This chapter quite likely contains some of both, so read the chapter, absorb the material, and take with you as much or as little as you like.

The primary requirement that SOA imposes on a system is that its business functionality must be accessible through more than one type of interface and through more than one kind of transport protocol. Enterprise developers have long understood the need to separate out business functionality into a dedicated set of components. In Chapter 3, the StockTrader Web service implemented its business logic directly, based on an IDC file (defined in a separate, though embedded, class file). This approach is incorrect from an SOA perspective for two reasons:

Web services should not implement business logic directly in their methods: They should delegate this processing to dedicated business assemblies. This is because you cannot assume that the business logic will always be accessed through a Web service. What happens, for example, when a new requirement comes through asking you to implement an alternate interface that cannot or will not interact with a Web service? You need to have a separate, ready-to-use assembly for the business logic.

Web services and their associated WSDL documents should not be the original reference points for interface definitions: Certainly, a WSDL document must conform to an established interface definition, but it should not be establishing what that definition is. This information belongs in a dedicated reference assembly, and should be stored as an interface definition that can be implemented in different kinds of components.

The previous version of the StockTrader Web service is not compatible with SOA because it prevents common functionality from being accessible via multiple interfaces. To put it in blunt terms, the StockTrader Web service is simply incompatible with SOA because it is not abstract enough. What it needs to do instead is to act as a trusted interface to a back-end StockTrader business component. It cannot directly contain implementation for the Stock-Trader functions (such as getting quotes and placing trades). Instead, it must delegate this functionality to a back-end business component and focus on its primary role of authenticating and authorizing incoming service requests and then relaying these service requests to the back-end business component. In conjunction to this, the Web service is also responsible for relaying responses back to the client.

Consider another aspect to this architecture: type definitions. If you separate out common functionality across multiple components, how do they maintain a common understanding of type definitions? For example, how does every component maintain the same understanding of the Quote and Trade data types? XML Web services and their clients can share XSD schema information for custom data types via the service's published WSDL document. But this is not an efficient way to share type information between a middle-tier business component and a Web service, especially when the Web service is delegating requests to the business component. The more efficient approach is to generate a dedicated assembly that encapsulates the data type definitions as custom classes, and to include a reference to this assembly from wherever the custom data types are needed.

I have covered several challenging conceptual points, so now let's move on to code, and actually build a service-oriented Web service. Figure 4-2 is an architecture (and pseudo-UML diagram) that provides an alternate architecture for the original StockTrader Web service, one that will enable it to participate better in a larger SOA. Notice that the type definitions and interface definitions have been broken out into a separate assembly called StockTraderTypes, which is referenced by several components in the architecture.

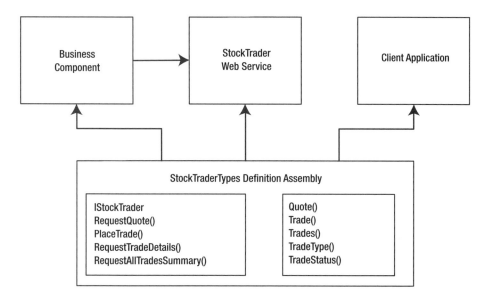

Figure 4-2. *Revised architecture for the StockTrader Web service showing how several components reference the common StockTraderTypes definition assembly*

Based on this UML diagram, there are six steps involved in building a message-oriented Web service that is compatible with SOA.

Step 1: Create a Dedicated Type Definition Assembly

Create a dedicated definition assembly for interfaces and type definitions. This assembly will be referenced by any component, service, or application that needs to use the interfaces or types.

Step 2: Create a Dedicated Business Assembly

Create a dedicated business assembly that implements logic for established interfaces and type definitions. This business assembly must reference the definition assembly from step 1. This ensures that the business assembly implements every available method definition.

Once this step is complete, you have the flexibility to build any kind of *n*-tier solution using the definition and business assemblies. This chapter focuses on building a service-oriented application that includes a Web service. But you could just as easily go a different route and build any kind of *n*-tier solution using the definition and business assemblies developed so far.

This point underscores the fact that in an SOA, Web services are simply a gateway to a set of methods and types that are controlled by other assemblies. The Web service itself merely provides a set of SOAP-enabled endpoints that are accessible over one or more transport protocols.

Step 3: Create the Web Service Based on the Type Definition Assembly

In the previous version of the StockTrader Web service, the definition information for the Web method implementations came from a dedicated IDC file, which provided abstract class definitions and class-based type definitions. But now this file is no longer needed because you have a dedicated definition assembly. The new Web service simply needs to import the definition assembly to have access to the required types and to the required interface.

Step 4: Implement the Business Interface in the Web Service

The Web service needs to import the business assembly so that it can delegate incoming service requests. Remember, the current architecture calls for a different level of abstraction, whereby the Web service itself does not control its interface, its data types, or the processing of business logic. Instead, it relies on other assemblies for this reference information and for this processing capability.

By implementing the interface, you ensure that you will not miss any methods because the project will not compile unless every interface method is implemented in the Web service. So, the definition assembly provides the interface definition, while the business assembly provides the processing capability for each method. All incoming Web service requests should be delegated to the business component, rather than implementing the business logic directly in the Web service.

The methods in this class file must be decorated with any required reflection attributes, such as WebMethod and SoapDocumentMethod. You always had to do this, so this is not new. But there is added importance now because many of these attributes will not be decorated elsewhere. Or if they are, they will not propagate to your class file. For example, the SoapDocumentMethod attributes are not included in the interface definition assembly (although the XML serialization attributes are). These attributes are not automatically carried over to the class file when it implements the definition assembly. As a matter of practice, we make sure that the interface definition assembly is decorated with the required serialization attributes, but we leave out attributes that relate to WebService and WebMethod attributes. This approach is implementation agnostic, meaning that it makes no assumptions about what kind of class file will implement the interface definition assembly.

■**Note** Reflection attributes provide additional metadata for your code. The .NET runtime uses this metadata for executing the code. Class members are said to be decorated with attributes. Reflection attributes are a powerful tool because they enable the same code listing to be processed in different ways, depending on how it is decorated. Chapter 3 has a more complete discussion of reflection attributes, and Table 3-1 provides detailed property descriptions for the SoapDocumentMethod attribute.

Step 5: Generate a Web Service Proxy Class File Based on the WSDL Document

Proxy class files can still be generated directly from the Web service WSDL document, so this step does not have to change with a revised architecture in order to still work. However, the autogenerated proxy class file will not automatically utilize the dedicated definition assembly. This creates a significant issue because the proxy class file maintains its own type and interface definitions. Your goal is to have a central repository for this information. So in the interest of type fidelity, you need to modify the autogenerated proxy file to utilize the definition assembly rather than a separate copy of the same information.

Separate copies can be modified, and there is nothing to stop you from altering a proxy file so that it can no longer call the Web service it is intended for. This is why it is good to derive all types and interfaces from a common source.

Step 6: Create a Web Service Client

The Web service client uses the generated proxy class file from step 5 to set a reference to the new Web service. The client must also reference the type definition assembly from step 1, so that both the client and the Web service have a common understanding of the data types that are used by the Web services and its associated business assembly.

Some readers may see a red flag here because this approach creates a very tight coupling between the client and the Web service due to their mutual dependence on the same reference assembly. In contrast, it would be much easier to create a loosely coupled client that autogenerates a proxy file itself, using the Web service WSDL document. This autogenerated proxy file would include both methods and data types, so it would deviate from the more abstract approach that we are presenting here—namely, the approach of separating type definitions and method definitions into a dedicated assembly.

I am not advocating that you should always enforce this level of tight coupling between a Web service and its client. By definition, Web services are loosely coupled to their clients. This alternate approach is simply that—an alternate approach that can be implemented if the scenario is appropriate. In some cases, this approach will not even be feasible because the client may not have access to a dedicated assembly. But this approach may be warranted in other cases, particularly when you have a sensitive business workflow and you want to prevent any kind of miscommunication between a service and a client.

So, as with all the material in this book, absorb the information, consider the different approaches, but then decide which approach is most appropriate for your business requirements.

Design and Build a Service-Oriented Web Service

This section provides the information that you need to build a message-oriented Web service for use in an SOA. It is organized along the same six steps presented earlier and provides both conceptual information and implementation information.

Create the Definition Assembly (Step 1)

The definition assembly provides two important sets of information:

- Class definitions for all custom types that are exchanged in the system

- Interface definitions for each operation that the system supports

In this sense it is not unlike the autogenerated IDC file from Chapter 3. Recall that the type information in this file (StockTraderStub.cs) is autogenerated from an XSD schema file using the xsd.exe tool. The operations are manually inserted as abstract class methods that must be overridden by whatever class implements this file.

There are two differences between the definition assembly and the IDC file:

The operations are documented as interfaces rather than abstract class methods. This is because a given class can only derive from one other class at a time. Web service classes, for example, must derive either directly or indirectly from the System.Web.Services. WebService class. The Web service class cannot implement an additional interface unless it is provided as an invariant interface.

The definition assembly does not include Web service and SOAP-related attribute decorations. This is because it will be referenced from a variety of different assemblies, some of which have nothing to do with Web services. However, the definition assembly can still include XML serialization attributes.

Figure 4-3 shows a UML class diagram for the definition assembly. Notice the following two important points:

1. The type definitions are encapsulated in dedicated classes (e.g., Quote).

2. The method definitions are contained within an interface class called IStockTrader.

It is possible for a client project to reference the StockTraderTypes assembly solely for the purpose of accessing the custom data type definitions. The client does not need to implement the interface class, just because it is included in the assembly. But of course if they do, they will be required to implement every member of the interface.

To create the definition assembly, start by creating a new Class Library project in Visual Studio 2005 called StockTraderTypes, and add to it a single class file also called StockTraderTypes.

Listing 4-1 shows high-level pseudocode for the StockTraderTypes definition assembly.

Listing 4-1. *Pseudocode Listing for the StockTraderTypes Definition Assembly*

```
namespace StockTraderTypes
{
    public interface IStockTrader {}
    public class Quote {}
    public class Trade {}
    public class Trades {}
    public enum TradeStatus {}
    public enum TradeTypes {}
}
```

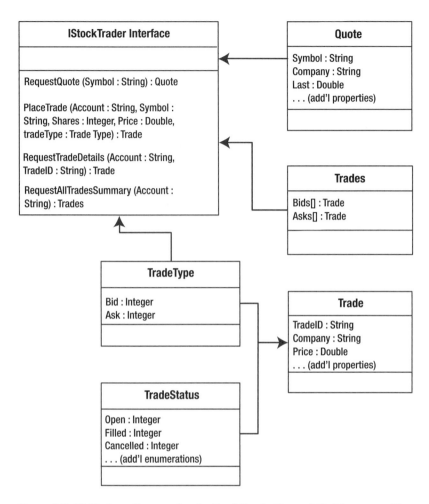

Figure 4-3. *UML class diagram for the StockTraderTypes definition assembly*

Listing 4-2 presents a more detailed code listing, excluding XML serialization attributes. These attributes are important because they directly relate the code elements to XML elements in the associated XSD schema (which is assigned to a qualified namespace at http:// www.bluestonepartners.com/schemas/StockTrader/).

Listing 4-2. *Detailed Code Listing for the StockTraderTypes Definition Assembly*

```
using System;
using System.Xml.Serialization;

namespace StockTraderTypes
 {
  public interface IStockTrader
  {
    Quote RequestQuote(string Symbol);
```

```
    Trade PlaceTrade(string Account, string Symbol, int Shares, ➥
        System.Double   Price, TradeType tradeType);
    Trade RequestTradeDetails(string Account, string TradeID);
    Trades RequestAllTradesSummary(string Account);
}

public class Quote
{
  public string Symbol;
  public string Company; // Additional type members not shown
}

public class Trade
{
  public string TradeID;
  public string Symbol; // Additional type members not shown
}

public class Trades
{
  public string Account;
  public Trade[] Bids;
  public Trade[] Asks;
}

public enum TradeStatus
{
  Ordered,
  Filled, // Additional type members not shown
}

public enum TradeType
{
  Bid,
  Ask
}

}
```

This is all the work that is required to create a definition assembly that can be reused across other components, services, and applications.

Create the Business Assembly (Step 2)

The business assembly implements the IStockTrader interface that is defined in the Stock-TraderTypes definition assembly. This logic was previously implemented directly in the Web service class file. But this design is very limiting because it isolates the business logic inside a specialized class file. The business assembly provides a standard middle-tier component that can be referenced and invoked by a wide variety of consumers, not just Web services.

Creating the business assembly requires three steps:

1. Create a new Class Library project in Visual Studio 2005 called StockTraderBusiness, and add to it a single class file also called StockTraderBusiness.

2. Set a reference to the StockTraderTypes assembly. For now you can create all projects in the same solution, and then set a reference to the StockTraderTypes project (from the Projects tab in the Add Reference dialog box).

3. Import the StockTraderTypes namespace into the StockTraderBusiness class file and implement the IStockTrader class. Implement code for each of the interface operations. You will get compiler errors if you attempt to build the solution without implementing all of the operations.

Listing 4-3 displays the pseudocode listing for the StockTraderBusiness business assembly.

Listing 4-3. *Pseudocode Listing for the StockTraderBusiness Business Assembly*

```
using System;
using StockTraderTypes;

namespace StockTraderBusiness
{

  public class StockTraderBusiness : StockTraderTypes.IStockTrader
  {
    public Quote RequestQuote(string Symbol)
    {
        // Implementation code not shown
    }
    public Trade PlaceTrade(string Account, string Symbol, int Shares, ➡
        System.Double Price, TradeType tradeType)
    {
        // Implementation code not shown
    }
    public Trade RequestTradeDetails(string Account, string TradeID)
    {
        // Implementation code not shown
    }
    public Trades RequestAllTradesSummary(string Account)
    {
        // Implementation code not shown
    }
  }

}
```

The business assembly is the sole location for implemented business logic and the final destination for incoming service requests. The previous listing looks very spare because it does not show the implementation code for any of the methods. You can refer to the sample project to view the full code listing. Very little implementation code is shown in this chapter because it is of secondary importance. It is more important that you feel comfortable with the interfaces and the architecture of the components.

Create the Web Service (Steps 3–5)

The previous version of the StockTrader Web service implemented an IDC file for operations and types. This file is no longer needed because the same information is now provided by the definition assembly.

Create a new Web service project named StockTraderContracts in the Visual Studio 2005 solution, and rename the .asmx file to StockTraderContracts. Use the Add Reference dialog box to set references to the StockTraderBusiness and StockTraderTypes assemblies.

Listing 4-4 displays the pseudocode listing for the StockTraderContracts Web service.

Listing 4-4. *Pseudocode Listing for the StockTraderContracts Web Service*

```
using System.Web;
using System.Web.Services;
using System.Web.Services.Protocols;
using System.Web.Services.Description;

using StockTraderTypes;
using StockTraderBusiness;

namespace StockTrader
{

    public class StockTrader : System.Web.Services.WebService, ➥
        StockTraderTypes.IStockTrader
    {

    [WebMethod]
    [SoapDocumentMethod(RequestNamespace= ➥
        "http://www.bluestonepartners.com/schemas/StockTrader/",
        ResponseNamespace="http://www.bluestonepartners.com/schemas/StockTrader/",
        Use=SoapBindingUse.Literal, ParameterStyle=SoapParameterStyle.Bare)]
    [return: System.Xml.Serialization.XmlElement("Quote", Namespace=
        "http://www.bluestonepartners.com/schemas/StockTrader/")]
    public Quote RequestQuote(string Symbol)
    {
        // Implementation code not shown
    }
     [WebMethod]
    //XML and SOAP serialization attributes not shown
    public Trade PlaceTrade(string Account, string Symbol, int Shares, ➥
```

```
          System.Double Price, TradeType tradeType)
     {
          // Implementation code not shown
     }
      [WebMethod]
     //XML and SOAP serialization attributes not shown
     public Trade RequestTradeDetails(string Account, string TradeID)
     {
          // Implementation code not shown
     }
      [WebMethod]
     //XML and SOAP serialization attributes not shown
     public Trades RequestAllTradesSummary(string Account)
     {
          // Implementation code not shown
     }

     }

}
```

The Web service methods no longer implement their own business logic. Instead, every method must delegate incoming requests to the business assembly. For example, Listing 4-5 shows how the RequestQuote Web method delegates an incoming service request to the RequestQuote method in the business assembly.

Listing 4-5. *Delegation in the RequestQuote Web Method*

```
[WebMethod]
// XML and SOAP attributes not shown
public Quote RequestQuote(string Symbol)
{
     StockTraderBusiness b = new StockTraderBusiness();
     Quote q = b.RequestQuote(Symbol);
     return q;
}
```

The code is extremely simple because the Web service and the business assembly share the same type definitions and implement the same interface. The communication between the parties is seamless because they share a common vocabulary.

Figure 4-4 shows the Solution Explorer window for the project, with the References nodes expanded so that you can see how the assembly references are configured in each of the projects: StockTraderTypes, StockTraderBusiness, and StockTraderContracts. In addition, this figure includes the client console application, StockTraderConsole, which is described in step 6.

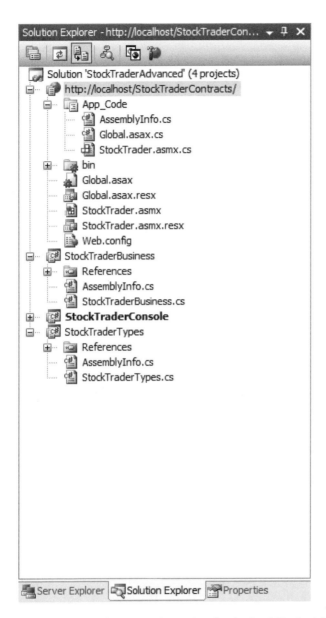

Figure 4-4. *The Solution Explorer view for the StockTraderAdvanced solution*

Create the Web Service Client (Step 6)

In this example, you are going to see how to build a tightly coupled Web service client that references the same definition assembly as the Web service itself. But as we clarified earlier, it is often advisable to implement a loosely coupled Web service client, whereby the client generates its own proxy file based on the Web service WSDL document and its associated XSD schemas. In fact, SOA promotes loose coupling between Web services and consumers.

As we stated earlier, our purpose in building a tightly coupled Web service client is to show you an alternate approach to building clients. In some cases, you will want to build a tightly coupled Web service client in order to prevent any miscommunication or misunderstanding between the Web service and its client as to what methods and types are supported. Certainly, type definitions can change, and so tight coupling can add an additional burden to the developer of the client. However, WSDL definitions can also change just as easily, and there is no clear way for a Web service to communicate interface changes to its clients.

Ultimately, we advocate the design approach of loose coupling between a Web service and its clients. The alternative tightly coupled approach that we are presenting here simply has the Web service itself referencing a type definition assembly and delegating all of its business logic to a dedicated business assembly. Technically, this is tight coupling between the Web service and client, as opposed to the traditional loose coupling between client and service, where the proxy class is generated as needed based on the current Web service WSDL specification. The material in this chapter provides everything you need to understand and implement both loosely coupled and tightly coupled designs. We will look at both approaches next.

Build a Loosely Coupled Web Service Client

Add a new console application named StockTraderConsole to the Visual Studio 2005 solution, and then do one of the following:

- Generate the proxy class manually with the wsdl.exe command-line utility applied to the Web service WSDL document.

- Use the Add Reference wizard in Visual Studio 2005 to automatically generate the proxy class in the client project.

Once you have generated the proxy class, you simply reference it directly from the client code, as shown in Listing 4-6.

Listing 4-6. *Web Service Consumer Code*

```
// Create an instance of the Web service proxy
StockTraderProxy serviceProxy = new StockTraderProxy();

// Retrieve the Web Service URI from app.config
serviceProxy.Url = ConfigurationSettings.AppSettings["remoteHost"];

// Call the Web service to request a quote
Quote q = serviceProxy.RequestQuote("MSFT");

// Display the Quote results in the form
Console.WriteLn("\t:Company:\t " + q.Company);
Console.WriteLn("\t:Symbol:\t " + q.Symbol);
Console.WriteLn("\t:Last:\t " + q.Last.ToString());
Console.WriteLn("\t:Prev Close:\t " + q.Previous_Close.ToString());
```

For more information on building loosely coupled clients, please refer to Chapter 3.

Build a Tightly Coupled Web Service Client

Autogenerated proxy class files are completely self-contained and essentially provide the client with a separate local copy of the interface and type definitions that the Web service supports. If the Web service interface changes, the client will not automatically pick up on these changes unless they clear the existing Web reference and regenerate the proxy class. You can manage this risk by modifying the autogenerated proxy class to conform to the standard interface and type definitions that are contained in the StockTraderTypes assembly.

Add a new console application project named StockTraderConsole to the Visual Studio 2005 solution file and copy over the proxy class file from the previous chapter's StockTrader Web service. Alternatively, you can autogenerate the proxy class from within the StockTrader-Console project as follows:

Step 1: Use the Add Web Reference Wizard to autogenerate the proxy class for the StockTraderContracts Web service at `http://localhost/StockTraderContracts/StockTrader.asmx`.

Step 2: The autogenerated proxy class file is called Reference.cs and is stored in the solution under the Web References\[Reference Name]\Reference.map subproject folder. (If you do not see this file, you can use the Project ➤ Show All Files menu option to expand all files.)

Step 3: Open the Reference.cs file and copy the entire code listing over to a new C# class file called StockConsoleProxy.cs.

Rename the proxy class file to StockConsoleProxy, and then do the following:

Step 1: Add a reference from the StockTraderConsole project to the StockTraderTypes assembly.

Step 2: In the StockConsoleProxy class, import the StockTraderTypes namespace and add the IStockTrader interface to the StockConsoleProxy interface list immediately following SoapHttpClientProtocol.

Step 3: Comment out all of the type definitions in the StockConsoleProxy class. These include Quote, Trade, Trades, TradeType, and TradeStatus. They are now redundant because the definition assembly contains the same type definitions.

The pseudocode for the proxy class now reads as shown in Listing 4-7 (modifications from the previous, or autogenerated, proxy classes are shown in bold).

Listing 4-7. *The Proxy Class for the StockTraderContracts Web Service, Modified to Reference the Type Definition Assembly StockTraderTypes*

```
using System.Web.Services;
using System.Web.Services.Protocols;

using StockTraderTypes;
```

```
[System.Web.Services.WebServiceBindingAttribute(Name="StockTraderServiceSoap",
    Namespace="http://www.bluestonepartners.com/schemas/StockTrader")]
public class StockConsoleProxy : SoapHttpClientProtocol, ➥
    StockTraderTypes.IStockTrader
{

    // Pseudo-code only: implementations and attributes are not shown
    public Quote RequestQuote() {}
    public System.IAsyncResult BeginRequestQuote() {}
    public System.IAsyncResult EndRequestQuote() {}

    // Additional operations are not shown
    // These include PlaceTrade(), RequestTradeDetails(),
    // and RequestAllTradesSummary()

    // Type definitions are commented out of the proxy class
    // because they are redundant to the type definition assembly
    // These include Quote, Trade, Trades, TradeType, and TradeStatus

}
```

These are trivial modifications because the proxy class already implements all of the IStockTrader interface members. The benefit of explicitly adding the IStockTrader interface is to ensure that the proxy class remains constrained in the way it implements the StockTrader operations. You could modify the proxy class in many other ways, but as long as the Stock-Trader operations remain untouched (interfacewise at least), the client application will compile successfully.

Once the proxy class has been modified, the client code can be implemented in the console application. The StockTraderTypes namespace must be imported into the client class file so that the client can make sense of the type definitions. No additional steps are required to use the definitions assembly. Listing 4-8 shows the client code listing for calling the RequestQuote operation.

Listing 4-8. *Client Code Listing for Calling the RequestQuote Operation*

```
using StockTraderTypes;

namespace StockTraderConsole2
{
class StockTraderConsole2
{

[STAThread]
static void Main(string[] args)
{
StockTraderConsole2 client = new StockTraderConsole2();
client.Run();
}
```

```
public void Run()
{
// Create an instance of the Web service proxy
StockConsoleProxy serviceProxy = new StockConsoleProxy();

// Configure the proxy
serviceProxy.Url = ConfigurationSettings.AppSettings["remoteHost"];

// Submit the request to the service
Console.WriteLine("Calling {0}", serviceProxy.Url);
string Symbol = "MSFT";
Quote q = serviceProxy.RequestQuote(Symbol);

// Display the response
Console.WriteLine("Web Service Response:");
Console.WriteLine("");
Console.WriteLine( "\tSymbol:\t\t" + q.Symbol );
Console.WriteLine( "\tCompany:\t" + q.Company );
Console.WriteLine( "\tLast Price:\t" + q.Last );
Console.WriteLine( "\tPrevious Close:\t" + q.Previous_Close );
}


}
}
```

Figure 4-5 displays a client console application that interfaces to the StockTraderContracts Web service using the modified proxy class. Please refer to the sample application (available from the Source Code/Download section of the Apress web site at http://www.apress.com) for full code listings.

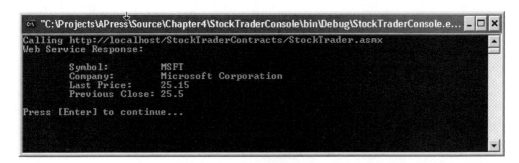

Figure 4-5. *Client console application for the StockTraderContracts Web service*

This concludes the overview of how to build a tightly coupled Web service client. Again, we would like to emphasize that this approach is not consistent with a pure SOA environment where the clients remain completely decoupled from the Web services they consume. However, it is always useful to consider alternative approaches and to realize new possibilities even if they never make it into a production environment.

Next, we will discuss a type of component that is unique to the service-oriented environment: the service agent.

Design and Build a Service Agent

Service agent components are essentially translator components that act as the intermediary between a business component and an external Web service. By *external*, we mean external to the domain where the business object is located. Service agents were discussed in some detail in Chapter 1 and are included in Figure 4-1 in this chapter. Briefly, the purpose of a service agent is to eliminate complexity in a business component by managing all interactions with an external service. If service agents did not exist, the business component would need to implement proxy classes and all of the associated error handling logic for working with external services. Clearly, this adds an undesirable layer of code and complexity to the business component that is superfluous because the business client will never call this code directly.

For example, consider Company A, which has built a business component that processes stock trades and provides stock quotes. In order to provide this functionality, the business component uses an external Web service that is provided by a premier brokerage company, Company B. Company A uses its own custom data types, which are encapsulated in the Stock-TraderTypes assembly. Company B, however, defines its own data types that are equivalent but not the same as Company A's. For example, Company A uses a Quote data type that defines a property called Open, for the day's opening share price. Company B uses a Quote data type that defines an equivalent property called Open_Ext. Company A uses strings for all of its custom data type properties, whereas Company B uses a mix of strings, floats, and dates.

Given these differences, Company A's service agent will perform two important functions:

1. It will implement the infrastructure that is required to communicate with Company B's external service. It will be responsible for the maintenance work that will be required if the external service updates its interface.

2. It will translate the responses from the external service and will relay them back to Company A's business component using a mutually understood interface.

The benefits of a service agent are clear: the service agent eliminates complexity for Service A's business component because it encapsulates all of the implementation details for interacting with the Web service and relays the requests back in the format that the business component wants. Figure 4-6 provides a schematic representation of this architecture.

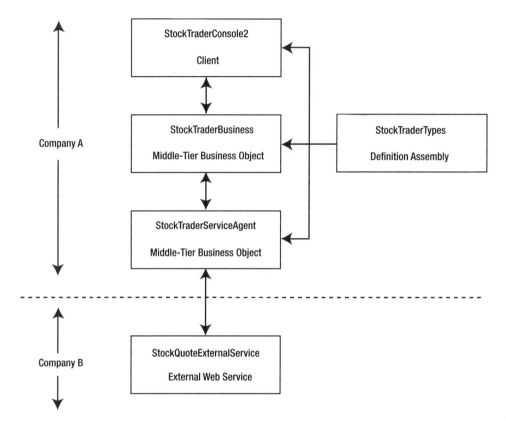

Figure 4-6. *SOA with a service agent*

Now let's look at how you implement this architecture in code.

Implement the StockTrader SOA Application Using a Service Agent

The StockTrader Web service has evolved in this chapter to where it delegates all requests to a business assembly (StockTraderBusiness). If a client contacts the Web service to request a stock quote, the Web service delegates the request to the business object's RequestQuote method. The Web service does not know or care how this method returns a stock quote, but it does expect to receive one every time it makes a request.

For the next evolution of the StockTrader Web service, your company signs a partnership agreement with another company that is a premier provider of stock quotes. You decide that going forward the StockTraderBusiness assembly will delegate all stock quote requests to this external service. The StockTrader Web service will continue to delegate requests to the business assembly, but the business assembly, in turn, will delegate the requests again, this time to an external Web service. You decide to build a service agent to minimize any change to the business assembly. Figure 4-7 shows the Solution Explorer for the solution that you are going to build, with selective References nodes expanded so you can see the relationships between the different components.

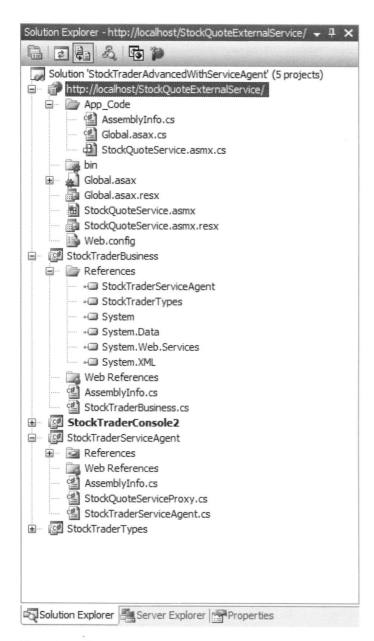

Figure 4-7. *Solution Explorer for the StockTrader SOA application, including a service agent*

The five components in this application are as follows:

1. *StockTraderConsole2*: The client application, providing a user interface

2. *StockTraderBusiness*: The middle-tier business component that handles processing for the client

3. *StockTraderServiceAgent*: The service agent used by the business component for communicating with external services

4. *StockTraderTypes*: The common type definition assembly, which is referenced by the three preceding components

5. *StockQuoteExternalService*: The external Web service

If this gets confusing, you can consult either Figure 4-6 or Figure 4-7, which include all five of these components. Let's look at how to build each component in turn, going from bottom to top, in the order of the service request workflow, starting with the external StockQuoteExternalService Web service.

The External Web Service (StockQuoteExternalService)

StockQuoteExternalService is a simple Web service that provides a single Web method for requesting stock quotes (RequestQuoteExt), and it returns its own equivalent to the StockTraderTypes.Quote type, which is named QuoteExt. The Quote and QuoteExt types are equivalent, but they differ from each other in three ways:

1. The QuoteExt type conforms to a different qualified namespace from the Quote type. Each type conforms to its own XSD schema file.

2. The QuoteExt type does not contain equivalents to the Quote type's Change and Percent_Change properties.

3. The QuoteExt type provides a time stamp property named DateTime_Ext, which is of type System.DateTime. The Quote type provides an equivalent time stamp property named DateTime that is of type String.

These are admittedly minor differences, but they illustrate the point. When you call an external service, it is unlikely that their type definitions will be equivalent to yours. You have to be prepared for some manual work to translate the differences.

In real life, of course, you would not have to create the external service yourself, but for the purposes of this demonstration you do.

The Service Agent (StockTraderServiceAgent)

The service agent implements the same interface and type definitions as the business assembly by referencing the StockTraderTypes assembly (as shown in Figure 4-6). The service agent also includes a proxy class for the StockQuoteExternalService external Web service.

Listing 4-9 shows the code listing for the service agent, including the complete listing for its RequestQuote method.

Listing 4-9. *The StockTraderServiceAgent Code Listing*

```
using System;
using StockTraderTypes;

namespace StockTraderServiceAgent
{
    public class StockTraderServiceAgent : StockTraderTypes.IStockTrader
    {
    public StockTraderServiceAgent(){}

    public Quote RequestQuote(string Symbol)
    {
        Quote q = null;

        // Request a Quote from the external service
        QuoteExt qe;
        StockQuoteService serviceProxy = new StockQuoteService();
        qe = serviceProxy.RequestQuoteExt("MSFT");

        // Create a local Quote object (from the StockTraderTypes namespace)
        q = new Quote();

        // Map the external QuoteExt object to the local Quote object
        // This requires some manual work because the types
        // do not map exactly to each other
        q.Symbol = Symbol;
        q.Company = qe.Company_Ext;
        q.DateTime = qe.DateTime_Ext.ToString("mm/dd/yyyy hh:mm:ss");
        q.High = qe.High_Ext;
        q.Low = qe.Low_Ext;
        q.Open = qe.Open_Ext;
        q.Last = qe.Last_Ext;
        q.Previous_Close = qe.Previous_Close_Ext;
        q.Change = (qe.Last_Ext - qe.Open_Ext);
        q.PercentChange = q.Change/q.Last;
        q.High_52_Week = qe.High_52_Week_Ext;
        q.Low_52_Week = qe.Low_52_Week_Ext;

        return q;
    }

    public Trade PlaceTrade(string Account, string Symbol, int Shares, ➥
        Double Price, TradeType tradeType)
    {
        // Implementation not shown
    }
```

```
    public Trades RequestAllTradesSummary(string Account)
    {
        // Implementation not shown
    }

    public Trade RequestTradeDetails(string Account, string TradeID)
    {
        // Implementation not shown
    }


    }
}
```

The code listing is very straightforward and shows how the service agent delegates its RequestQuote method to the external service's RequestQuoteExt method. The service agent performs some manual translations to map between its native Quote type and the external QuoteExt type. Finally, the agent returns a native Quote object to the consuming application, which in this case is the business assembly.

The Business Assembly (StockTraderBusiness)

The business component sets references to both the service agent assembly and the definition assembly of custom types. Listing 4-10 shows how the business component calls the service agent.

Listing 4-10. *The StockTrader Business Component Calling the Service Agent*

```
using System;
using StockTraderTypes;
using StockTraderServiceAgent;

namespace StockTraderBusiness
{
    public class StockTraderBusiness : StockTraderTypes.IStockTrader
    {
        public StockTraderBusiness() {}

    public Quote RequestQuote(string Symbol)
    {

        // Create a new Quote object
        Quote q = new Quote();

        // Call the service agent
        StockTraderServiceAgent sa = new StockTraderServiceAgent();
        q = sa.RequestQuote(Symbol);
```

```
        return q;
    }


    }
}
```

As you would expect, the listing is very simple because the business assembly no longer has to provide its own implementation of the Quote request logic.

In summary, service agents are an elegant solution when you need to interface with one or more external services and wish to isolate the code that handles the communication. Service agents provide stability to a business assembly by bearing the responsibility of ensuring successful calls to external services and returning results in a form that the business assembly natively understands. Service agents can also act as intermediaries between two or more Web services.

This concludes the discussion of how to build basic service-oriented Web services.

Summary

In this chapter, we expanded on the previous discussion of message-oriented Web services and showed you a six-step process for designing and building a service-oriented Web service from scratch:

Step 1: Create a dedicated type definition assembly.

Step 2: Create a dedicated business assembly.

Step 3: Create the Web service using the type definition assembly.

Step 4: Implement the business interface in the Web service.

Step 5: Delegate processing logic to the business assembly.

Step 6: Create a Web service client.

You saw how to build both tightly coupled clients and loosely coupled clients. In most SOA applications you will want to build loosely coupled clients, but under some circumstances you may want a higher level of control over the type definitions. Tightly coupled clients reference the same type definition as the assembly rather than generating their own using a proxy class.

Finally, we discussed the service agent component, which is a special feature of service-oriented applications. The service agent manages communication between a business assembly and an external Web service. It can also act as the intermediary between two or more Web services.

The goal of this chapter is to help you rethink your approach to Web services design so that you can start thinking in terms of SOA.

CHAPTER 5

■■■

Web Services Enhancements 3.0

Web services technology has evolved rapidly since its debut a few years ago. Businesses were initially reluctant to fully adopt the technology because of a lack of industry-standard specifications to govern such important issues as message security and reliable delivery. Businesses will not send sensitive information across the wire if it is vulnerable to detection. And they will not implement large-scale distributed systems with this technology if the reliability of the messages cannot be guaranteed.

This chapter lays the groundwork for the second half of the book, where we will focus intensively on how to implement WS- specifications using Microsoft's Web Services Enhancements 3.0 for .NET. This chapter includes the following:

- Overview of the WS- specifications

- Introduction to Web Services Enhancements (WSE) 3.0

- Installing and configuring WSE 3.0, including the test certificates

- Using the WSE 3.0 utilities

This chapter is a must-read in order to get the most out of the second half of the book. It will help you to understand the WS- specifications and how WSE fits into the context of SOA. It will also get you started with installing and configuring WSE 3.0, including the test certificates, which are required for many of the code samples.

Overview of the WS- Specifications

Web services technology was initially tailored toward point-to-point communication, based on the familiar HTTP request/response model in which a client request generates a timely server response. This model works well for Internet browsing, but it proves to be very limiting for distributed service applications. Web services that are involved in business processing cannot always generate a timely response. The business process may be long-running, or a required back-end system may be offline.

In addition, the point-to-point communication model proves to be overly limiting for executing complex distributed business processes. It is unlikely that one Web service has the ability to execute a business process 100 percent of the time. More likely it needs to interact with other systems and perhaps even with other Web services. Clearly, it is a problem if a Web service receives a request message but is then unable to forward it on to other services for additional processing.

Industry leaders have been working together for several years to address the current limitations with Web services technology. Standards committees have formed to bring a sense of order to the wide variety of available technologies and versions. In Chapter 1, we discussed the WS-I Basic Profile, which outlines a set of Web-related technologies by version number and groups them together into a standard profile. You are considered to be in compliance with this standard if you are implementing the exact technology versions in this profile. In addition, nonprofit organizations such as OASIS are important forums where companies are actively cooperating in the development and advancement of new standards and specifications.

Companies, including Microsoft, IBM, BEA Systems, and VeriSign, are working on a set of specifications called the Web service specifications (WS-*) that are based on XML, SOAP, and WSDL extensibility models. Together these specifications define a set of composable features to make Web services "secure, reliable, and transacted," as the standard tag line often reads. Composability refers to the fact that you can pick and choose the selected specifications that apply to your particular business scenario. None of the specifications are ever required, even the security specifications, though as they become more widely accepted, it is likely that a subset of the specifications will be required in any robust, business-quality Web service.

Business Significance of the WS- Specifications

The WS- specifications are incredibly important to the future of Web services technology and to SOA. Microsoft provides a set of tools for .NET called Web Services Enhancements (WSE). WSE includes managed APIs for implementing selected WS- specifications in a composable manner. We say *selected* because the WS- specifications continue to evolve, and it will take time for all of the current standards to be submitted, accepted, and then incorporated into WSE. New WS- specifications continue to be released, so the future promises to hold many interesting and important developments in this evolving technology.

The purpose of the WS- specifications is to establish a set of standards for enterprise-level, service-oriented Web services. The focus of the specifications is on Web services in general, and on messages in particular, because messages are the essential aspects of an SOA. Without messages, Web services cannot communicate. And without secure, reliable messages, businesses will never trust that they can send sensitive information between Web services. The integrity of the message is the key to gaining acceptance for Web services as a robust business solution.

Each of the WS- specifications addresses a different business-critical issue. For example, WS-Security addresses how to implement digital signing and encryption technology in Web services. WS-Reliable Messaging addresses how to ensure that messages are always delivered, even if one part of the system is temporarily unavailable. Each specification is recorded directly in the header of the applicable SOAP message, using a dedicated XML schema. Some specifications, such as WS-Security, also modify the body of the SOAP message for encryption.

Listing 5-1 shows one example of a SOAP message that implements multiple specifications, including WS-Addressing, WS-Security, and WS-Reliable Messaging. Notice that the message header is divided into distinct parts and that the individual specification schemas do not overlap. This is known as *composability* because the individual specifications may be added or removed from the message header as needed.

Listing 5-1. *SOAP Message Illustrating Web Service Composability*

```
<s:Envelope xmlns:S="http://www.w3.org/2002/12/soap-envelope"
    xmlns:wsa=http://schemas.xmlsoap.org/ws/2003/03/addressing
        xmlns:wsse=http://schemas.xmlsoap.org/ws/2003/03/security
        xmlns:wrm="http://schemas.xmlsoap.org/ws/2003/03/reliablemessaging">

<s:Header>

<!--WS-Addressing -->
<wsa:From>
    <wsa:Address>http://www.bluestonepartners.com/Buyer</wsa:Address>
</wsa:From>
<wsa:ReplyTo>
    <wsa:Address>http://www.bluestonepartners.com/Broker</wsa:Address>
</wsa:ReplyTo>
<wsa:To>http://www.bluestonerealty.com/Seller</wsa:To>
<wsa:Action>http://www.bluestonerealty.com/MakeOffer</wsa:Action>

<!--WS-Security -->
<wsse:Security>
    <wsse:BinarySecurityToken ValueType="wsse:X509v3"
        EncodingType="wsse:Base64Binary">
            JKH8dH7SJa8.......SKJa87DJsAK3
    </wsse:BinarySecurityToken>
</wsse:Security>

<!--WS-ReliableMessaging -->
<wrm:Sequence>
    <wsu:Identifier>http://www.bluestonerealty.com/mls123</wsu:Identifier>
    <wrm:MessageNumber>32<wrm:MessageNumber>
</wrm:Sequence>

</s:Header>

<s:body xmlns:po=
    "http://www.bluestonerealty.com/PurchaseHouse">
    <po:PurchaseHouse>
    ...
    </po:PurchaseHouse>

</s:body>

</s:Envelope>
```

As you can see, each of the specifications is encapsulated within the SOAP header and each supports distinctive element tags so that no specification information can conflict. Web service composability is essential for allowing developers to choose which specifications are important for their Web services. In addition, this feature keeps message payloads smaller in size by not including element tags for unused specifications.

Introducing the WS- Specifications

Instead of simply listing the various WS- specifications, it is more useful to present them in the context of the framework's goals. There are different perspectives on what the full set of goals are because the specifications are always evolving and are being drawn together by diverse coalitions of companies and organizations. But in our minds, there are six primary goals for the WS- specifications.

Interoperability

Web services must be able to communicate even if they are built on and operated on different platforms. Web service messages must use standard protocols and specifications that are broadly accepted, such as the WS-I Basic Profile, which includes XML, SOAP, and WSDL. Interoperability is the key to widespread acceptance of Web services for handling critical business processes.

Composability

This is a design principle that is fundamental to the WS- specifications. The term *composability* alludes to the fact that many of the WS- specifications are independent of each other and that a given Web service may not need to implement them all. For example, one Web service may require security but not reliable messaging. Another Web service may require transactions, but not policy. Composability allows a developer to implement only those specifications that are required. The WS- specifications support this because they are implemented as discrete sections within the SOAP message header (see Listing 5-1 for an example).

Security

Protocol-level security mechanisms such as HTTPS are currently in wide use, but they are designed for point-to-point security rather than message-oriented security, which is much more dynamic. The WS-Security specification is a message-oriented security solution that supports the dynamic nature of messages. With WS-Security, the security information is stored directly in the message header, so it stays with the message, even if the message gets routed to more than one endpoint. Messages must carry their security information with them so they can remain dynamic. The WS-Trust and WS-Secure Conversation specifications enable you to create a secure token service that procures security tokens for the duration of a specific conversation between a client and a Web service.

Description and Discovery

Web services may be accessed from different clients across different domains. Web services must therefore be capable of publishing their metadata so that potential clients know how to call them. The WSDL document publishes supported types, operations, and port information. The WS-Policy specification documents and enforces usage requirements and preferences for a Web service. For example, WS-Policy will enforce that incoming SOAP requests must be signed and encrypted with digital certificates only, rather than any type of security token. The UDDI specification aims to provide a mechanism for clients to look up Web service metadata in a centralized directory.

Messaging and Delivery

The biggest vulnerability for a message besides security is the risk that it may never reach its intended destination—or worse, that not only does the message fail to reach the destination, but the sender is also unaware that it never arrived. You cannot correct a problem if you do not know it occurred. The WS-Reliable Messaging specification establishes a framework that is designed to keep all parties informed of where messages are and whether they arrived. This is critical in an architecture where a message may get routed between multiple endpoints. Failure at one endpoint should not bring down the entire workflow that the message is a part of.

Transactions

Transaction processing is a way of orchestrating multiple related business operations so that they succeed or fail together, and thereby preserve the integrity of the overall workflow. Transaction management is an extremely difficult challenge in an SOA. Web services are inherently disconnected stateless components that do not by nature participate in broadly distributed transactions. The WS-Coordination, WS-Atomic Transaction, and WS-Business Activity specifications are designed to address the challenge of implementing transactions across distributed Web services.

The WS- Specifications Covered in This Book

The WS- specifications will allow developers to build Web services that are interoperable, reliable, secure, and transacted. Ultimately, the overarching goal is for Web services technology to make it into the business mainstream and to be considered as good of a business solution as more established technologies.

This book does not cover all of the available WS- specifications for two reasons: First, it is impractical because some of the specifications are too new or too poorly established to be useful to most people. Second, it is problematic because WSE implements only a few of the available WS- specifications, albeit many of the most important ones.

With these points in mind, here is a list of the WS- specifications we will be covering in this book:

- WS-Security

- WS-Policy

- WS-Secure Conversation

- WS-Addressing

- WS-Reliable Messaging

Perhaps the most glaring omission from the current WSE 3.0 is the absence of the transaction-related family of specifications, including WS-Coordination and WS-Atomic Transaction. But many other important specifications are present, most notably WS-Security, WS-Policy, and the WS-Addressing specifications. Omissions in WSE do not equate to insufficiency because it continues to evolve along with the WS- specifications themselves. WSE 3.0 will be subsumed in the future into the Windows Communication Foundation (WCF), formerly code-named *Indigo*, which will provide integrated support for message-oriented technology directly in the operating system, including greatly expanded infrastructure support. Many of the tasks that we must write complex code for today will become simpler in WCF. You can read more about WCF in Chapter 9.

Appendix A lists a number of useful references for learning more about the WS- specifications. Surprisingly, the original WS- specifications documents are highly readable and very informative. They do not, of course, cover any vendor-specific developer toolkit, such as WSE. But they provide clear definitions and explanations of the specifications, along with examples and references on how specifications are encoded within a SOAP message.

■Tip You can find links to the original WS- specifications documents at `http://www-106.ibm.com/developerworks/webservices/standards/`.

One last thing to keep in mind is that just because a specification is absent from WSE does not mean that you cannot implement it yourself using custom code. The .NET Framework gives you support classes for working with XML, SOAP, and Web services, namely most of the core Web services technologies. In a sense, WSE provides you convenience, which you would like to have but can also live without if you have to. Developers already have a natural instinct to be self-motivated and to build custom solutions when nothing else is readily available. We are not advocating that you find your own way to implement something that should be standard. In the absence of a canned solution, you still have the tools to build a credible alternative solution yourself. However, be prepared for considerable complexity!

In general, this book will remain focused on implementing solutions using the WSE support classes. But at times, we will show you ways to make up for deficiencies in WSE so that you can remain true to the spirit of the specification while using additional support technologies. As a .NET developer, you will find that the current version of WSE, along with a measure of creative thinking, will bring a heightened maturity to your Web services development efforts. WSE enables you to implement many of the features that a robust, business-oriented solution should include.

Welcome to the dynamic, evolving world of SOA with WSE.

Introducing Web Services Enhancements 3.0

WSE generally refers to both a software development toolkit and an add-on processing infrastructure for implementing the WS- specifications in .NET projects. From an infrastructure perspective, WSE is basically a processing engine for applying the WS- specifications to SOAP messages. As you have seen, WS- specifications are stamped across different parts of a SOAP message. All of the WS- specifications append to the SOAP message header, while some of them also modify the SOAP message body directly (such as the WS-Security specifications). WSE automatically modifies SOAP messages to implement the WS- specifications. It also provides the infrastructure for processing these SOAP messages. In this sense it is similar to the ASP.NET Web services infrastructure, which provides SOAP and communications infrastructure support for the Web services you create using a friendlier API. Overall, the goal of WSE is to save developers from having to write custom code to implement basic required Web service infrastructure (such as security and policy).

WSE 3.0 is an SDK package for Microsoft .NET developers that includes the following:

The Microsoft.Web.Services3 assembly: This provides an API and includes several support classes, such as SOAP extensions and custom handlers.

Documentation and help files: These show you how to use and configure the WSE API and utilities.

QuickStart samples: These show you how to code with WSE.

Configuration Editor: This utility provides a GUI interface for configuring WSE in your .NET projects.

X.509 Certificate Tool: This utility helps you work with X.509 digital certificates.

Policy Wizard: This utility provides a GUI for generating XML policy expression files (located inside the Configuration Editor).

How the WSE Processing Infrastructure Works

WSE installs a set of filters that intercept and process inbound and outbound SOAP request messages, as shown in Figure 5-1. The WSE filters work together inside a processing pipeline that also integrates with the ASP.NET processing pipeline. When a client application generates a SOAP request that includes WS enhancements, it specifies these in code using the API provided by WSE. When the message is sent out, it goes through a set of WSE filters that translate the code into SOAP extensions that are then applied directly to the SOAP message.

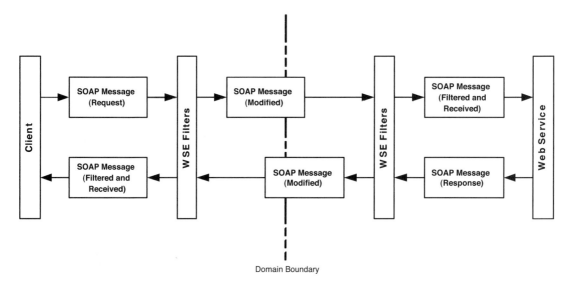

Figure 5-1. *WSE processing of SOAP messages*

The WSE filters are dedicated to specific WS- specifications, or to groups of related specifications, including

- Security (including WS-Security)

- Policy (including WS-Policy and WS-Policy Attachments)

- Messaging (including WS-Addressing)

WSE is an extension to the existing ASP.NET framework and is dedicated to modifying and processing SOAP messages. WSE must be configured to work with a project. Even if it is installed on your machine, it will not automatically apply to your projects unless they are configured to use it. When you use WSE in a project, you register one of its assembly types as a SOAP extension class.

When you want to use WSE in a project, you must add a reference to the Microsoft.Web.Services3 project. You must also register the Web services configuration class in the project's web.config file, as shown in Listing 5-2.

Listing 5-2. *The WSE Configuration Class*

```
<configuration xmlns="http://schemas.microsoft.com/.NetConfiguration/v2.0">
  <configSections>
    <section name="microsoft.web.services3"
        type="Microsoft.Web.Services3.Configuration.WebServicesConfiguration,
        Microsoft.Web.Services3, Version=3.0.0.0, Culture=neutral,
        PublicKeyToken=31bf3856ad364e35" />
  </configSections>
</configuration>
```

If the project is an ASP.NET Web service or application, you must also register the WSE SOAP extension classes in the web.config file, as shown in Listing 5-3.

Listing 5-3. *The WSE SOAP Extension Type*

```
<system.web>
    <webServices>
        < soapServerProtocolFactory ➠
type="Microsoft.Web.Services3.WseProtocolFactory,
            Microsoft.Web.Services3, Version=3.0.0.0, Culture=neutral,
            PublicKeyToken=31bf3856ad364e35"/>
        </soapServerProtocolFactory>
        <soapExtensionImporterTypes>
            <add type="Microsoft.Web.Services3.Description.WseExtensionImporter,
                Microsoft.Web.Services3, Version=3.0.0.0, Culture=neutral,
                PublicKeyToken=31bf3856ad364e35"/>
        </soapExtensionImporterTypes>
    </webServices>
</system.web>
```

This step instructs WSE to process the project's SOAP messages through its filters. By default, WSE automatically applies all of its filters to SOAP messages. However, you can optimize the process by turning off selected filters. For example, if you do not implement routing and referral, you can turn off the related filters. This simply means that WSE will stop looking for these related elements when it processes incoming and outbound SOAP messages.

Note WSE 3.0 ships with a utility called the Configuration Editor, which will automatically generate for you the configuration XML in Listing 5-2 and Listing 5-3. These listings are the same in every project, so you should not have to manually enter them. The Configuration Editor is reviewed later in this chapter in the section titled "Install and Configure WSE 3.0."

How WSE Works with ASP.NET

WSE provides an API for applying WS- specifications to SOAP messages. The key player in the WSE class framework is the SoapContext class, which directly records the Web specification options and then later makes them available to the WSE filters for processing. The SoapContext class is a member of the Microsoft.Web.Services3 namespace and applies to both request and response messages and provides you with a programmatic window to examine the contents of a SOAP message, including its envelope, header, and body contents. The SoapContext class is similar to the HTTPContext class, which encapsulates all HTTP-specific information about an individual HTTP request. Listing 5-4 shows you one example of using the SoapContext class to examine the security elements in a SOAP message.

Listing 5-4. *Examining Message Security Elements Using the SoapContext Class*

```
using Microsoft.Web.Services3;
using Microsoft.Web.Services3.Security;
using Microsoft.Web.Services3.Security.Tokens;

SoapContext requestContext = RequestSoapContext.Current;

foreach (ISecurityElement objElem in requestContext.Security.Elements)
{
if (objElem is MessageSignature)
{
MessageSignature clientSignature = (MessageSignature)objElem;

if (clientSignature.SignatureToken is X509SecurityToken)
{
// Add code to process the X509SecurityToken
}
else if (clientSignature.SignatureToken is UsernameToken)
{
// Add code to process the UsernameToken
}
}
}
```

Table 5-1 provides a summary of important SoapContext class properties. Many of these properties provide access to specialized classes with their own nested API. For example, the Security property provides access to the SoapHeader class called Security, which provides support members for examining existing security information and for appending new security information to the SOAP message header.

Table 5-1. *The SoapContext Class Properties*

Property	Description
Addressing	Provides access to the collection of WS-Addressing elements assigned to the SOAP message via the AddressingHeaders class.
Envelope	Provides direct access to the SOAP envelope via the SoapEnvelope class. This class provides several additional classes and properties that are useful for retrieving the contents of the SOAP envelope and body via classes and properties or directly as XML.
IsInbound	Indicates whether the SOAP message is incoming (true) or outbound (false).
Referrals	Provides the collection of referral elements assigned to the SOAP message via the ReferralsCollection class.
Security	Provides the security headers for the ultimate recipient of the SOAP message via the Security class.

As you look through the table, remember that the SoapContext class is always referenced in context, meaning that when you reference it in code, it will always be holding the contents of an active request or response message. By definition, there is no such thing as stand-alone or disconnected SoapContext. So it is useful to explore this class by setting a breakpoint in your code and examining the various member properties and their settings in the Immediate debug window. Also, the WSE 3.0 documentation contains a detailed class reference for the member classes. You can learn a lot about how WSE works by examining the various classes and properties and learning how they interact with each other.

The Microsoft.Web.Services3 assembly provides a large number of namespaces that cover several different WS- specifications. These are summarized in Table 5-2, along with a brief description of which WS- specifications they apply to. As you begin coding with the various WS- specifications, you will need to import one or more of these namespaces into your Web services project.

Table 5-2. *Namespaces in WSE 3.0 Microsoft.Web.Services3 Assembly*

Namespace	Description
(Root)	Provides support classes for working with SOAP request and response messages, including the important SoapContext class.
.Addressing	Provides support for the WS-Addressing specification, which enables the SOAP message to contain its own addressing, destination, and routing information.
.Configuration	Provides support for processing the WSE configuration settings.
.Configuration.Install	Provides support functions to manage the installation of WSE.
.Diagnostics	Provides tracing support to log diagnostic information on a SOAP message before and after processing by the WSE filters.
.Messaging	Provides support for WS-Messaging, which enables you to process SOAP messages for transport with the HTTP or TCP protocols. The classes support SOAP formatting and serialization.
.Messaging.Configuration	Provides support for working with configuration elements that relate to the WS-Messaging specification.
.Design	Provides classes for processing policy expression files.
.Referral	Provides support for WS-Referral, which enables the routing of SOAP messages across multiple endpoints.
.Security	Provides support for WS-Security, including attaching security elements to SOAP messages and processing them.
.Security.Configuration	Provides support for working with configuration elements that relate to the WS-Security and WS-Secure Conversation specifications.
.Security.Cryptography	Provides support functions for processing cryptographic operations.
.Security.Policy	Provides support for the WS-Security Policy specification, which supports security-specific policy assertions.
.Security.Tokens	Indicates specialized classes for working with security tokens.

Continued

Table 5-2. *Continued*

Namespace	Description
.Security.Tokens.Kerberos	Indicates specialized classes for working with security tokens that are associated with Kerberos tickets.
.Security.X509	Indicates specialized classes for working with X.509 digital certificates. Note that this namespace provides utility classes for working with the classes in namespace .Security.Cryptography.X509Certificate.X509Certificate2.
.Security.Utility	Specifies generic classes for working with security-oriented properties, such as the creation and expiration time stamp information for a SOAP message.
.Security.Xml	Indicates specialized classes for working with XML signatures, which are an important support technology for digital signatures.
.Xml	Specifies general support classes for working with XML, particularly as it relates to the XML that is generated by the WS- specifications. These classes are used in conjunction with other XML classes in the .NET Framework.

WSE provides programmatic hooks in the specifications that automatically generate the required SOAP elements for you, so you do not have to construct them manually. The WSE API is accessed differently by Web services vs. Web service clients. Let's briefly look at the differences.

■Note With Visual Studio 2005, Web services can now be hosted under console applications through simple configuration entries in the application configuration file. This chapter focuses on Web services that are hosted under IIS, because it is currently a more common implementation scenario for .NET developers.

Web Service Access to the WSE API

Web services can access the SoapContext for either request or response SOAP messages using specialized classes called RequestSoapContext and ResponseSoapContext. These classes provide direct access to SOAP messages, and they support messages that are transported over different protocols, including the HTTP and TCP protocols. Each of the classes provides a static property called Current, which furnishes a reference to the SoapContext class.

For request messages, the SoapContext class is accessed using

```
SoapContext requestContext = RequestSoapContext.Current;
```

RequestSoapContext is a class provided by the WebServicesClientProtocol, and Current is a static property that returns the SoapContext class.

For response messages, the SoapContext class is accessed using

```
SoapContext responseContext = ResponseSoapContext.Current;
```

Once the client references the SoapContext for the request message, it can reference or assign WS- specifications with the WSE API. For example, if the incoming request message requires digital signing with a certificate, the Web service can inspect the attached digital signatures using SoapContext (as shown previously in Listing 5-4). The Web service can also use SoapContext to modify outgoing response messages.

Unlike the service proxy class (described in the next section), the Web service itself does not need to derive from a specialized class in order to access the WSE functionality. However, you need to make sure the WSE support assemblies are correctly registered in the service's web.config file.

■**Note** The SoapContext.Current static class creates a blocking risk because it interacts directly with the Web service context. For this reason, a Web service wrapper class (that invokes the Web service proxy) should never be created as a singleton; otherwise, multiple calls to the wrapper will result in blocked calls. Here is an example of what not to do:

```
Public Class webservicewrapper (singleton)
{
    Private webserviceproxy _myProxy;

    Public void dosomething
    {
        _myProxy.DoSomething();
    }
}
```

Web Service Client Access to the WSE API

A Web service client interacts with a Web service via a proxy class. WSE provides a new base class for this proxy class to inherit from

```
Microsoft.Web.Services3.WebServicesClientProtocol
```

Without WSE installed, proxy class files inherit from

```
System.Web.Services.Protocols.SoapHttpClientProtocol
```

If WSE 3.0 is installed and a reference is set to Microsoft.Web.Services, two classes will be generated. One class will be derived from SoapHttpClientProtocol and will be named after the service (e.g., MyServiceClass). The second generated class will derive from WebServicesClientProtocol and will be named after the service name, with "WSE" appended to it (e.g., MyServiceClassWSE). The WebServicesClientProtocol class provides access to the SoapContext class for both request and response messages via the proxy class. Listing 5-5 shows an example of a Web client that is digitally signing a SOAP request message before sending it out to a service. The listing shows how you reference the SoapContext and then use it to assign the digital signature to the SOAP request message.

Listing 5-5. *Digitally Signing a SOAP Request Message via the SoapContext*

```
using Microsoft.Web.Services3;
using Microsoft.Web.Services3.Security;
using Microsoft.Web.Services3.Security.Tokens;

// Retrieve the SoapContext for the outgoing SOAP request message
StockTraderServiceWse serviceProxy = new StockTraderServiceWse();

// Retrieve the X509 certificate from the CurrentUserStore certificate store
X509SecurityToken token = GetSigningToken();

// Add signature element to a security section on the request to sign the request
serviceProxy.RequestSoapContext.Security.Tokens.Add( token );
serviceProxy.RequestSoapContext.Security.Elements.Add( ➥
    new MessageSignature( token ) );
```

This concludes the introduction to the WSE 3.0 API. The remainder of this chapter focuses on installation and configuration options for WSE 3.0. The subsequent chapters in the book are dedicated to showing you how to use the WSE API to implement the WS- specifications in your own service-oriented applications.

Install and Configure WSE 3.0

WSE 3.0 is easy to install and to configure. You must install Visual Studio 2005 prior to installing WSE 3.0, since WSE 3.0 will not install with earlier versions. You can install Visual Studio 2005 side by side with Visual Studio .NET 2003 if required.

WSE 3.0 is a package of QuickStart sample applications and documentation that shows you how to use the various classes in the WSE assembly. But the engine of WSE 3.0 is a single assembly called Microsoft.Web.Services3.dll, which is installed by default under C:\Program Files\Microsoft WSE\v3.0. In addition, this assembly gets automatically registered in the Global Assembly Cache (GAC).

In order to use the new assembly in your Web services projects, you will need to register it as a SOAP extension within either the machine.config or web.config files. If you update the machine.config file, the assembly will automatically be registered for all future Web services projects. Otherwise, you will need to update the web.config files for each new project individually.

Listing 5-6 shows the two additional elements that you must update in the web.config file in order for your project to use WSE. You may actually require additional entries, but these are specific to individual WS- specifications such as WS-Security and are only required as needed. Note that you must include each individual element on a single line. In Listing 5-6, elements such as <section> are broken out on multiple lines for clarity only. They must, however, be entered as single lines in the actual web.config file.

Listing 5-6. *The web.config Updates for a WSE-Enabled Web Service Project*

```
<configuration xmlns="http://schemas.microsoft.com/.NetConfiguration/v2.0">
  <configSections>
    <section name="microsoft.web.services3"
        type="Microsoft.Web.Services3.Configuration.WebServicesConfiguration,
        Microsoft.Web.Services3, Version=3.0.0.0, Culture=neutral,
        PublicKeyToken=31bf3856ad364e35" />
  </configSections>
<system.web>
    <webServices>
        < soapServerProtocolFactory type="Microsoft.Web.Services3.WseProtocolFactory,
                Microsoft.Web.Services3, Version=3.0.0.0, Culture=neutral,
                PublicKeyToken=31bf3856ad364e35"/>
        </soapServerProtocolFactory>
        <soapExtensionImporterTypes>
            <add type="Microsoft.Web.Services3.Description.WseExtensionImporter,
                Microsoft.Web.Services3, Version=3.0.0.0, Culture=neutral,
                PublicKeyToken=31bf3856ad364e35"/>
        </soapExtensionImporterTypes>
    </webServices>
  </system.web>
</configuration>
```

Web service client projects do not need to register the SOAP extension, but they do need to register the WebServicesConfiguration class. In addition, the client's Web service proxy class must inherit from

```
Microsoft.Web.Services3.WebServicesClientProtocol
```

Without WSE, the proxy class file inherits from

```
System.Web.Services.Protocols.SoapHttpClientProtocol
```

This change is required so that Web service requests get routed through the WSE filters rather than through the standard HTTP-based SOAP filters.

■**Note** If you want to update the machine.config file, simply copy the <section> element from Listing 5-2 into the machine.config file, under the <configSections> node.

If you prefer to not type these entries manually (and we certainly do!), then you can use the convenient Configuration Editor that ships with WSE 3.0. This tool provides a tabbed GUI interface in which you specify configuration settings for a project and then automatically apply the settings without having to write the code manually. The tool can be accessed directly from within your Visual Studio .NET project, as shown in Figure 5-2.

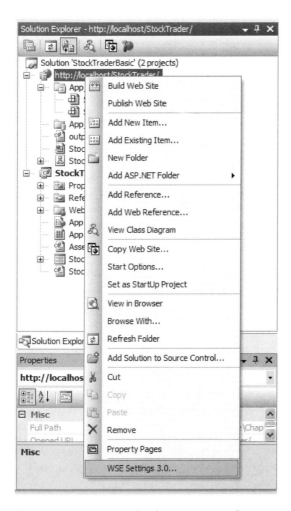

Figure 5-2. *Menu access for the WSE 3.0 Configuration Editor*

Figure 5-3 shows how you can use the editor to implement the basic settings we have covered so far. You can use the editor for all .NET project types. If you are using it for an ASP.NET Web application or service project, it gives you an additional option to register the SOAP extension class. Otherwise, the second check box in the GUI interface is disabled. The editor settings shown in Figure 5-3 will generate the web.config settings that are shown in Listing 5-6. This is not bad for two simple check box clicks!

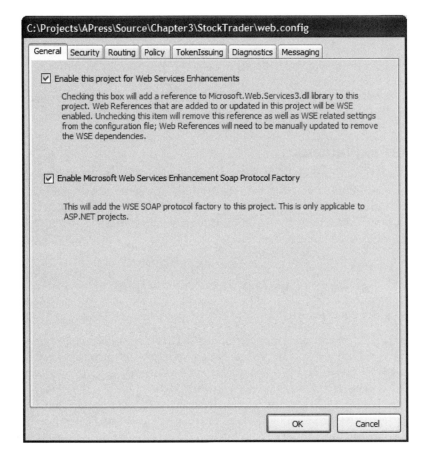

Figure 5-3. *The WSE 3.0 Configuration Editor*

When you create a new client application for your WSE-enabled Web service, you can generate the proxy class in two ways. You can either generate it manually from the WSDL document, or you can generate it using Visual Studio .NET's Add Web Reference Wizard. If you use the wizard, keep in mind that the generated proxy file will contain two separate proxy classes. One inherits from the WebServicesClientProtocol class, which is provided by the Microsoft.Web.Services3 assembly. The other class inherits from the traditional SoapHttpClientProtocol class, which is provided by the System.Web.Services assembly.

■**Note** The Configuration Editor provides helpful configuration support for several of the WS- specifications, as you can tell from the additional tabs in Figure 5-3. We will discuss the additional support that the Configuration Editor provides in the relevant chapters.

X.509 Certificate Support

Several of the upcoming sample solutions in this book use X.509 digital certificates, which can be used to digitally sign and encrypt SOAP messages (with the help of WSE). In addition, WSE 3.0 uses X.509 digital certificates in its QuickStart sample applications. Certificate installation and configuration can be quite complex, so we felt it was important to provide a section on how to install and configure the X.509 sample certificates.

X.509 Certificates Explained

X.509 digital certificates are widely used as a basis for securing communication between separate endpoints. For example, they are used to support the HTTP Secure Sockets Layer (SSL) protocol, otherwise known as HTTPS.

You will be working directly with the X.509 test certificates that ship with WSE 3.0. You actually have several options for obtaining test certificates:

- Use the WSE 3.0 test certificates (the most convenient option).

- Use the makecert.exe command-line utility to generate test certificates.

- Obtain a test certificate from VeriSign.

Digital certificates are used for asymmetric encryption, also known as *public-key encryption*. The certificate is used to generate a public-private key pair, whereby the private key is known only to one party, while the public key may be distributed to anyone.

In a service-oriented application that includes a client and a Web service, it is the client that typically procures the certificate and the public-private key pair. This is the model that the sample applications use, so it is important to understand how it works. In an SOA application, certificates and keys are used as follows:

- The client uses the certificate to digitally sign an outgoing SOAP request message (to the Web service).

- The Web service uses the public key to encrypt the outgoing SOAP response message (to the client).

- The client uses the private key to decrypt the incoming SOAP response message (from the Web service).

Chapter 6 provides detailed explanations of how encryption and digital signing work under the hood; but for now this is all you need to know, because it helps you to understand where the certificates and keys need to be registered.

Installing the X.509 Test Certificates

Web servers such as IIS provide good support tools for installing digital certificates that will be used to support HTTPS. In addition, Windows operating systems provide a Microsoft Management Console (MMC) snap-in called the Certificate Manager for working with certificates.

The sample applications in this book use the X.509 test certificate to support public-key encryption and to support digital signing; therefore, not only do you need the certificate itself, but you also need a public-private key pair that has been generated from the certificate. Luckily, WSE 3.0 ships with these keys already generated, so you are saved one more manual step.

■**Caution** WSE 3.0 test certificates should not be used in production applications. Their keys are well-known, so they will not provide any effective security in production applications.

The digital certificate and the keys need to be stored in a location called the *certificate store*, which you can access using the Certificate Manager snap-in. For testing purposes, most of us use the same machine to run the Web service and the client applications. This requires you to update two certificate stores:

- *The Local Computer certificate store*: Used by the Web service, this location should store the public key.

- *The Current User certificate store*: Used by the client, this location should store the certificate and the private key.

You can install the certificates manually, or you can run a preset batch script called Setup.bat that ships with WSE 3.0 and is available in the folder C:\Program Files\Microsoft WSE\v3.0\Samples. The batch script is the easiest way to install the test certificates; however, you will need to know how to install them manually as well for your own development work outside of the QuickStart samples or the code samples that accompany this book.

Here are the installation steps to manually install the certificates:

1. Open a new MMC console by typing **mmc** in the Run dialog window.

2. Select File ➤ Add/Remove Snap-In. Click the Add button and then select Certificates from the available list. You will be prompted to select the type of account that will manage the certificates. Select My User Account and click Finish.

3. Repeat step 2, but this time when you are prompted for an account, select Computer Account and click Finish. Click OK to close out the dialog box for adding certificate stores. You should now be looking at an MMC console view that displays the Current User and the Local Computer certificate stores, as shown in Figure 5-4.

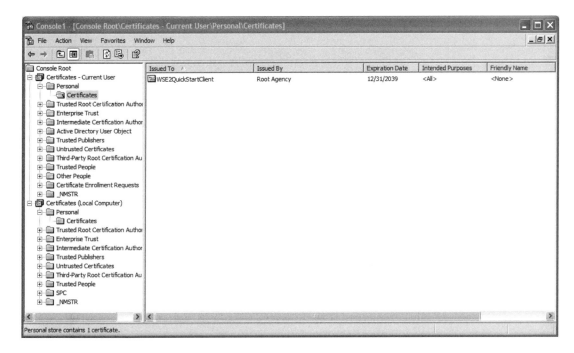

Figure 5-4. *MMC console displaying the Current User and the Local Computer certificate stores*

4. Expand the Personal folder of the Current User certificate store and then right-click it to select the All Tasks ➤ Import menu option. Import the sample personal information exchange file titled Client Private.pfx. The sample certificates and private keys are installed with WSE 3.0, and their default location is C:\Program Files\Microsoft WSE\v3.0\Samples\Sample Test Certificates\. Client Private.pfx is the private key that the Web service client will use to encrypt requests to the Web service. Note that you will be prompted to enter a password for the private key during the import. For the WSE 3.0 test certificates, you can locate this password in a file called readme.htm, which is located in the same folder as the test certificates.

5. Right-click again the Personal folder of the Current User certificate store and select the All Tasks ➤ Import menu option. Import the sample test certificate titled Server Public.cer. This is the public key that the client uses to digitally sign requests for the Web service.

6. Expand the Personal folder of the Local Computer certificate store and import the sample test certificate titled Server Public.cer. This is the public key that the Web service uses to decrypt the client's request.

This completes the installation of the certificates. But in order to use them from within ASP.NET, you will need to adjust permission levels for the ASP.NET worker process.

Set ASP.NET Permissions to Use the X.509 Certificates

WSE 3.0 ships with a useful utility called the X.509 Certificate Tool. You can use this tool for several purposes:

- Browse installed certificates in the Current User and Local Computer certificate stores.

- Set permissions on the keys in the MachineKeys folder, which provides access to Local Computer certificates.

- Retrieve the base64 key identifier for installed certificate keys.

Figure 5-5 shows the X.509 Certificate Tool with a selected certificate, which in this case is the private key certificate for the Local Computer user.

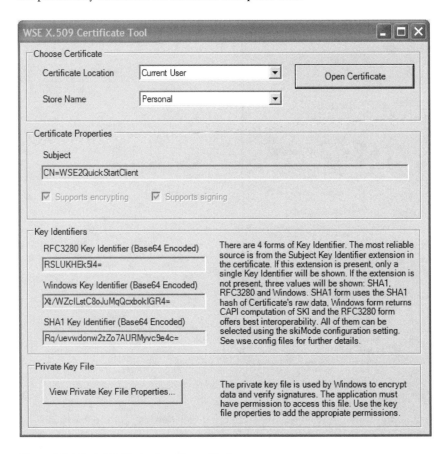

Figure 5-5. *The WSE X.509 Certificate Tool*

The ASP.NET worker process needs Full Control security-level access to the folder that stores the Local Computer certificates. Click the lower button in the X.509 Certificate Tool page that is labeled View Private Key File Properties to open property pages for the folder. Switch to the Security tab to display the list of users who have access to the folder. Add the account that is assigned to the ASP.NET worker process and give it Full Control permissions. By default, on Windows XP/2000 under IIS 5.0, the worker process runs under a machine account called ASP.NET. On Windows Server 2003 the worker process usually runs under the NETWORK SERVICE account. Figure 5-6 shows what the Security tab looks like once you have added the ASP.NET worker process account.

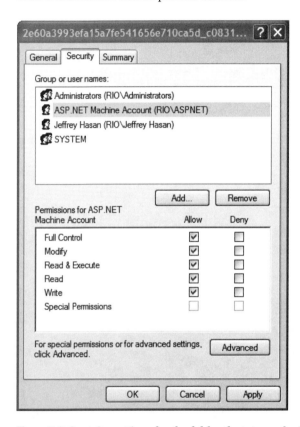

Figure 5-6. *Security settings for the folder that stores the Local Computer certificates and keys*

The X.509 Certificate Tool provides the base64-encoded key identifier for the certificate. You will need this identifier in the code listings in order to retrieve the correct certificate. Listing 5-7 shows you how to retrieve a certificate from the certificate store using its key identifier.

Listing 5-7. *Retrieving a Certificate from the Local Computer Certificate Store Using Its Key Identifier*

```
using Microsoft.Web.Services3.Security.X509;

private X509SecurityToken GetSigningToken()
{
// NOTE: If you use the WSE 3.0 sample certificates then
// you should not need to change these IDs
string ClientBase64KeyId = "Xt/WZcILstC8oJuMqQcxbokIGR4=";

X509SecurityToken token = null;

// Open the CurrentUser Certificate Store
X509CertificateStore store;
store = X509CertificateStore.CurrentUserStore( X509CertificateStore.MyStore );
if ( store.OpenRead() )
{
X509CertificateCollection certs = store.FindCertificateByKeyIdentifier( ➥
    Convert.FromBase64String( ClientBase64KeyId ) );

if (certs.Count > 0)
{
// Get the first certificate in the collection
token = new X509SecurityToken( ((X509Certificate) certs[0]) );
}
}
return token;
}
```

Certificates require some effort to install and to configure, but it is well worth it. Certificates are easy to use once they are installed and you get a high level of security from asymmetric encryption compared to other methods. Asymmetric encryption does have the drawback of being more processor-intensive than other methods, so it can suffer in performance compared to other methods. But there are workarounds to this. For example, you can implement WS-Secure Conversation, which optimizes the performance of encrypted communication between a Web service and client. WS-Secure Conversation is covered in Chapter 7. Finally, you will learn a lot more about using certificates in your solutions by reading Chapter 6, which focuses on the WS-Security specification.

Final Thoughts on WSE

WSE is an evolving product that implements only a subset of the available ratified WS- specifications. Microsoft has done a good job of implementing the more popular WS- specifications, including security and policy. But the WSE product cannot keep pace with the rapid change of the WS- specifications. Existing specifications continue to change and new ones continue to be released. Even within a given specification, WSE will probably only cover a subset of what is available. This is in fact why Microsoft develops WSE on a separate release schedule from the .NET Framework.

Summary

This chapter introduced you to the Web services specifications, or *WS- specifications*, which provide a framework for building secure, reliable, service-oriented Web services. The WS-specifications provide the following benefits when they are implemented in Web services:

- Interoperability

- Composability

- Security

- Description and discovery

- Messaging and delivery

- Transactions

Microsoft Web Services Enhancements 3.0 is a software developer kit for implementing the WS- specifications in .NET applications. It includes the Microsoft.Web.Services3 assembly, configuration tools, QuickStart application samples, and documentation. WSE is an excellent productivity tool that implements many of the important WS- specifications. The current version of WSE does have gaps, most notably in its support for transactions. Developers will need to build some aspects of the WS- specifications manually for now.

This chapter lays the groundwork for the rest of the book, which explores several of the WS- specifications in detail.

CHAPTER 6

■■■

Secure Web Services
with WS-Security

Companies have started the adoption of Web service technology and the WS-Security specification as an approach to ensure the integrity of transmitted messages and data. The WS-Security specification is a joint effort by Microsoft, IBM, and VeriSign to address this most important issue. The WS-Security specification is designed to provide an extensible security implementation that will evolve as Web services technology becomes more sophisticated.

The WS-Security Specification

What do we actually mean when we talk about *security*? In broad terms, we are talking about authentication, authorization, data integrity, and confidentiality.

Authentication: This is the process of identifying a user based on credentials. In SOA, the user is not necessarily a person; it can be an application that is making a remote call from the intranet or Internet. This application must be able to identify itself by providing the required credentials. These credentials can be in the form of a username and password, also known as Username Token, or a digital certificate, such as an X.509 certificate or a Kerberos token.

Authorization: This is the process of validating whether an already authenticated user has access to a particular resource. For example, a Web service can perform multiple operations and they might only be available to a limited group of users or roles. Together, authentication and authorization provide a security model that allows you to identify users and then give them selective access to resources.

Integrity: This means that the message was not tampered during transit. A digitally signed message helps us ensure that the content of a message hasn't been modified before reaching its destination. Digital signatures work by generating a short string based on the content of the message. This short string or *hash* is most likely unique, and a single change made to the content of the message would generate a different hash value.

Confidentiality: This is the process that guarantees that only authorized individuals have access to a message. In order to protect a message, its contents must be encrypted. An encrypted message would not be readable by intruders that do not possess the key to decrypt the message. There are two types of encryption: *symmetric* and *asymmetric*.

- *Symmetric encryption*: In this scenario the client and the service use the same key to encrypt and decrypt the message.

- *Asymmetric encryption*: In this scenario one party encrypts the message using one key and the other party decrypts it using a different key. This is also known as *public key encryption*. These two keys are also known as the *public/private key pair*. The public key is available to anyone who wants to communicate with the service, and the client uses this key to encrypt the messages. The private key is used by the service to decrypt the messages encrypted with the public key.

The prime currency in SOA applications is SOAP messages, because they are the means by which requests are made and responses are received from Web service methods. The WS-Security specification provides a way for you to protect the integrity and confidentiality of messages and to implement authentication and authorization models in your Web services. The WS-Security specification enables you to implement the following protections in your Web service calls:

Authentication: Security credentials, or tokens, may be exchanged between a client and a Web service to validate the identity of the caller. The tokens are added directly to the header of the SOAP message.

Digital signing: Digital signing creates a cryptographic signature attached to the message that uniquely identifies the sender. The receiver can check this signature to verify the identity of the sender and the integrity of the message. A SOAP exception is raised on the receiving end if the contents of a SOAP message have been tampered with. Digital signing is especially important in an SOA where a single SOAP message may be routed through multiple SOAP endpoints and across multiple servers. Message integrity is essential in any Web service–based architecture, but especially in an SOA.

Encryption: This encodes a SOAP message to ensure its confidentiality. A number of available encryption algorithms are available. In addition, you can encrypt a SOAP message based on an X.509 certificate.

The goal of this specification is to provide mechanisms that will enable businesses to exchange SOAP messages in a secure environment. The specification does not intend to replace previous security specifications; on the contrary, it leverages existing security standards such as SSL, X.509, and Kerberos.

The WS-Security specification is platform-independent and transport-neutral, as are all of the other WS- specifications. Security information is generated by the client and stored within the envelope of the SOAP request message. The Web service in turn will deserialize this information; verify its validity, and then process the requested operation. In the event that the message security does not pass verification, the Web service will return a SOAP fault back to the client.

Listings 6-1 and 6-2 compare two SOAP request messages for the same Web service method. The Web service is StockTrader.asmx, and the requested method is RequestQuote, which accepts a single stock ticker symbol as an input parameter. Listing 6-1 is an unsecured Web method call, while Listing 6-2 is secured and implements digital signing and encryption (based on an X.509 certificate). The listings are greatly simplified for clarity and for length and were originally created using the trace files generated by WSE 3.0.

Listing 6-1. *Unsecured SOAP Request Message (Simplified for Clarity)*

```
<soap:Envelope>

<soap:Header>
    <wsa:Action>
        http://www.bluestonepartners.com/schemas/StockTrader/RequestQuote
    </wsa:Action>
    <wsa:MessageID>Message ID</wsa:MessageID>
    <wsa:ReplyTo>
    <wsa:Address>
        http://schemas.xmlsoap.org/ws/2004/08/addressing/role/anonymous
    </wsa:Address>
    </wsa:ReplyTo>
    <wsa:To>
        http://localhost/StockTraderContracts/StockTrader.asmx
    </wsa:To>
    <wsse:Security>
        <wsu:Timestamp>
            Message Creation/Expiration TimeStamps
        </wsu:Timestamp>
    </wsse:Security>
</soap:Header>

<soap:Body>
    <Symbol>
        MSFT
    </Symbol>
</soap:Body>

</soap:Envelope>
```

Listing 6-2. *Digitally Signed and Encrypted SOAP Message with Highlighted Differences from an Unsigned SOAP Message (Simplified for Clarity)*

```
<soap:Envelope>

<soap:Header>
    <wsa:Action>
        http://www.bluestonepartners.com/schemas/StockTrader /RequestQuote
```

```
        </wsa:Action>
        <wsa:MessageID>
            Message ID
        </wsa:MessageID>
        <wsa:ReplyTo>
            <wsa:Address>
                http://schemas.xmlsoap.org/ws/2004/08/addressing/role/anonymous
            </wsa:Address>
        </wsa:ReplyTo>
        <wsa:To>
            http://localhost/StockTraderContracts/StockTrader.asmx
        </wsa:To>
        <wsse:Security soap:mustUnderstand="1">
            <wsu:Timestamp>
                Contains Message Creation/Expiration TimeStamps
            </wsu:Timestamp>
            <wsse:BinarySecurityToken>
                Represents an X.509 security token
            </wsse:BinarySecurityToken>
            <xenc:EncryptedKey>
                <xenc:EncryptionMethod>
                    Specifies the algorithm that is used to encrypt a SOAP message
                </xenc:EncryptionMethod>
                <xenc:CipherData>
                    <xenc:CipherValue>Encrypted key</xenc:CipherValue>
                </xenc:CipherData>
            </xenc:EncryptedKey>
            <wssc:DerivedKeyToken>
                Represents a security token whose key is cryptographically derived
                from the key of another security token
            </wssc:DerivedKeyToken>
            <Signature>
                Represents the name of the element that defines a signature
            </Signature>
        </wsse:Security>
    </soap:Header>

    <soap:Body>
        <xenc:EncryptedData >
            <xenc:EncryptionMethod/>
            <KeyInfo>
                <wsse:SecurityTokenReference>
                    <wsse:Reference/>
                </wsse:SecurityTokenReference>
            </KeyInfo>
            <xenc:CipherData>
                <xenc:CipherValue>
```

```
            Encrypted message body
        </xenc:CipherValue>
      </xenc:CipherData>
    </xenc:EncryptedData>
</soap:Body>

</soap:Envelope>
```

The main difference between Listing 6-1 and Listing 6-2 is the addition of WS-Security tags in the request header and an encrypted message body. You can notice that the value of the symbol parameter is not readable in Listing 6-2.

This is a clear example of Web service composability, where additional specifications may be added or subtracted to a SOAP message as needed. WSE provides the API for implementing WS-Security in .NET-based Web services and client applications. The API allows you to write code to format secured SOAP request messages in the client and to process secured messages within a Web service.

Secure Web Services in an SOA

Security in an SOA presents several challenges. Traditional security mechanisms do not provide a comprehensive solution because most of them depend on a well-defined boundary that limits the enforcements of their rules. Plus, our industry has been shaped by companies that have developed products that do not necessarily integrate well with each other or that do not integrate at all. If we add the fact that hacker attacks occur on a daily basis, and that they could even come from someone within your organization, we have a not-so-pleasant picture that requires well-designed security strategies.

Before we look at some of these strategies, let's review the most important challenges involved in securing an SOA:

Interoperability and policies: There are several encryption and signing mechanisms and there are several platforms with different security models. A service and their consumers need to be able to implement the same standard in order to establish a successful communication.

Message security: A SOAP message crosses domain boundaries, and it might go through intermediaries. Traditional security models are designed to work within a controlled environment, but in the case of SOA there are messages that will be transmitted across multiple environments, and the integrity and confidentiality of the message still needs to be guaranteed.

Identity and trust: Both the client and the server need to know that they can rely on the other party. Each one of the systems that consume or expose a Web service might be under a different security model, and users will still need to be authenticated and authorized to perform a particular task.

WSE 3.0 provides us with the tools required to address most of these concerns without having to manually build the messages that will be compliant with the WS-Security specification. You might be thinking that all you need to secure your services is to enable SSL on your web application, but that is only the tip of the iceberg when it comes to a robust security implementation. There are several disadvantages of securing communication at the transport level and it will not always be the best option for your particular needs.

■**Note** *Transport level security* is the term used when data protection is provided by securing the communication channel itself. The most common example is the HTTPS channel that secures connections between browsers and web servers. HTTPS is based on the SSL protocol.

Existing security technologies, such as SSL, have limitations. We will address this particular topic in this chapter because it will help you understand why the WSE toolkit plays such an important role in the development of a secure Web service. These limitations are in the following areas:

Point-to-point security: SSL does not allow your message to go through intermediaries that might need to read the message or parts of the message and then forward it to a third-party entity.

Wire protection: Messages are only protected while they are on the wire. If the message reaches its destination and it gets stored it will be saved as plain text. This means that the message could be accessible to unauthorized users if the application is not properly configured to guarantee the message confidentiality.

Transport level encryption: You can't encrypt only a fragment of a message when you use transport level encryption. This is limiting because there are some cases where not all the information in the message needs to be protected, and you could reduce some of the encryption/decryption overhead by encrypting only the message elements that are confidential.

The WSE toolkit provides a solution for each one of these restrictions. Let's take a closer look at WSE 3.0 to see how it can be used to build a secure Web service based on the needs of your deployment scenario.

Implement WS-Security Using the WSE 3.0 Toolkit

One of the main design goals behind WSE 3.0 was to create a better product that allowed software developers to easily build secure Web services. The feedback obtained after releasing WSE 1.0 and 2.0 allowed the identification of common security scenarios.

You can find that your problem at hand is similar but not identical to one of these security scenarios. If that is the case, you can still leverage the portion of the scenario that matches your particular needs.

Public Web service: An application accesses a Web service provided by a third party. In this scenario the users are authenticated by sending a username and a password to the Web service. The Web service decrypts this data and validates it against a local identity store. The information that is transmitted needs to be protected, so the client and the server communicate using HTTPS. The service is accessed via the Internet, as shown in Figure 6-1.

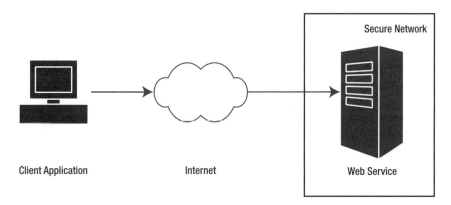

Figure 6-1. *A public Web service*

Intranet Web service: An organization exposes a Web service that provides business operations. In this scenario the messages are always within the boundaries of an organization that uses Active Directory to manage the network security. Active Directory supports the Kerberos protocol which provides the authentication, encryption, and message signing mechanisms required to guarantee a secure communication. This Web service is accessed by internal applications through the intranet, as shown in Figure 6-2.

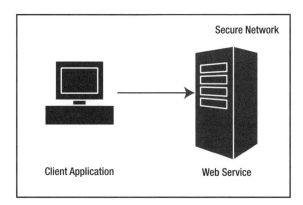

Figure 6-2. *An intranet Web service*

Internet B2B: Messages flow within an organization and between businesses. This scenario requires two different solutions: one for the client application that communicates with the internal Web service, and another one to secure the communication between two Web services that are hosted by different organizations. For the internal communication, the chosen solution is implemented using the Kerberos protocol. For the communication between businesses, X.509 certificates are used to provide mutual authentication, data protection, and data authenticity. Figure 6-3 shows a Web service that uses one security protocol for messages that are sent within the organization, and a different one for messages that are transferred between businesses.

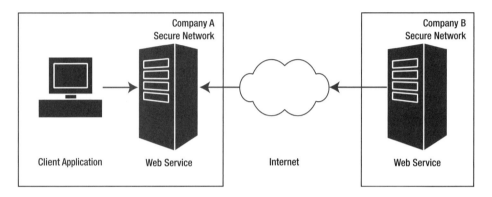

Figure 6-3. *A B2B Web service*

Multiple Internet Web services: These services are exposed by organizations whose policies require single sign-on capabilities (SSO). In this scenario the web application needs to access several services provided by an organization that stores user credentials in a database. The web application uses a secure channel to communicate with a Security Token Service (STS) that generates a secure token. This secure token can be used to interact with Web services A and B. This model provides a performance benefit because the authentication of the user is done only once: at the beginning of the session. The rest of the service calls are done using the secure token provided by the STS. Figure 6-4 illustrates a highly utilized web application that needs to access more than one external service.

These common security scenarios helped Microsoft define a set of core strategies that allow software developers to easily secure a Web service. These strategies are called *turnkey security assertions* and they are available in WSE 3.0 as a group of predefined policies that can be configured using the WSE 3.0 Settings Tool, or manually via code or a configuration file. Before we discuss these turnkey assertions, let's review the policy framework provided by WSE. This will help you understand the way that messages get processed when they are being sent or received by a client or a service.

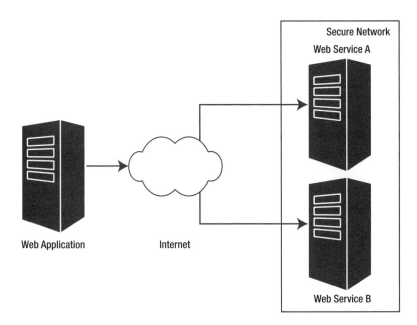

Figure 6-4. *A multiple Internet Web service*

WSE 3.0 Security Policies

WSE provides a set of classes that allow you to define your security requirements by declaring a policy using an XML configuration file. This file can be edited manually or using the WSE Settings Tool. Later in this chapter you will have the opportunity to use this tool to implement security policies for a client and service project. Each policy file can contain multiple policies, which gives you the flexibility to enforce different security restrictions within the same application.

You can also define your policies directly in the code. This could be a good option if you don't want to have the flexibility to add the policy definition without having to recompile your application. We recommend using policy files, since they will give system administrators the ability to modify the policy depending on the characteristics of the deployment environment. If you separate the security policy from the code you will increase the maintainability of your system and it will make your application easier to secure.

A policy is a group of policy assertions that map directly to a class. These classes get instantiated at runtime by the WSE framework and they are responsible for processing the SOAP messages and applying digital signatures, encryption, or any other custom processing that you might need, such as writing the content of the message to trace log.

■Note WSE 3.0 has greatly simplified the policy model, compared to the one provided by WSE 2.0. In this new version of WSE, the declarative model and the imperative programming model have been aligned so that you can use policy files to implement the same security restrictions that you could define via code.

Listing 6-3 shows a simplified policy file that defines that SOAP messages should be secured using Kerberos. The name of the class that implements the assertion is shown in bold.

Listing 6-3. *Policy File Showing an Empty Kerberos Assertion*

```
<policies xmlns="http://schemas.microsoft.com/wse/2005/06/policy">
    <extensions>
        <extension name="kerberosSecurity"
            type="Microsoft.Web.Services3.Design.KerberosAssertion,
            Microsoft.Web.Services3, Version=3.0.0.0, Culture=neutral,
            PublicKeyToken=31bf3856ad364e35" />
    </extensions>
    <policy name="MyKerberosPolicy">
        <kerberosSecurity />
    </policy>
</policies>
```

You can assign a policy to a Web service by using the Policy attribute, as shown in the following example:

```
[Policy("MyKerberosPolicy")]
public class Service : System.Web.Services.WebService
{
    public Service () {}
     [WebMethod]
    public string HelloWorld() {
        return "Hello World";
    }
}
```

You can do the same at the client side by applying the Policy attribute to the proxy class autogenerated by WSE 3.0. When you use WSE 3.0, your proxy file will contain a couple of classes that you can use to communicate with the service. One of them inherits from SoapHttpClientProtocol and it doesn't provide the extended capabilities offered by WSE. The second one inherits from WebServicesClientProtocol and this is the class that allows you to benefit from the features of the WSE framework. You could apply the Policy attribute to the second class, but this file is autogenerated and you would lose your changes if you update the Web reference.

For this reason, the best way to apply a policy at the client side is using the SetPolicy method of the WSE-enabled proxy class.

```
MyService.ServiceWse myService = new MyService.ServiceWse();
myService.SetPolicy("MyKerberosPolicy");
```

You can think of policies and their assertions as a pipeline where the assertions are executed in the order in which they are listed. Each policy assertion generates SOAP filters that are responsible for inspecting and modifying the SOAP messages. The methods that apply these filters are defined as abstract methods in the PolicyAssertion class and they are overridden by each policy assertion implementation.

```
public abstract SoapFilter CreateClientInputFilter(FilterCreationContext context);
public abstract SoapFilter CreateClientOutputFilter(FilterCreationContext context);
public abstract SoapFilter CreateServiceInputFilter(FilterCreationContext context);
public abstract SoapFilter CreateServiceOutputFilter(FilterCreationContext context);
```

Not all the assertions will implement all the methods; for example, a replay detection policy would need to process incoming messages only. These methods process the SOAP message and then return a SoapFilterResult instance that determines if the execution must continue or if it needs to be terminated.

Figure 6-5 represents how policy filters are applied to incoming and outgoing messages that flow between a service and a client.

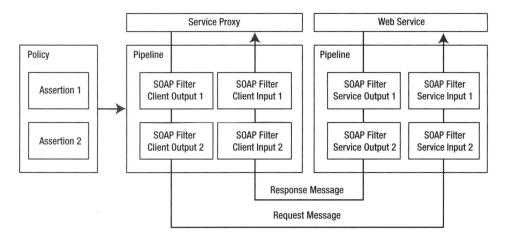

Figure 6-5. *Policies applied in the order in which they are defined*

This overview of the policy framework will now allow us to discuss the six turnkey security assertions provided by WSE 3.0. These six assertions are nothing else but predefined policies that cover the most frequent deployment scenarios that Microsoft has identified in existing Web service implementations.

Turnkey Security Assertions

The turnkey security assertions are a set of core strategies that allow software developers to easily secure a Web service. We present a brief definition of each one of them; most of them will be covered in detail later in this chapter and also in Chapter 7.

UsernameOverTransportSecurity: This strategy can be used when there is an existing secure channel, such as the one provided by SSL. The Web service client will send a Username Token to the server as a way to prove its identity. The server will be responsible for the validation of the token information, which contains the username and password. Upon successful validation of the credentials, the server might check whether the user is authorized to access the requested resources. In this scenario the client and the server trust each other enough to share a secret that will be used for authentication. This shared secret is the user's password that is received by the server and validated against a local database, a legacy application, LDAP, or Active Directory.

UsernameForCertificateSecurity: This assertion also uses a username and password to identify the Web service consumer, but it encrypts the content of the message using an X.509 certificate at the message level and not at the transport level. The main difference between these first two assertions is that in the first one, there must be an existing secure channel, such as HTTPS. In the second one, the client uses the public portion of the server's certificate to encrypt the message before sending it through the wire. In this case, the message might be sent via HTTP, but it is still protected because a hacker who could intercept the message won't be able to read it because the message was previously encrypted by the client.

AnonymousForCertificateSecurity: In this scenario, the server does not need to determine the identity of the Web service consumer. Any client application that has access to the certificate's public key will be able to communicate with the server. If needed, the identity of the caller could be determined by sending their credentials as part of the data contained in the message (not as part of a secure token).

MutualCertificate10 and MutualCertificate11: In these two assertions, the client and the server use certificates to prove their identity and to secure the messages. They provide similar implementations, except that one of them adheres to the WS-Security 1.0 standard and the other one follows the WS-Security 1.1 specification. There are other assertions that also use X.509 certificates to encrypt messages, but in these assertions in particular, the certificates are not only used for data encryption, they are also used to identify the other party by accessing the signature portion of the message. This signature is encrypted by the client using its private key, and decrypted by the server using the client key. The same applies when the server provides its credentials back to the client. The server signs the message using its private key and the client uses the server public key to decrypt it. This is why these patterns are named *mutual certificate*, because both the client and the server must prove its identity.

KerberosSecurity: This strategy is best suited for intranets where the messages flow between one or more Windows domains that use Active Directory. One of the biggest advantages of using this assertion is that it provides single sign-on features and better performance than X.509 certificates. This assertion provides tight integration with the Windows security model. This means that you will be able to use features such as impersonation and delegation when making a remote service call. In this scenario the management of user identities is greatly simplified because you can leverage the tools provided by Windows security.

WSE 3.0 is not limited to these six security assertions. Developers can create custom assertions that better meet their needs; however, in the majority of the cases, your deployment configuration will fall within one of these predefined categories.

Securing the StockTrader Application Using WSE 3.0

The turnkey assertions described in the previous section should help as a guide to choosing the best security mechanisms to protect your SOAP messages. We would like to emphasize that these decisions should be made based on the characteristics of the environment where your application will run, as opposed to the particular features provided by the service. This is what allows for great flexibility in your systems, where you can have a base set of features and multiple policy files that get used depending on the deployment scenarios.

We will now take a look at the first sample implementation of the turnkey security assertions.

Getting Started with the Sample Solution

The sample solution that is presented here shows you how to secure an application using the UsernameForCertificate assertion.

Figure 6-6 shows the Solution Explorer window for the Visual Studio .NET solution that we will use in this chapter. It is based on the StockTrader application presented in Chapters 3 and 4 and includes the following:

- A Web service called StockTraderSecure, which provides methods for requesting stock quotes and executing trades.

- A client console application called StockTraderClient, which invokes the StockTrader Web service via a proxy class.

- A reference assembly called StockTraderTypes, which provides code definitions for the custom types that are used by the StockTrader Web service. (The source project is included in this chapter's solution for clarity. However, future chapter projects will simply reference the compiled StockTraderTypes assembly instead.) The type definitions are contained in a separate assembly in order to be accessible to any application that wants to interact with the StockTrader Web service. (Recall that these custom types are based on the StockTrader XSD schema, which is presented in Chapter 3.)

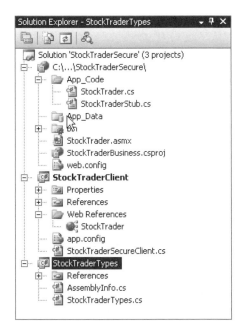

Figure 6-6. *The StockTraderSecure .NET solution, containing three projects*

Note There will be some cases where a client application and a service application will not be able to share the assembly that contains the data type definitions. For example, you will not be able to reference the StockTraderTypes assembly directly if you build your client application using Java. For these cases, you can rely on the data types exposed by the autogenerated proxy class. As you will see later, we will be using the Quote object exposed by the proxy class and not the one provided by the StockTraderTypes assembly. This approach has an important benefit, which is that you do not need to redistribute the data types DLL to your client applications. Keep in mind that using this approach does not mean that the developers building the Web service are free to change the data type definitions at any time. If they do this, they will generate compatibility issues between the client and the service. Having this flexibility doesn't exempt a developer from carefully managing changes to the definition of a Web service.

The StockTraderSecure Web service is a copy of the StockTrader Web service presented in Chapter 3 with additional code for processing SOAP request messages that have been digitally signed and encrypted. To get started with building the solution, you need to perform the following steps:

1. Install and configure the WSE toolkit (refer to Chapter 5 for detailed instructions).

2. Install and configure the X.509 test certificates (refer to Chapter 5 for detailed instructions).

3. Create a new ASP.NET Web service by clicking the File ➤ New ➤ Web Site menu option in Visual Studio 2005. Choose the File System Location option to create the project in a new folder named StockTraderSecure.

4. Delete the Service1.asmx and Service1.cs files from the project.

5. Copy the existing files StockTrader.asmx, StockTrader.cs, and StockTraderStub.cs from the original StockTrader project over to the new StockTraderSecure project. Add these files to the new project by right-clicking the App_Code folder and selecting the Add Existing Item menu option. (You do not need to modify namespace information in the newly added files.)

6. Add the StockTraderTypes reference assembly or project to the solution. Again, you can obtain this reference project from the Chapter 3 sample files. Alternatively, you can just copy the StockTraderTypes.dll compiled assembly over to the \bin directory of the StockTraderSecure Web service project. Use the Project ➤ Add Reference menu option to set a reference to the StockTraderTypes assembly or project from the StockTrader-Secure Web service project.

Create the Web Service Client

So far the StockTraderSecure solution only contains a Web service; and you have not yet modified the Web service code to handle digitally signed SOAP messages. First you will write a Web service client that generates SOAP request messages. The steps are as follows:

1. Add a new Console Application project to the solution called StockTraderClient.csproj.

2. Rename the default C# class file to StockTraderSecureClient.cs.

3. Add a Web reference to the StockTraderSecure Web service from the console application project using the Project ➤ Add Web Reference menu option. Give this reference the name StockTraderProxy. This will autogenerate a proxy class file called Reference.cs under the Web References\[Reference Name]\Reference.map subproject folder. (If you do not see this file you can use the Project ➤ Show All Files menu option to expand all files.)

■**Note** In Chapter 4 we showed you how to build the StockTraderConsole client by adding a reference to the StockTraderTypes DLL. In many cases it won't be possible to share the data type definition files between the Web service and the Web service consumer. For example, there will be cases where the service is built using .NET, and the consumer is built using Java. In this type of scenario, the Web service consumer would need to rely on the information provided by the WSDL in order to create classes that would store the values returned by the Web service calls.

---

4. Create a method in the default class that contains the code shown in Listing 6-4.

Listing 6-4. *Basic Unsecured Code Listing for the Web Service Client*

```
// Create an instance of the Web service proxy
StockTraderProxy.StockTrader serviceProxy = new StockTraderProxy.StockTrader();

// Call the service
Console.WriteLine("Calling {0}", serviceProxy.Url);
string Symbol = "MSFT";
StockTraderProxy.Quote q = serviceProxy.RequestQuote(Symbol);

// Show the results
Console.WriteLine("Web service Response:");
Console.WriteLine("");
Console.WriteLine( "\tSymbol:\t\t" + q.Symbol );
Console.WriteLine( "\tCompany:\t" + q.Company );
Console.WriteLine( "\tLast Price:\t" + q.Last );
Console.WriteLine( "\tPrevious Close:\t" + q.Previous_Close );
```

Compile and run the project to make sure that everything is working correctly. At this point you are calling the Web service using a proxy that derives from the System.Web.Services. Protocols.SoapHttpClientProtocol class.

Secure the StockTrader Web Service

Enable the Web service project for WSE 3.0 by following the next steps:

1. Right-click the StockTraderSecure project and select the WSE Settings Tool. On the General tab, check the Enable This Project for Web Services Enhancements box and the Enable Microsoft Web Service Enhancements Soap Protocol Factory box.

■**Note** The Soap Protocol Factory is only needed when accessing ASP.NET Web services that run under IIS.

---

2. Click the Security tab and check the Allow Test Roots box. The certificates used in this sample are not created by a certification authority and they will be rejected if you do not check this box. You should be careful not to allow test roots in the configuration of a production application.

3. Click the Diagnostics tab and check Enable Message Trace. This will allow you to examine SOAP messages like the ones in Listings 6-1 and 6-2.

4. Click OK to accept the changes and close the dialog. All the changes made by the WSE Settings Tool are saved in the web.config file, as shown in Listing 6-5.

Listing 6-5. *Changes Made by the WSE Configuration Tool*

```
<configuration>
    <configSections>
        <section name="microsoft.web.services3"
            type="Microsoft.Web.Services3.Configuration.WebServicesConfiguration,
                Microsoft.Web.Services3, Version=3.0.0.0, Culture=neutral,
                PublicKeyToken=31bf3856ad364e35" />
    </configSections>
    <system.web>
        <webServices>
            <soapExtensionImporterTypes>
                <add ➥
type="Microsoft.Web.Services3.Description.WseExtensionImporter,
                    Microsoft.Web.Services3, Version=3.0.0.0, ➥
Culture=neutral,
                    PublicKeyToken=31bf3856ad364e35" />
            </soapExtensionImporterTypes>
            <soapServerProtocolFactory
                type="Microsoft.Web.Services3.WseProtocolFactory,
                    Microsoft.Web.Services3, Version=3.0.0.0, Culture=neutral,
                    PublicKeyToken=31bf3856ad364e35" />
```

```
        </webServices>
        <compilation debug="true">
            <assemblies>
                <add
                      assembly="Microsoft.Web.Services3,
                      Version=3.0.0.0, Culture=neutral,
                      PublicKeyToken=31BF3856AD364E35" />
            </assemblies>
        </compilation>
    </system.web>
    <microsoft.web.services3>
        <diagnostics>
            <trace
                enabled="true"
                input="InputTrace.webinfo"
                output="OutputTrace.webinfo" />
        </diagnostics>
        <security>
            <x509 allowTestRoot="true" />
        </security>
    </microsoft.web.services3>
</configuration>
```

Create a Security Policy

Now, implement the UsernameForCertificate assertion by making the following changes to StockTraderSecure and StockTraderClient:

1. Enable the Web service project for WSE 3.0, either manually or with the WSE Settings Tool.

2. On the WSE Settings Tool, click the Security tab and check the Allow Test Roots box. This should only be done in a development or test environment. If you enable this feature you will be able to use test X.509 certificates as if they were valid certificates.

3. Click on the Diagnostics tab and check the Enable Message Trace box. This feature will generate a couple of files where incoming and outgoing messages will be logged as they get processed by the WSE 3.0 pipeline.

4. Go to the Policy tab, click Add, and provide a name for this new policy. Enter the name **UsernamePolicy** and click OK. This will bring up the WSE Security Settings Wizard. This wizard will guide you through the process of defining a security policy for your service or client. The result of this wizard will be a configuration file that will be stored in the root folder of your application. This XML-based policy file can be easily modified after the wizard has been completed.

5. Click Next in the wizard's welcome screen. The first decision is to choose whether you want to secure a client or a service application. In this case, you are securing a service application. The second question prompts you to choose a client authentication method. In this example, you want to secure your service using a username and password. As you can see, there are other options available that resemble the different security turnkey assertions described previously. For the current example, choose the Username radio button and click Next.

6. Leave the Perform Authorization box unchecked and click Next. We will discuss authorization in the "Authorization" section later in this chapter. In this first example you will not perform authorization checks. This means that you will not make an additional security check to verify if a user is authorized to execute a particular task. You will assume that once a user is authenticated they can access the operations provided by the service.

7. The username and password will help the service authenticate the user, but we still need to define a way to encrypt the information that will be sent in the message. The current step in the wizard allows you to choose the level of protection by providing the following options:

- *None*: This option relies on transport level protection; for example, this can be used if the communication channel will be secured using SSL.

- *Sign*: This option signs the message. In other words, a hash is created that can be used to determine whether the message was tampered with while in transit.

- *Sign and Encrypt*: This option signs the message and its contents are encrypted. Even if a nonauthorized user has access to the message, they won't be able to read its contents.

- *Sign, Encrypt, and Encrypt Signature*: This option signs the message and both the signature and the message itself are encrypted. This is the most secure option, but it also incurs additional overhead.

For this sample, choose Sign and Encrypt. Also, uncheck the Secure Session box, a feature that is discussed in Chapter 7.

8. The wizard will now show a screen where you can choose the X.509 certificate for encryption and signing. Select the WSE2QuickStartServer certificate and click Next.

9. The last step of the wizard shows you a summary of the decisions that you made. The name of the assertion is located in the second row of the summary pane. The questions asked by this security wizard will vary significantly, depending on the approach that you want to follow to secure your messages. However, at the end of the wizard you will notice that your decisions can be summarized as one of the six turnkey scenarios defined by Microsoft, as shown in Figure 6-7.

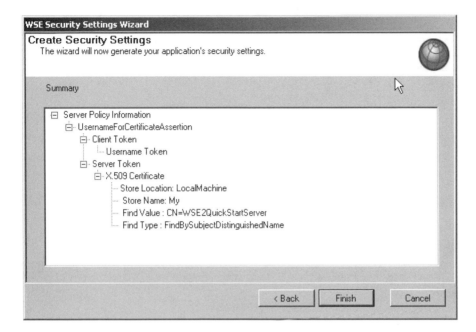

Figure 6-7. *Summary of the policy defined using the WSE Security Settings Wizard*

The wizard will generate a new file in the root directory of your project. The name of the file is wse3policyCache.config and it contains the definition of the policy that you just created. Listing 6-6 shows the policy file generated based on the options you chose in the WSE Security Settings Wizard.

Listing 6-6. *Policy File Generated by the WSE Security Settings Wizard*

```
<policies xmlns="http://schemas.microsoft.com/wse/2005/06/policy">
  <extensions>
    <extension name="usernameForCertificateSecurity"
        type="Microsoft.Web.Services3.Design.UsernameForCertificateAssertion,
        Microsoft.Web.Services3, Version=3.0.0.0, Culture=neutral,
        PublicKeyToken=31bf3856ad364e35" />
    <extension name="x509" type="Microsoft.Web.Services3.Design.X509TokenProvider,
        Microsoft.Web.Services3, Version=3.0.0.0, Culture=neutral,
        PublicKeyToken=31bf3856ad364e35" />
    <extension name="requireActionHeader"
        type="Microsoft.Web.Services3.Design.RequireActionHeaderAssertion,
        Microsoft.Web.Services3, Version=3.0.0.0, Culture=neutral,
        PublicKeyToken=31bf3856ad364e35" />
  </extensions>
```

```
<policy name="UsernamePolicy">
  <usernameForCertificateSecurity establishSecurityContext="false"
        renewExpiredSecurityContext="true" requireSignatureConfirmation="false"
        messageProtectionOrder="SignBeforeEncrypt" requireDerivedKeys="true"
        ttlInSeconds="300">
    <serviceToken>
      <x509 storeLocation="LocalMachine" storeName="My"
            findValue="CN=WSE2QuickStartServer"
            findType="FindBySubjectDistinguishedName" />
    </serviceToken>
    <protection>
      <request signatureOptions="IncludeAddressing, IncludeTimestamp,
            IncludeSoapBody"
            encryptBody="true" />
      <response signatureOptions="IncludeAddressing, IncludeTimestamp,
            IncludeSoapBody"
            encryptBody="true" />
      <fault
            signatureOptions="IncludeAddressing,
            IncludeTimestamp, IncludeSoapBody"
            encryptBody="false" />
    </protection>
  </usernameForCertificateSecurity>
  <requireActionHeader />
</policy>
</policies>
```

The web.config file is also modified by the wizard by the addition of one line that references the new policy file. That line is under the <Microsoft.web.services3> section:

```
<policy fileName="wse3policyCache.config" />
```

Reference the Security Policy from Code

Open the StockTrader.cs file and make the following changes:

1. Add a using directive for the Microsoft.Web.Services3 namespace.

2. Add the following reflection attribute to the definition of the StockTrader class:
   [Policy("UsernamePolicy")].

Implement a Custom Username Token Manager

The default behavior of the UsernameTokenManager class is to authenticate the user against an Active Directory or a local Windows account. In this example, we are going to override the default behavior of this class by creating a custom username token manager. To accomplish this, you will need to create a new class file named UsernameTokenManager.cs, and type in the code shown in Listing 6-7.

Listing 6-7. *A Custom Username Token Manager*

```
using System;
using System.Xml;
using Microsoft.Web.Services3.Security;
using Microsoft.Web.Services3.Security.Tokens;

namespace StockTraderSecure
{

    public class CustomUsernameTokenManager : UsernameTokenManager
    {

        public CustomUsernameTokenManager()
        {
        }

        public CustomUsernameTokenManager(XmlNodeList nodes) : base(nodes)
        {
        }

        protected override string AuthenticateToken(UsernameToken token)
        {

            // return the password, in this sample, the password is the same value
            // as the user name, but in upper case

            // In a production application, the password would be retrieved
            // from an external storage, such as a SQL Server database or
            // an LDAP directory.

            return token.Username.ToUpper();

        }

    }
}
```

The previous code uses a straightforward algorithm to obtain the user's password. It simply converts the username to uppercase. If you want the user to be authenticated successfully, you will need to build a client application that passes the same value as a username and password, with the second one containing only uppercase characters.

The last step is to modify the web.config file to specify the name of the user-defined class that will handle user authentication. The <securityTokenManager> section must be located under the <security> tag of the <microsoft.web.services3> section. Listing 6-8 shows a fragment of the web.config file that enables the service to use a custom security token manager.

Listing 6-8. *Fragment of the web.config File*

```
<securityTokenManager>
      <add
          type="StockTraderSecure.CustomUsernameTokenManager"
          namespace="http://docs.oasis-open.org/wss/2004/01/oasis- ➥
             200401-wss-wssecurity-secext-1.0.xsd"
          localName="UsernameToken" xmlns=""/>
</securityTokenManager>
```

Secure the Client Application

The client application will also be secured using the WSE Security Settings Wizard. The following steps will help you define a client security policy that will comply with the rules defined by the service policy.

1. Enable the StockTraderClient project for WSE 3.0 using the WSE Settings Tool. Enable Message Tracing in the Diagnostics tab, just like you did for the StockTraderSecure project.

2. In the WSE Settings Tool, choose the Policy tab, and select the Enable Policy check box.

3. Click Add and enter the name **UsernamePolicy** and click OK.

4. Click Next in the WSE Security Settings Wizard welcome screen.

5. Choose the option to secure a client application, select the Username radio button, and click Next.

6. Choose to specify the username and password in code. It is not recommended to store these credentials in a configuration file.

7. Choose the option to Sign and Encrypt the messages, just like you did when you defined the policy for the service. If you choose a different encryption level, the client will not be compliant with the policy defined by the service and you will get a SOAP exception during the service call. Uncheck the Secure Session box and click Next.

8. The wizard will now show a screen where you can choose the X.509 certificate that will be used for encryption and signing. Select the WSE2QuickStartServer certificate and click Next.

9. The last step of the wizard, shown in Figure 6-8, displays the summary of the security policy that you have created for the client application. Notice that these decisions can be grouped under the same turnkey scenario as the service application.

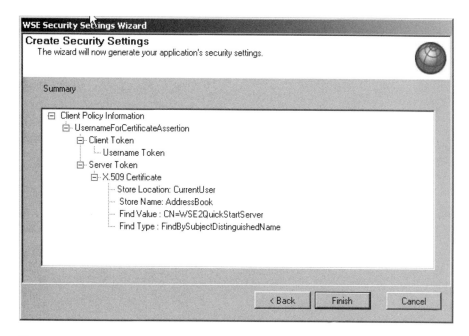

Figure 6-8. *Summary of the security policy*

Use the Proxy Class Generated by WSE

The next step is to regenerate the StockTraderProxy Web reference. Right-click it in the Solution Explorer and select the Update Web Reference command.

Open the Reference.cs autogenerated file, which is located under the StockTradeProxy/ Reference.map folder. Find the definition of the StockTraderWse class and you will see that it inherits from the Microsoft.Web.Services3.WebServicesClientProtocol class. The Microsoft. Web.Services3 namespace contains the core classes that are used by the WSE toolkit.

Now open the StockTraderConsole.cs class and modify it as follows:

1. Add a using directive for the Microsoft.Web.Services3.Security.Tokens namespace.

2. Modify the line that creates an instance of the Web service proxy by replacing the StockTrader class with the StockTraderWse class.

3. Create a Username Token. For sample purposes, the password value is the username in uppercase letters. The password is included as plain text in the token, which is encrypted using the X.509 certificate.

4. Append the token to the proxy.

5. Set the client policy.

Listing 6-9 shows the code after the previously described changes have been made.

Listing 6-9. *Secured Code Listing for the Web Service Client*

```
// Create an instance of the Web service proxy
StockTraderProxy.StockTraderWse serviceProxy = new ➥
    StockTraderProxy.StockTraderWse();

// Create user name token
UsernameToken token = new ➥
    UsernameToken("admin", "ADMIN", PasswordOption.SendPlainText);

// Append token to the proxy
serviceProxy.SetClientCredential<UsernameToken>(token);

// Set the client policy
serviceProxy.SetPolicy("UsernamePolicy");

// Call the service
Console.WriteLine("Calling {0}", serviceProxy.Url);
string Symbol = "MSFT";
StockTraderProxy.Quote q = serviceProxy.RequestQuote(Symbol);

// Show the results
Console.WriteLine("Web service Response:");
Console.WriteLine("");
Console.WriteLine( "\tSymbol:\t\t" + q.Symbol );
Console.WriteLine( "\tCompany:\t" + q.Company );
Console.WriteLine( "\tLast Price:\t" + q.Last );
Console.WriteLine( "\tPrevious Close:\t" + q.Previous_Close );
```

You can now run the application and use the trace files generated by WSE to examine the messages that are being sent and received by the service and the client applications. The trace file shows the messages at different steps of the SOAP filtering pipeline.

You can create new policies or modify the existing one and use this trace utility to see the effect that they have in the generated SOAP messages. For example, you can create a new policy where the content of the message is only signed but not encrypted. In this case you will be able to read the values of messages sent by looking at the unprocessed messages in the trace files. In the sample that you just created you won't be able to see the values passed between the client and the service due to the encryption mode that was set in the policy file.

Authorization

WSE 3.0 provides a framework to authorize users and roles. Similar to other security configuration features in WSE 3.0, you can do this using either a policy file or code.

Declarative Authorization

The StockTrader.asmx Web service authenticates users through a custom username token manager, but no further security checks are performed after the user is successfully identified.

You will now configure this Web service to validate whether the user is authorized to access the services provided by the StockTrader service. The simplest way to do this is through a policy file, as shown in the following steps:

1. In the wse3policyCache.config file, add the following elements under the <policy> section:

```
<authorization>
      <allow user="admin" />
      <deny user="*" />
</authorization>
```

2. In the same file, under the <extensions> section, add the following line:

```
<extension name="authorization"
      type="Microsoft.Web.Services3.Design.AuthorizationAssertion,
      Microsoft.Web.Services3,
      Version=3.0.0.0, Culture=neutral,
      PublicKeyToken=31bf3856ad364e35" />
```

The <authorization> tag allows you to grant or deny access to the service based on the user's name or role. You can test this by modifying the code in the console application to use a different username, such as "guest." If you run the application, it will throw an exception that displays the message "Microsoft.Web.Services3.Security.SecurityFault: User 'guest' is not authorized to access the service."

■Note In this sample we chose to implement a very simple custom username token manager. If we had used the default username token manager or a Kerberos token, we could have used Windows roles to allow or deny access to the service. In these two models, a successfully authenticated user is mapped to a Windows account using the Principal property of the current token.

Code-Based Authorization

There might be some cases where policy-based authorization is not what you need because it gets applied equally to all the methods available in the service. The following example shows you how to authorize a user at the method level:

1. Add a using directive for the Systems.Xml namespace and one for the Microsoft.Web.Services3.Security.Tokens namespace.

2. Add a private method in the StockTrader.cs file.

```
private void authorize()
{

    string username = ➡
        RequestSoapContext.Current.Credentials.UltimateReceiver. ➡
        GetClientToken<UsernameToken>().Username;

    if (username == "admin")
    {
        return;
    }
    else
    {
        throw new SoapException("Access denied.",
        new XmlQualifiedName("Authorization"));
    }
}
```

3. Add the following lines to the beginning of the RequestQuote method:

```
// Check if the user is authorized to access this method
authorize();
```

The previous changes reflect a scenario where only the "admin" user is authorized to access the RequestQuote operation. The authorize method will throw an exception if the user is not authorized, and the execution of the call will be aborted.

Summary

In this chapter we explained some important security concepts and we gave you an overview about why WS-Security and WSE 3.0 play such an important role when building .NET-based Web services or Web service consumers.

You learned about the common security scenarios that Microsoft has identified based on feedback from developers who implemented Web services using WSE 1.0 and WSE 2.0. Then you reviewed the six turnkey assertions that Microsoft built into the WSE Security Settings Wizard.

The second part of this chapter guided you through a simple example that secures the StockTrader application. We implemented the UsernameForCertificate assertion using the WSE Security Settings Wizard and we showed you how to create a custom username token manager. Finally, we showed you how to authorize a user using either code or a policy file.

You are now ready to jump into Chapter 7, where you will take a look at other turnkey assertions and review topics such as stateful sessions and replay attacks.

■ ■ ■

Extended Web Services Security with WS-Security and WS-Secure Conversation

In Chapter 6 you learned about the UsernameForCertificateSecurity assertion. In this assertion the client provides a username and a password as a means to prove its identity, and the content of the messages is encrypted using an X.509 certificate. In this scenario, the client and the service trust each other enough to establish direct communication without relying on a third party that proves their identities. This model is known as *direct authentication,* and it is the most basic authentication approach that can be used to establish a trust relationship. We begin this chapter by reviewing this authentication model as well as delving into the concept of *brokered authentication.*

Authentication Models

The characteristics of your deployment scenarios will give you the option to choose between different types of authentication mechanisms. Your decision will depend upon several factors, such as existing security infrastructure, interoperability requirements, and organizational boundaries. Let's review direct authentication and discuss brokered authentication, describing the main advantages and disadvantages of each.

Direct Authentication

In this model, the client provides its credentials and the service is responsible for the validation of the credentials against an identity store, such as LDAP or a SQL Server database. In the majority of cases, these credentials will be passed as a username and password and both the service and the client have the responsibility to maintain these credentials as confidential. If the client and the service do not manage these credentials appropriately the security of the information is compromised. For example, relying on a service to manage its own passwords using a SQL Server database leaves the door open for possible mistakes. The developer implementing the solution could choose to store the passwords in plain text format and someone who gains access to the database could read those credentials.

This model is most frequently used when there is no security infrastructure that can be used by both parties during the authentication process. The diagram in Figure 7-1 shows how the client, service, and identity store interact in order to validate a client request.

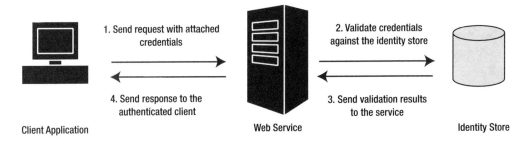

Figure 7-1. *A graphical representation of the direct authentication model*

Advantages and Disadvantages of Direct Authentication

The direct authentication model has several advantages and disadvantages. The advantages are as follows:

Simplicity: You don't need to rely on a public key infrastructure (PKI) or Active Directory in order to implement a secure Web service.

Flexibility: You can use almost any identity store to provide the authentication mechanism. For example, you can call a legacy system already used in the organization that can validate user credentials on your behalf.

The disadvantages are as follows:

Management overhead: Giving each service the ability to manage its own identity store could create a management nightmare when the number of Web services in the organization grows to support more business scenarios.

Shared-secret-based: Sharing a secret, such as a username and password, and using it to provide authentication is not the strongest form of security available in the industry. There are stronger security mechanisms such as X.509 or Kerberos. The reason shared secrets are not strong is because users tend to select passwords that are easy to guess. If a user selects a strong password he might write it down in a note and leave it next to his computer. This is a security risk not only for the system that is being attacked by a hacker but also for any other applications where the user has used the same login name and password.

Process-intensive: The client must authenticate itself every time it calls the service. This is a process-intensive operation due to the encryption and decryption steps executed both at the client and the service.

Implementation Options for Direct Authentication

If you wish to implement this security model you can rely upon two of the turnkey security assertions provided by WSE 3.0.

UsernameForCertificateSecurity: In this assertion, the message confidentiality is provided at the message level by encrypting the content of the message using an X.509 certificate.

UsernameOverTransportSecurity: This assertion relies on an existing secure channel that will prevent the message from being accessed by an unauthorized entity.

Brokered Authentication

In this model, the client and the service do not attempt to authenticate each other directly. They use an intermediary that validates the client's identity and then provides a security token as proof of successful authentication. The client attaches this token to the request and the service uses this token to authenticate the client. In the real world this is equivalent to a passport or a driver's license, which is tamperproof and secure enough to be trusted. There are government agencies responsible for the validation of the person's identity and, in the case of the driver's license, validation of the person's driving skills. These agencies require different documentation to validate the person's identity. Once the license or passport is issued, the person can use it to identify himself at places such as banking institutions.

Similar to this analogy, authentication brokers, such as VeriSign or Windows Active Directory, require the entity to provide enough information to validate its identity. In the case of VeriSign, it requires documentation to validate whether the organization is registered and legitimate and still active.

Security tokens have a duration period; some of them, such as X.509 certificates, can last years, and some others, such as Kerberos tickets, can last only minutes or hours.

The duration of an X.509 certificate depends on the criteria used by the certificate authority when it extends the certificate. In the case of VeriSign, it extends for a limited number of years, because with every renewal it wants to reverify whether your corporation is in good standing. An Active Directory Kerberos ticket has a default duration of ten hours; this value can be modified using the Group Policy Object Editor at the domain level.

The diagram in Figure 7-2 shows a client that requests a security token and then uses it to communicate with two services. You can notice that the client only needs to request the token once during this session, which helps reduce the transaction time. Another important aspect of the diagram is that two services are using the same authentication broker. This is one of the main advantages of this model, because it provides a centralized authentication authority and it allows for easier management of the identity store.

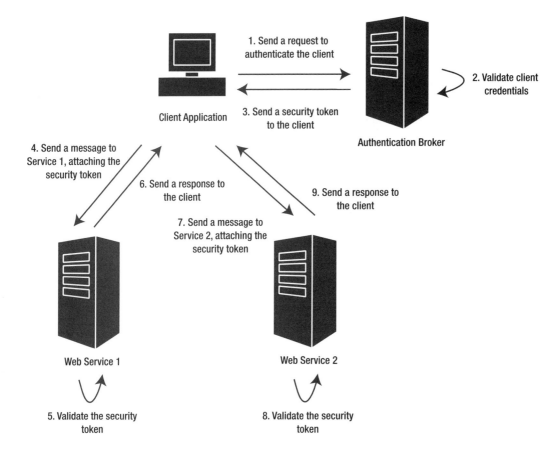

Figure 7-2. *A brokered authentication model*

Advantages and Disadvantages of Brokered Authentication

The main advantages of brokered authentication are as follows:

Centralized authentication: Having a single source for authentication simplifies the management of the identity information. The services won't need to create and manage their own set of users; they can rely upon the centralized identity broker to perform these tasks.

Single sign-on (SSO) capabilities: This model allows clients to authenticate once and then use the same token for different services within the organization.

Stronger security: Brokered authentication relies on robust authentication mechanisms such as X.509 certificates and Kerberos. The storage of passwords and the protection mechanisms are more reliable than those that could be implemented by a developer that follows a direct authentication pattern.

Direct trust: In this scenario the client and the service don't need to trust each other directly. This means that the services can rely on somebody else to add, remove, and update the identity information from their client base.

The main disadvantages of brokered authentication are as follows:

Single point of failure: If for any reason the authentication broker is not available or its security is compromised there could be a negative effect on the clients and services that rely upon it for identity management. This means that while the broker is not available, all the services that depend on it for authentication will not be accessible to process secure messages. This risk can be mitigated by having a backup server. If the security of the broker is compromised, the client or the service could be tricked to believe that it is communicating with an authorized entity.

Existing infrastructure: Using brokered authentication requires existing infrastructure such as Active Directory or a PKI. If an organization does not have access to these resources it will need to obtain it before the implementation of this security model.

Implementation Options for Brokered Authentication

WSE 3.0 provides three brokered authentication options:

Kerberos: This option is ideal for organizations that manage their network security using Windows domains and Active Directory. This protocol allows you to take full advantage of the security features provided by Windows, such as impersonation and delegation.

X.509 certificates: Certificates provide a robust solution for inter-organization communication and securing messages that go across multiple platforms.

Custom security token: This option requires the implementation of a Security Token Service (STS). The STS authenticates a client and it then issues a custom token, such as an XML-based Security Assertion Markup Language (SAML) token. This is a good pattern for inter-organization communication where all parties can agree on a standard implementation of the STS.

Implementing Brokered Authentication

Let's take a look at a couple of examples that implement the brokered authentication pattern.

Brokered Authentication Using Mutual Certificates

Here we are going to use the client's X.509 certificate to provide the credentials needed by the server to authenticate the caller. As we discussed previously, usernames and passwords are not the strongest form of security, and X.509 certificates provide an alternate authentication mechanism.

We are going to use the solution created in Chapter 6. This solution shows the implementation of the UsernameForCertificateSecurity assertion.

How Mutual Certificate Authentication Works

Let's walk through the list of steps that need to take place in order to establish a secure communication between a Web service and a client that follow the MutualCertificate10 or MutualCertificate11 patterns.

Infrastructure Prerequisites

As we discussed earlier, the brokered authentication model requires infrastructure that might or might not be in place in your organization, or in the organizations that you are doing business with. In the case of the mutual certificate model, both the service and the client need to have a valid X.509 certificate. These certificates can be generated by any of these three approaches:

- Use the Makecert tool that is available as part of the WSE 3.0 toolkit. This is only a valid option if you are in a development or test environment.

- Use Windows 2003 Certificate Services.

- Use a certificate authority, such as VeriSign and Digicert.

■**Note** Windows 2003 has the capability to act as a certificate authority. This gives you the ability to generate your own certificates and maintain your own PKI. New features, such as autoenrollment for users, give you the ability to automatically deploy a certificate with no user intervention.

Here we are using the WSE2QuickStartClient and the WSE2QuickStartServer. You need to make sure that these certificates are properly installed in your computer. In order to do this, you can open the Certificates tool provided by the WSE 3.0 toolkit, or you can use the Certificates snap-in within the Microsoft Management Console.

Let's use the Certificates tool in this exercise. As you already know, this tool is available via the Programs menu, under the Microsoft WSE 3.0 group. After you open the tool you can select the Current User location and Personal for the store name to find the WSE2QuickStartClient certificate. After you choose this certificate from your personal store, the tool will display the screen shown in Figure 7-3.

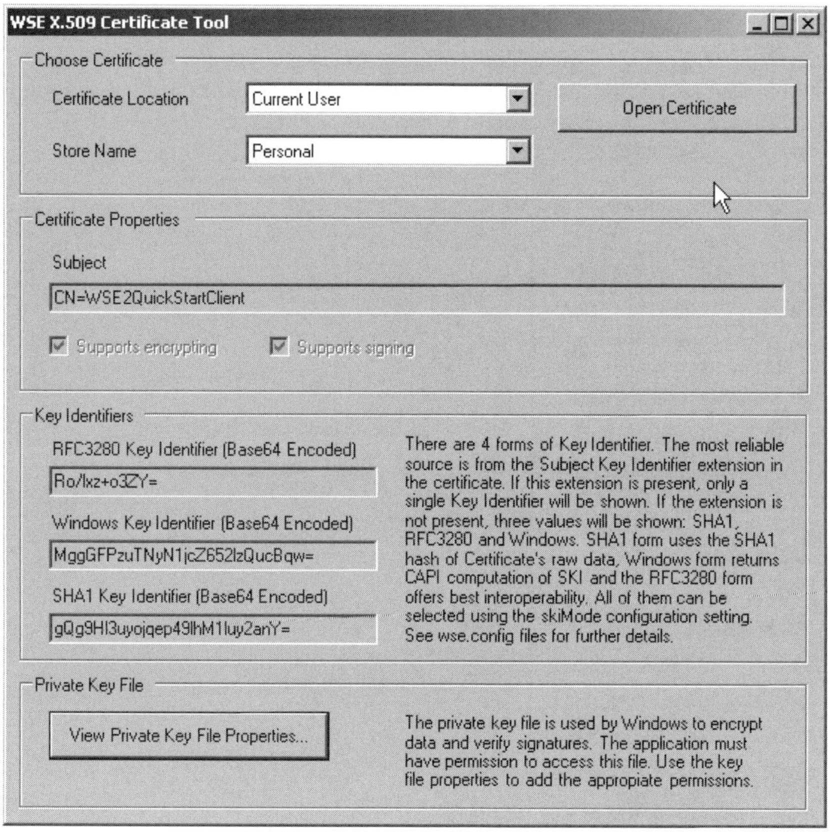

Figure 7-3. *The properties of the WSE2QuickStartClient certificate*

Now choose the Local Computer certificate location and the Personal store to find the WSE2QuickStartServer certificate. If both certificates are there it means that you either installed them automatically through a setup file, or manually, following the instructions in Chapter 5. The certificates must be installed correctly in order to run this sample. If you get any exceptions during the execution of this sample, you should go back to Chapter 5 and review the installation instructions to make sure you didn't miss any important steps. Another option is to run the setup.bat file that is located under the Sample directory of the %Program Files%\Microsoft WSE\v3.0 directory.

Message Flow

Before the communication takes place, the client must have access to its own certificate, plus the public portion of the server's certificate. The server only needs to have access to its own certificate, because the client will attach the public portion of the client certificate to the request. The diagram in Figure 7-4 shows a simplified representation of the steps.

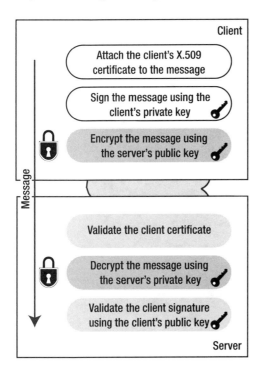

Figure 7-4. *Mutual certificate assertion message flow*

The following steps occur when the client makes a call to the service using the mutual certificates pattern:

1. *Attach X.509 certificate*: The client assumes that the server does not have access to its certificate in a local store. It attaches the certificate information to the outgoing message.

2. *Sign the message*: The client uses its private key to sign the message. This signature will allow the server to validate the message origin and its integrity.

3. *Encrypt the message*: The client uses the server public key to encrypt the message. This will prevent nonauthorized users from accessing the content of the message while it is in transit.

4. *Validate client certificate*: The server checks that the certificate has not expired, that it has not been tampered with, and that it is issued by a certificate authority that is trusted by the server. It also checks the certificate revocation list (CRL) to see if the certificate is included in the list. The check can be performed online or against a local CRL. The default mode is to check online and this can be modified in the Security tab of the WSE 3.0 Settings Tool.

5. *Decrypt the message*: After the certificate is validated, the server proceeds to decrypt the message using its private key.

6. *Validate the signature*: The last step is to validate the client signature using the client public key. This helps the service validate whether the message is coming from the right client and has not been altered while in transit.

Secure the Web Service

The following steps show you how to secure a Web service using X.509 certificates:

1. In the StockTraderSecure project, open the WSE 3.0 Settings Tool.

2. In the Policy tab, click the Add button. You should see the UsernamePolicy in the list of existing Application Policies.

3. Name this policy *MutualCertificatePolicy* and click OK.

4. Click Next in the welcome screen and choose to secure a service in the Authentication Settings step. Select Certificate as the authentication method and click Next.

5. The Authorized Clients step allows you to choose one or many certificates that are allowed to access the service. In this example we are going to uncheck this box, and we will configure Authorization later, making changes directly to the configuration files.

6. This step prompts you to select the message protection level, just as you have already seen in Chapter 6. Leave the WS-Security 1.1 Extensions box checked. You would uncheck this box if you need to interact with clients that do not support WS-Security 1.1. Choose Sign and Encrypt, uncheck the Secure Session box, and click Next.

7. Click the Select Certificate button and choose the WSE2QuickStartServer from the list. Click Next to continue.

■**Note** The client will also have access to the WSE2QuickStartServer certificate and it will use its public key to encrypt the message. When the service receives the message, it will use this certificate's private key to decrypt it. If the service sends a response to the client, it will use the certificate's private key to sign the message.

---

8. Review the settings of the MutalCertificatePolicy to make sure that you selected the right options during this process. The summary should look like the screen shown in Figure 7-5.

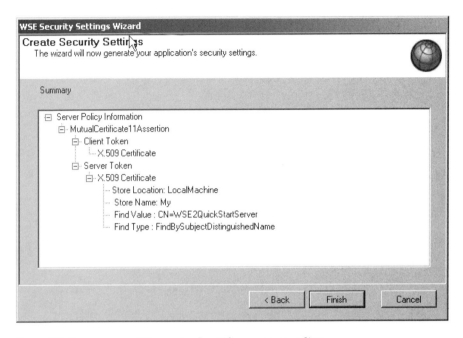

Figure 7-5. *A summary of the mutual certificate server policy*

9. Click Finish to complete the process and open the wse3policyCache.config policy file to see the new settings.

The wizard adds the following elements to the existing policy file. You can see that the definition UsernamePolicy is still in there, which means that you can select to use it or the MutualCertificatePolicy in your project. Listing 7-1 shows the changes to the policy file after adding the MutualCertificatePolicy.

Listing 7-1. *The Policy File After Adding the MutualCertificatePolicy*

```
<policy name="MutualCertificatePolicy">
    <mutualCertificate11Security
        establishSecurityContext="false"
        renewExpiredSecurityContext="true" requireSignatureConfirmation="true"
        messageProtectionOrder="SignBeforeEncrypt" requireDerivedKeys="true"
        ttlInSeconds="300">
        <serviceToken>
            <x509 storeLocation="LocalMachine" storeName="My"
                findValue="CN=WSE2QuickStartServer"
                findType="FindBySubjectDistinguishedName" />
        </serviceToken>
```

```
        <protection>
            <request signatureOptions="IncludeAddressing, IncludeTimestamp,
                IncludeSoapBody" encryptBody="true" />
            <response signatureOptions="IncludeAddressing, IncludeTimestamp,
                IncludeSoapBody" encryptBody="true" />
            <fault
                signatureOptions="IncludeAddressing,
                    IncludeTimestamp, IncludeSoapBody"
                encryptBody="false" />
        </protection>
    </mutualCertificate11Security>
    <requireActionHeader />
</policy>
```

In this policy file you can see that the WSE 3.0 security wizard identifies our scenario as falling within the MutualCertificate11Security assertion. If you look closer at these elements you will see that each one of your decisions is reflected here and you can make changes manually if required.

To demonstrate how easy it is to make changes, we are going to add an authorization section to this policy. The authorization rules will only grant access to those clients that are authenticated using the WSE2QuickStartClient certificate. Copy these lines of code under the start of the Policy tag in the policy file:

```
<authorization>
    <allow user="CN=WSE2QuickStartClient"/>
    <deny user="*"/>
</authorization>
```

The last step before we move to the client project is to apply this policy to the service. You can do this by finding the place in the StockTrader class where you applied the Username-Policy and modify the policy name to say MutualCertificatePolicy. After this change, the class definition should look like the following:

```
[Policy("MutualCertificatePolicy")]
public class StockTrader : StockTraderStub
```

Secure the Client Application

In order to secure the StockTraderClient application you will follow similar steps to the ones you executed in Chapter 6. The fact that these steps are similar is one of the main benefits of using WSE 3.0. It gives you the ability to concentrate more on decisions to secure your application than on putting the security implementation in place.

We are going to abbreviate some of the instructions, given that you have been through this wizard a couple of times already:

1. Open the WSE 3.0 Settings Tool, go to the Policy tab, and click the Add button.

2. Name this policy *MutualCertificatePolicy* and click OK.

3. In the Authentication Settings step, choose Secure a Client Application and choose Certificate and click Next.

4. In the Client Certificate step, choose the X.509 certificate named *WSE2QuickStart-Client* from the CurrentUser store and click Next. This is the certificate that will be used to sign the message using the certificate private key. The service will use this certificate public key to validate the integrity of the message.

5. The Message Protection screen gives you the options that you are already familiar with. Since you selected to use WS-Security 1.1 in the service, you will need to do the same in the client. The protection order for the message should also match the service protection order requisites, which are *Sign* and *Encrypt*. Remember to uncheck the Secure Session box. We will talk about the benefits provided by this feature in the section "Establish Trusted Communication with WS-Secure Conversation" later in this chapter. Click Next once you have provided all the answers required in this step.

6. In this screen you are asked to select one more certificate. Select the LocalMachine store, click Select Certificate, and choose the WSE2QuickStartServer certificate from the list. This is the server certificate that will be used to encrypt the message. The client application must have access to this certificate before you make this first call. In a production scenario, you can achieve this by including the public portion of the certificate as part of the installation package. Click Next and review the policy summary. It should look like the one shown in Figure 7-6. Click Finish to complete the process.

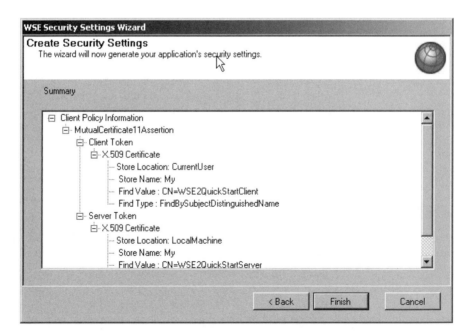

Figure 7-6. *A summary of the mutual certificate client policy*

Let's take a look at Listing 7-2 to review the changes made to the wse3policyCache.config file. The MutualCertificatePolicy has been added and you can see that it references both the client token and the server token.

Listing 7-2. *Changes to the Client Policy File After Adding the MutualCertificatePolicy*

```
<policy name="MutualCertificatePolicy">
    <mutualCertificate11Security establishSecurityContext="false"
        renewExpiredSecurityContext="true" requireSignatureConfirmation="true"
        messageProtectionOrder="SignBeforeEncrypt" requireDerivedKeys="true"
        ttlInSeconds="300">
        <clientToken>
            <x509 storeLocation="CurrentUser" storeName="My"
                findValue="CN=WSE2QuickStartClient"
                findType="FindBySubjectDistinguishedName" />
        </clientToken>
        <serviceToken>
            <x509 storeLocation="LocalMachine" storeName="My"
                findValue="CN=WSE2QuickStartServer"
                findType="FindBySubjectDistinguishedName" />
        </serviceToken>
        <protection>
            <request signatureOptions="IncludeAddressing, IncludeTimestamp,
                IncludeSoapBody" encryptBody="true" />
            <response signatureOptions="IncludeAddressing, IncludeTimestamp,
                IncludeSoapBody" encryptBody="true" />
            <fault signatureOptions="IncludeAddressing, IncludeTimestamp,
                IncludeSoapBody" encryptBody="false" />
        </protection>
    </mutualCertificate11Security>
    <requireActionHeader />
</policy>
```

The final change to the sample solution is to modify the code in the StockTraderConsole.cs class. You need to remove the lines that create the Username Token and append it to the proxy class. You also need to change the name of the policy from UsernamePolicy to MutualCertificatePolicy.

Running the Sample Solution

Now you can run the sample solution to test the implementation of the mutual certificate pattern. Try to access the client certificate at the service by using the following property:

```
RequestSoapContext.Current.Credentials.UltimateReceiver. ➥
GetClientToken<X509SecurityToken>().Certificate
```

You can use this property to obtain the identity of the caller and log every incoming call for audit purposes.

Brokered Authentication Using Kerberos

Now we are going to take a look at another form of brokered authentication. Kerberos is the security protocol that Microsoft chose to implement distributed security in its Windows 2000 and 2003 domains. Prior to Windows 2000, Microsoft relied on NTLM, which stands for Windows NT LAN Manager. NTLM is a proprietary security protocol, as opposed to Kerberos, which is an open standard created by the Massachusetts Institute of Technology (MIT) and published by the Internet Engineering Task Force (IETF) as RFC 1510 and later deprecated by RFC 4120. NTLM is still supported in order to provide backward compatibility, and it is also used to authenticate a user that logs into a computer using a local account.

Let's review a few basic concepts of the Kerberos protocol. This is an extensive topic and we are only going to cover the areas that will help you understand how WSE 3.0 and Kerberos can help you secure your Web services.

The Kerberos Protocol

The fact that Kerberos is based on open standards and that Microsoft has chosen it to be its default network authentication protocol makes it an essential topic of discussion in this book. The benefits provided by this protocol make it an ideal candidate for Web service security in scenarios where you want to take full advantage of the features provided by Windows implementation of the Kerberos protocol.

These are some of the terms that will help you understand the description of the Kerberos protocol:

Security principal: This is an entity in a Windows domain that can be uniquely identified. It can be a user, services, or a machine.

Active Directory: This is an LDAP implementation that is used to store information about the security principals and their relationships.

Long-term keys: These are cryptographic keys that are persisted in the identity store. Each key is associated with a security principal.

Authenticator: This contains information about the client, such as IP address, username, message time stamp, and Kerberos protocol version.

Session keys: These are keys associated to security principals and they only last a few minutes or hours. They are used to encrypt the authenticators.

Service principal names: These are unique identifiers that can be used to obtain a security token without having to use the name of the account that is running the service.

KDC: This is the Kerberos Key Distribution Center. It is composed of the Authentication Service and the Ticket Granting Service.

■**Note** Some of these terms are specific to the Microsoft implementation of the Kerberos protocol.

How Kerberos Works

Kerberos uses shared secrets as an authentication mechanism. A user defines a password when his account is created in the identity store, which in this case is Active Directory. These passwords can't be stored or transmitted in clear text, because this would make them vulnerable to attacks. For this reason, a symmetric key is used to encrypt these passwords. After they have been encrypted they can be referred to as a *long-term key*. Not only users have associated long-term keys; these are also created for services and computers that join a Windows domain.

When a user logs in, the client encrypts the password using a symmetric key and sends a request to the KDC for a Ticket Granting Ticket (TGT). If the key matches the value stored in Active Directory the KDC returns the TGT and a session key. This session key is encrypted by the KDC using the user's long-term key; we will refer to it as session key #1. The TGT is encrypted using the KDC secret key. The client computer stores this information in memory and it is used to request service tickets. Figure 7-7 shows the process that takes place when the user logs into the domain.

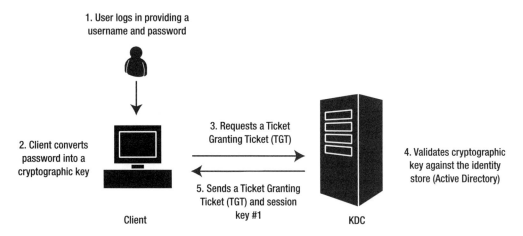

Figure 7-7. *The TGT request process*

The next step takes place when the client attempts to access a service. The client will send a request to the KDC. The request is composed by the TGT and an authenticator. The authenticator includes client information such as the username, a machine IP address, and a time stamp. The authenticator is encrypted with session key #1.

The KDC receives this request, decrypts the TGT with its long-term key, and decrypts the authenticator using the session key that it sent to the client at login. If all the information is valid, the KDC creates another session key (session key #2) and a service ticket. The KDC will encrypt the service ticket using the server's long-term key. It will also encrypt the session key using session key #1.

■**Note** The KDC doesn't send the service ticket to the server because it is not guaranteed that the service ticket will get to the server faster than the client request. There are also other implications, such as the need to maintain a state for each service ticket in order to allow the server to be ready for the time when the client request arrives.

When the client receives the service ticket and session key #2 from the KDC, it decrypts session key #2 using session key #1. The client then creates a new authenticator with a time stamp and information about the client, such as the IP address and username. This authenticator is encrypted using session key #2 and it is sent to the server along with the service ticket.

The server receives the request that has the Kerberos security token attached to it. This token contains the authenticator and the service ticket. The service uses its long-term key to decrypt the service ticket. The service ticket has session key #2 in it. The server will use this session key to decrypt the authenticator.

After the client is successfully validated, the service can provide mutual authentication by encrypting the time stamp found in the authenticator and sending it back to the client. This time stamp is encrypted using session key #2. Figure 7-8 shows the steps executed after the client obtains the TGT from the KDC.

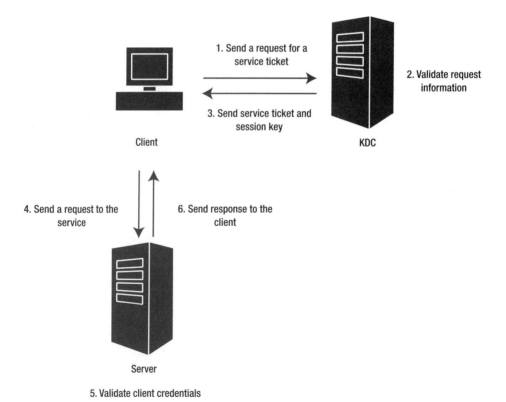

Figure 7-8. *Steps for obtaining the TGT from the KDC*

Advantages and Disadvantages of Using Kerberos

Using the Kerberos protocol offers several advantages and disadvantages. The advantages include the following:

Mutual authentication: Kerberos provides a simple mechanism for mutual authentication. As you saw in the previous pages, the server just needs to encrypt the time stamp included in the client authenticator and send it back as a proof of its identity. When the client receives the message and decrypts it with the session key, it can easily validate whether the service is who it claims to be.

Improved performance: The identity of the client only needs to be verified once during the duration of the session. After the TGT is generated, the client no longer needs to access the authentication service.

Integration with Windows: If your organization already relies on Active Directory you can benefit from this existing infrastructure and implement a protocol that benefits from the impersonation, delegation, authorization, and audit capabilities provided by Windows.

Interoperability: Kerberos is a protocol that has been adopted by other important players in the IT industry, so you don't have to worry about being limited using it within a Windows domain.

SSO: The fact that Kerberos is based on security tokens makes it an ideal candidate for SSO scenarios. The user only needs to provide its credentials once at the beginning of a session, and a TGT can be used to provide multiple session tickets to access different network resources.

The main disadvantages of using the Kerberos protocol include the following:

Requires additional infrastructure: If your organization does not use Active Directory, you will need to incur the additional expense of setting it up. You will also need to consider the investment for maintaining an Active Directory implementation.

Requires online access: The client needs to have online access to the KDC; otherwise it won't be able to retrieve the service ticket and make a call to the server.

Limited to a domain or trusted domains: This authentication mechanism does not work outside the boundaries of the domain or the trusted domains.

Now let's modify our sample application to use Kerberos authentication. You can continue the same solution that you used to implement mutual certificates and the Username Token assertions. You will see how easy it is to switch between one security model and another when using WSE 3.0.

Set Up the Environment

Follow these steps to make sure that your computer is configured correctly in order to secure the sample application using the Kerberos security turnkey assertion:

1. Log on to a Windows domain. You will need to log in to your computer using a domain account.

2. Use IIS instead of the ASP.NET Development Server. If you are using Windows XP and have been running your samples using the ASP.NET Development Server you will need to create a virtual directory in IIS that points to the StockTraderSecure folder. You don't need to make any changes in Visual Studio 2005. You can continue to work using the ASP.NET development server. You will access the Web service via IIS at runtime only.

3. Map a domain account. If you are using Windows XP, you will need to use a domain account to run the ASP.NET process. In order to do this, you need to open the machine.config file and modify the following line:

```
<processModel autoConfig="true" userName="domain\username"
password="userpassword" />
```

You will need to make sure that the username and password attributes match with those of a domain account. By default, the ASP.NET process runs under the local ASPNET account. A local computer account cannot be validated against Active Directory and this would not allow you to implement brokered authentication.

If you are using Windows 2003 you don't need to make any changes to the machine.config file. This is because the ASP.NET process runs under a service account that can be validated against Active Directory.

4. Configure the SPN. SPNs can be used to uniquely identify a service. Each SPN is linked to an Active Directory account. When a client requests a Kerberos token using an SPN, Active Directory obtains the information about the associated Windows account, which allows the authentication process to be executed.

SPNs can be managed using a utility named setspn.exe. This utility is available on Windows 2003 servers and it can be downloaded from the Microsoft site if you are using Windows 2000 or Windows XP.

In the following sample, we are going to create new SPNs and link them to the domain account that you are using to run the ASP.NET process. The syntax to create the new SPNs is the following:

```
Setspn.exe -a stocktrader/host1 domain\username
Setspn.exe -a stocktrader/host1.domain.com domain\username
```

Verify whether the SPNs were added successfully by running the following line:

```
Setspn.exe -l domain\username
```

The utility will return the names of the two SPNs that you just added. The result should look like the following:

```
stocktrader/host1.domain.com
stocktrader/host1
```

Secure the Web Service

Now that you have configured your environment, you are ready to modify the StockTrader application. You are going to begin by securing the service, just like we did in the previous samples.

1. In the StockTraderSecure project, open the WSE 3.0 Settings Tool.

2. In the Policy tab, click the Add button. Name this policy *KerberosPolicy* and click OK.

3. Click Next in the welcome screen.

4. In the Authentication Settings step, choose to secure a service application using Windows as the authentication method. Click Next to continue.

5. Add the user or users that will be authorized to access this service. Make sure that you add the domain account you used to log on to your computer. Click Next when you finish adding the authorized accounts.

6. In the Message Protection step, choose to Sign and Encrypt the message and uncheck the Establish Secure Session box. Click Next to continue.

7. Review the summary information of the new security policy, shown in Figure 7-9, and click Finish.

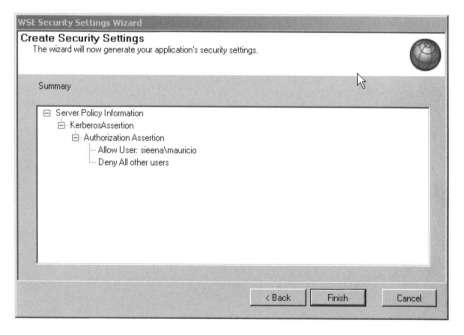

Figure 7-9. *A summary of the Kerberos server policy*

The new policy is added to the configuration file. As you can see in Listing 7-3, this policy does not make any particular reference to the KDC or the Active Directory that will be involved in the brokered authentication process. This information is obtained directly from the machine environment. This simplifies the deployment of Kerberos-based policies, because there aren't parameters to specify in the policy and you don't need to install a certificate as in the case of the MutualCertificatePolicy.

Listing 7-3. *Changes to the Service Policy File*

```
<policy name="KerberosPolicy">
    <authorization>
        <allow user="sieena\mauricio" />
        <deny user="*" />
    </authorization>
    <kerberosSecurity
            establishSecurityContext="false"
            renewExpiredSecurityContext="true"
            requireSignatureConfirmation="false"
            messageProtectionOrder="SignBeforeEncrypt"
            requireDerivedKeys="true" ttlInSeconds="300">
        <protection>
            <request signatureOptions="IncludeAddressing, IncludeTimestamp,
                        IncludeSoapBody" encryptBody="true" />
            <response signatureOptions="IncludeAddressing, IncludeTimestamp,
                        IncludeSoapBody" encryptBody="true" />
            <fault signatureOptions="IncludeAddressing, IncludeTimestamp,
                        IncludeSoapBody" encryptBody="false" />
        </protection>
    </kerberosSecurity>
    <requireActionHeader />
</policy>
```

The next step is to apply this policy to the service. You can do this by finding the place in the StockTrader class where you applied the MutualCertificate Policy and modify the policy name to *KerberosPolicy*. After this change, the class definition should look like the following:

```
[Policy("KerberosPolicy")]
public class StockTrader : StockTraderStub
```

Finally, before moving to the client project, you will need to add the following line in the web.config file, right under the <system.web> tag. This line will allow you to use Integrated Windows Authentication.

```
<authentication mode="Windows" />
```

Secure the Client Application

The followings steps show you how to secure a client application using the Kerberos security assertion:

1. Open the WSE 3.0 Settings Tool, go to the Policy tab, and click the Add button.

2. Name this policy *KerberosPolicy* and click OK.

3. Click Next in the welcome screen.

4. In the Authentication Settings step, choose to secure a client application using Windows as the authentication method. Click Next to continue.

5. The Kerberos Token step prompts you to enter the Service Principal Name. Type in **wse/host1**, where *host1* is the name of your computer. Choose Impersonation in the drop-down box and click Next.

6. In the Message Protection step, choose to Sign and Encrypt the message, and uncheck the Establish Secure Session box. Click Next to continue.

7. Review the policy summary, shown in Figure 7-10, and click Finish.

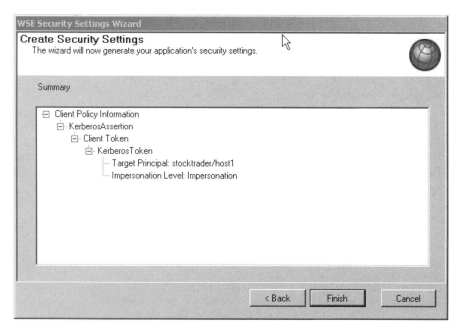

Figure 7-10. *A summary of the Kerberos client policy*

Listing 7-4 shows the configuration of the new policy. Pay special attention to the <token> element, where the target principal and the impersonation level are defined.

Listing 7-4. *Configuration of the KerberosPolicy*

```
<policy name="KerberosPolicy">
    <kerberosSecurity
        establishSecurityContext="false"
        renewExpiredSecurityContext="true"
        requireSignatureConfirmation="false"
        messageProtectionOrder="SignBeforeEncrypt"
        requireDerivedKeys="true" ttlInSeconds="300">
        <token>
            <kerberos targetPrincipal="stocktrader/host1"
                impersonationLevel="Impersonation" />
        </token>
        <protection>
            <request
                signatureOptions="IncludeAddressing,
                    IncludeTimestamp, IncludeSoapBody"
                encryptBody="true" />
            <response
                signatureOptions="IncludeAddressing,
                    IncludeTimestamp, IncludeSoapBody"
                encryptBody="true" />
            <fault
                signatureOptions="IncludeAddressing,
                    IncludeTimestamp, IncludeSoapBody"
                encryptBody="false" />
        </protection>
    </kerberosSecurity>
    <requireActionHeader />
</policy>
```

The last step is to modify the StockTraderConsole.cs class. The Run() method should look like the following:

```
public void Run()
{

    // Create an instance of the Web service proxy
    StockTraderProxy.StockTraderWse serviceProxy = ➥
        new StockTraderProxy.StockTraderWse();

    // Use the logged in user identity as the identity of the current thread.
    // You will need to add a using clause for the ➥
        System.Security.Principal namespace
    AppDomain.CurrentDomain.SetPrincipalPolicy(PrincipalPolicy.WindowsPrincipal);
```

```
    // Access the IIS based service
    serviceProxy.Url = "http://host1/StockTraderSecure/StockTrader.asmx" ;

    // Use the credentials of the current security context
    serviceProxy.UseDefaultCredentials = true;

    // Set the client policy
    serviceProxy.SetPolicy("KerberosPolicy");

    // Call the service
    Console.WriteLine("Calling {0}", serviceProxy.Url);
    string Symbol = "MSFT";
    StockTraderProxy.Quote q = serviceProxy.RequestQuote(Symbol);

    // Show the results
    Console.WriteLine("Web Service Response:");
    Console.WriteLine("");
    Console.WriteLine( "\tSymbol:\t\t" + q.Symbol );
    Console.WriteLine( "\tCompany:\t" + q.Company );
    Console.WriteLine( "\tLast Price:\t" + q.Last );
    Console.WriteLine( "\tPrevious Close:\t" + q.Previous_Close );

}
protected static void Error(Exception ex)
{
    Console.WriteLine("EXCEPTION!" + ex.Message + "\n" + ex.StackTrace);
}
```

The SetPrincipalPolicy method will assign the identity of the logged-on user to the current thread and the UseDefaultCredentials property will indicate the proxy to attach those credentials to the outgoing message.

Replace the host1 name of the server for the name of your local computer and run the application. If you get any security exceptions, review the instructions to set up the environment. It is important that you use a domain account and that you use the SPN name correctly. Kerberos authentication is an effective mechanism but you need to carefully configure the deployment environment in order to have a successful communication between the service and the client.

Impersonation

Let's take a look at how to impersonate the client user at the server by obtaining his identity from the Kerberos token. We are going to create a file in the server hard drive that only the client logged-in user has permission to access:

1. Create a new file under the C:\temp folder named Impersonation.txt.

2. Right-click the Impersonation.txt file and choose Properties.

3. Select the Security tab and click the Advanced button.

4. In the Advanced Security Settings dialog, uncheck the Inherit from Parent the Permission Entries box.

5. In the Security pop-up window, click the Remove button, shown in Figure 7-11.

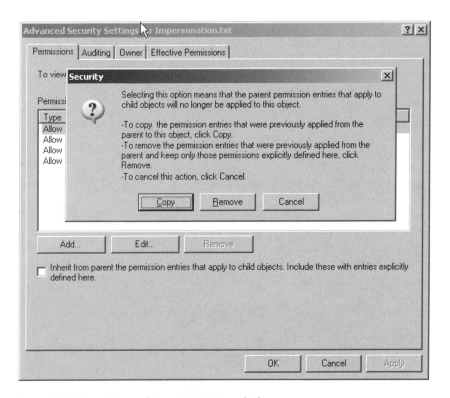

Figure 7-11. *The Advanced Security Settings dialog*

6. Click OK on the Advanced Security Settings dialog. You will get a prompt asking you if you want to remove all the users from the list. Click Yes. You are going to add a new user with read permissions in the next step.

7. In the Security tab, click the Add button and enter the name of the client user that you are going to authenticate at the server. Use the domain\username format.

8. Make sure the user has read access to the file and click OK.

This file will help you validate whether the impersonation is taking place. Remember that this service is running under a domain account different from the one that you used to log on to the client computer. So if impersonation doesn't take place, the following code will not be successful:

```
private void impersonate(KerberosToken token)
{
    if (token.Principal!=null && token.Principal.Identity is WindowsIdentity)
    {
        // Obtain user identity
        WindowsIdentity callerIdentity = ➥
            token.Principal.Identity as WindowsIdentity;

        // Initialize context object
        WindowsImpersonationContext context = null;

        try {

            // Impersonate the user
            context = callerIdentity.Impersonate();

            // Access a file that only this user has permissions to read
            FileStream x = File.OpenRead("c:\\temp\\Impersonation.txt");
            x.Close();

        }
        catch (Exception ex)
        {
            // rethrow the exception
            throw ex;
        }
        finally
        {
            context.Undo();
        }
    }
}
```

Add a line at the beginning of the RequestQuote method that passes the Kerberos token to the Impersonate method.

```
impersonate(RequestSoapContext.Current.Credentials.UltimateReceiver. ➥
GetClientToken<KerberosToken>());
```

This method starts by obtaining the user's identity from the Kerberos token, and then it impersonates the user by setting its identity in the current security context. After the user has been impersonated, the code opens the Impersonate.txt file and it immediately closes it. If the user is not impersonated successfully, this line will cause a SystemUnauthorizedAccess exception.

The impersonation code has to be implemented within a try, catch, finally block. The goal is to restore the original security context after the file has been read or after an unexpected error.

Impersonation can also be achieved by adding the following line at the web.config file. However, this applies to all the methods in the Web service and it doesn't allow you to impersonate a user only for a particular task:

```
<identity impersonate="true" />
```

Constrained Delegation

There is another feature provided by Kerberos that is named Constrained Delegation. This feature allows the impersonated client user to access a resource on a different machine. The service user that will be performing the delegation needs to be configured in Active Directory. This configuration consists of choosing a list of services that the user is authorized to delegate on. In Figure 7-12, the WSE user is authorized to delegate credentials to the HTTP server of the MTYSVR01 computer.

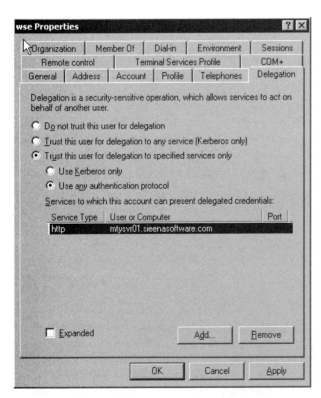

Figure 7-12. *Delegation properties tab in Active Directory*

You have the option to trust the user for delegation to any service. This is known as *Unconstrained Delegation* but it is not recommended because if the security of the service is compromised it means that all the services in the network are also compromised.

Prevent Replay Attacks Using Time Stamps, Digital Signatures, and Message Correlation

We will continue this chapter with a look at a different kind of security issue called *replay attacks*. A replay attack occurs when a client makes multiple Web service calls to the same service without waiting for a response from one or more previous requests. If enough of these calls are made, it is possible to overwhelm the Web service's hosting server, and to then cause the service to become unresponsive or to go offline. Replay attacks are at best a nuisance and, at worst, can cause critical system breakdowns.

The WS-Security specification mentions replay attacks and briefly describes a strategy for dealing with them. The key to preventing a replay attack is for a Web service to monitor the status of incoming messages and to verify their uniqueness. The Web service needs to verify that an incoming SOAP request message is unique and has not already been sent before the service starts processing the message.

▪**Note** You can eliminate replay attacks by unauthorized clients by using an encrypted communication channel such as Secure Sockets Layer (SSL). However, SSL provides no protection if the authorized client decides to conduct a replay attack. Other protective measures are required. The strategies that are outlined in this section assume that you want to prevent replay attacks by verifying request messages for uniqueness and verifying that they have not been tampered with.

Standard Web service calls are stateless, and SOAP messages are inherently stateless one-way communications. SOAP messages must therefore include extra information that tracks their uniqueness and thereby helps the service to verify whether a request message has already been received. There are three main ways to track this information and to enable message verification and protection against replay attacks:

- Message time stamps (including Created and Expires)

- Username Token nonce values

- Message correlation (including sequence numbers)

In the next sections we will consider each of these and how they can be used to secure SOAP messages, and Web services, against replay attacks.

Use Time Stamps for Message Verification

Message time stamps are added to an outgoing SOAP request message by the sender. They help in detecting unauthorized SOAP message requests. The client may choose to set an expiration date and time on the request message, which means that the message is only valid for a specific number of seconds after it is issued. This ensures that if the SOAP message is intercepted and re-sent by an unauthorized sender, it will only be useful to them for a limited amount of time. And, of course, if the message expiration is set short enough, there will not be time for an unauthorized party to intercept and reroute the message. Message time stamps and expiration are a useful first defense for preventing the unauthorized use of legitimate SOAP messages. As added protection, the client may digitally sign both the message body and the time stamp directly. This allows the receiving service to detect a scenario wherein the time stamp itself was tampered with and altered by an unauthorized user.

■**Note** SOAP message interception and tampering is a serious security issue that will become more widely understood (and worried about) once Web services become more commonly deployed and used by companies. If a thief steals your credit card or a document that contains your personal information, he has access to a legitimate source of credit, even though he is not an unauthorized user. SOAP message interception potentially creates the same security compromise scenario.

Once the service receives the request message, it can cache the SoapContext while it processes the message. Subsequent incoming request messages can then be compared against the cached SoapContext objects and rejected if the service detects that the request has already been received. Recall that the SoapContext is a WSE-specific class representation of a SOAP message and is a member of the Microsoft.Web.Services3 namespace. You can use the SoapContext class to programmatically access the properties of a SOAP message, including its headers and body.

There are no specific rules as to what kind of information you should use to correlate SoapContext information between messages. Basically, any unique identifying information makes for a good candidate, as long as it cannot be spoofed by an unauthorized third party. So you will want to choose a piece of information that can be digitally signed in the request message. Good candidates include addressing headers and security token IDs. In addition to addressing headers, you can correlate messages using specific contents of the SOAP message body, or any other header information that is uniquely set by the client. If the message uses a security token, the token itself can be used to uniquely identify a message.

Use Username Token Nonce Values for Message Verification

If you find yourself struggling to extract a unique piece of information from a message (using the SoapContext class), and the message includes a Username Token security token, you can use a nonce-based token ID as a unique identifier. A *nonce* is simply a random cryptographic string that can be assigned as the ID value for the Username Token security token. When the service receives a request message, it can extract the nonce value from the security token and cache the value for the duration of the request message. These ID values are part of the message signature and cannot be spoofed. And because they are nonce values, it is highly unlikely that two request messages will coincidentally share the same ID values. However, this could happen if you choose to rely on the autogenerated ID value for the security token.

Again, the burden remains on the service to cache information on incoming request messages. But if you need to take this approach, a nonce value is the simplest way to do so.

Listing 7-5 shows how the client can assign a nonce value to a Username Token security token.

Listing 7-5. *Assigning a Nonce Value to a Username Token Security Token*

```
using Microsoft.Web.Services3.Security;
using Microsoft.Web.Services3.Security.Tokens;

SecurityToken token = new UsernameToken(username, passwordEquivalent, ➥
    PasswordOption.SendPlainText);

// Assign a random nonce value to the security token
Nonce objNonce = new Nonce(34);
token.Id = objNonce.Value;
```

You may be wondering why nonce values apply specifically to the Username Token security token. This is because other security tokens are more sophisticated and do not require the additional guarantee of uniqueness that a nonce value provides. A Username Token security token is, after all, simply a hashed username-password combination, and there is nothing inherently unique about this combination. Usernames and passwords can be duplicated between users much more easily than cryptographic values can, especially if a malicious client is intentionally using another client's credentials.

If you use an alternate security token such as an X.509 certificate, you are automatically afforded some protection because the client and the service are using credentials that are not easily discovered. However, as we pointed out with SSL, this does not provide protection against replay attacks. You cannot assume that authorized clients will by their nature avoid carrying out a replay attack. For example, consider a client that autogenerates Web service calls in batch mode. If this client were to experience a system error or breakdown in business logic, it is conceivable that the client might generate duplicate request messages to the service. This is why you must tackle replay attacks at the message and service level. You cannot protect against replay attacks under the umbrella of a trusted relationship between client and service.

Use Message Correlation and Sequence Numbers for Message Verification

The key to preventing replay attacks is for the Web service to verify the uniqueness of incoming request messages. The WS-Addressing specification describes a GUID-based message ID that is one of several addressing headers that can be assigned to a SOAP message. WSE provides support for the WS-Addressing specification in general, and for addressing headers specifically. Once again, the burden is on the Web service to store message correlation information and to determine whether an incoming message has already been received. As with other kinds of identifiers, the message ID does not in and of itself prevent replay attacks, but it provides another simple, unique identifier for an incoming SOAP message.

Another type of message identifier is the sequence number, which stamps a message with the sequential role that it plays in a business process. Sequence numbers are part of the WS-Reliable Messaging specification and are designed to enable business orchestration, which refers to a business process or workflow that spans multiple components. In SOAs, sequenced messages are exchanged between multiple Web services, and the collective outcome represents the completion of the business workflow.

Sequence numbers provide an additional advantage for preventing replay attacks because a message that contains a duplicate sequence number is automatically suspect. Sequence numbers alone do not ensure uniqueness, but they will in conjunction with a message ID.

Establish Trusted Communication with WS-Secure Conversation

The WS-Secure Conversation specification allows Web services and clients to establish a token-based secure conversation for the duration of a session. It is analogous to the SSL protocol that provides on-demand secure communications over the HTTP transport channel. Secure conversations are essentially an efficiency mechanism to optimize the secure communication between a service and a client after the initial exchange of security credentials is over; this is known as the *handshake*. Secure conversations reduce the need for frequent authentication between client and service.

In previous chapters, you saw how the WS-Security and WS-Policy family of specifications combine to provide a comprehensive approach to securing Web services. Together these specifications provide an assortment of security options, including digital signatures, encryption algorithms, and custom authorization schemes. We discussed these technologies in the context of protective security, meaning that they protect messages in transit and keep unwanted eyes from discovering sensitive information. This is certainly an important application of these technologies and it needs no further explanation. But for the purpose of this chapter, we need to expand the context within which to view these technologies. They are no longer needed just for protective security; in a broader context, they are needed for establishing trusted communications.

In the discussions so far, we have made the big assumption that the client and the Web service automatically trust each other. By this, we mean the assumption that they both have an equivalent confidence in the integrity of the security tokens they are using to sign, encrypt, and otherwise secure their communications. For example, if a client and a Web service agree to encrypt their messages using a digital X.509 certificate, they must both trust the source of the certificate, and must be comfortable using the private and public keys that are generated from the certificate. In a sense, both the client and the Web service have come to a mutual agreement that they will offload the burden of proving trust to a (trusted!) third-party source, which issues a digital certificate to act as the tangible record of that trust.

Of course, the issue is more complex than this. When it comes to certificates, for many of us they are a necessary requirement for trusted communication. As clients, we may have all the trust in the world in a service provider, but we still need to use a digital certificate for the mechanics of signing and encrypting shared messages. We happen to be comfortable with digital certificates for most communication requirements because they represent certified trust. However, other client-service communications may be just as well off using a simpler Username Token security token, which is based on a simple username-password combination that gets hashed during transit. Luckily, the WSE implementation of the WS-Security specification is flexible, and you have a choice of security token types to use for conducting trusted communication.

The point is that your preferred security tokens and your preferred hashing and encryption algorithms are simply a means to a bigger goal of establishing trusted communication, otherwise known in the Web services world as *secure conversation*. There is no single correct choice of technologies that you should always use. Instead, you need to be using those technologies that are appropriate for establishing a trusted, secure conversation between a given client and a Web service. The rules can change depending on who is doing the communicating.

This chapter focuses on how you establish session-oriented, trusted communications using the WS-Secure Conversation specification. The great thing about the WS- specifications is that many of the concepts complement each other and build on each other. The understanding that you now have about WS-Security and WS-Policy will translate directly into the concepts behind WS-Secure Conversation. By the end of this chapter, you will have a good understanding of what constitutes secure conversation, and a broader appreciation for the usefulness of the WS-Security family of specifications.

Overview of Secure Conversation

The WS-Secure Conversation (and WS-Trust) specification provides the means for a client and a service to establish an optimized secure communication channel for a session, that is, an established duration of time. Secure conversation uses a security token that is procured by a service token provider following the initial handshake, or exchange of original security tokens, by the service and client. The security token is used to encrypt and sign all subsequent SOAP messages that are exchanged between the service and client. This process involves an initial amount of overhead, but once the channel is established, the client and service exchange a lightweight, signed security context token, which optimizes message delivery times compared with using regular security tokens. The security context token enables the same signing and encryption features that you are used to with regular security tokens.

Secure conversation is analogous to communications over the HTTPS protocol. HTTPS establishes a secure channel for the duration of a session and ceases to be in effect once that session is over. The classic example is an e-commerce transaction, in which you browse a catalog over an unsecured channel, but then you establish a secure channel for the purpose of completing a sales transaction with the vendor. The communication needs to be secure because sensitive payment and order information is being exchanged, so the client and the vendor need to establish a secured channel for as long as it takes to complete the transaction. For performance reasons, the client does not need or even want to establish a continuous secure session for every interaction with the vendor. HTTPS is useful for providing on-demand secure communication for exactly as long as it is needed.

■**Note** HTTPS and WS-Secure Conversation differ in one important way: HTTPS is not typically used for client authentication, whereas secure conversation is.

A secure conversation has the following characteristics:

- It is based on established security tokens, including Username Tokens and X.509 certificates.

- It uses a dedicated service token provider to generate a signed service context token, which is a lightweight security proxy.

- It provides a secure communication channel for the duration of the session.

- It provides optimized performance for session-oriented communications with multiple round trips (by using the security context token).

The difference between secure conversation and standard secure message exchange (with WS-Security and WS-Policy) is that a standard security policy framework establishes a fixed security policy that all service clients must adhere to. However, secure conversation has a more dynamic aspect. The client and service can initiate a secure channel as needed, rather than one based on an established policy framework. Secure conversation uses security tokens that are issued for the purpose of a specific communication. The service itself can act as the provider of these security tokens. Alternatively, this responsibility can be offloaded to a third-party service token provider, which is a dedicated resource that acts as a trusted intermediary between clients and services, and the issuer of security tokens for their secure conversations. Figure 7-13 provides an architecture diagram for typical secure conversation solutions.

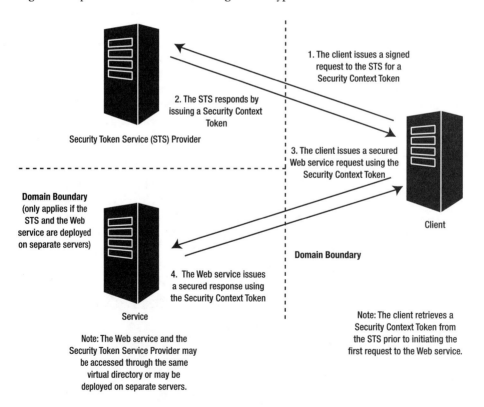

Figure 7-13. *Architecture diagram for a secure conversation solution*

In WSE 3.0 solutions the Web service will typically also act as the secure token service provider. Figure 7-13 shows the secure token service provider as a separate third-party service in order to distinguish this functionality from that of the Web service itself.

A secure conversation is initiated by a client that requires an on-demand secure communication session with a Web service. The session may be required for the duration of one request, or for several back-and-forth requests and responses between the client and the Web service.

The workflow for establishing and conducting a secure conversation as presented in Figure 7-13 typically follows four steps:

1. The client initiates the secure conversation by issuing a signed request to the STS provider for a security context token. The client may sign the request with any standard security token, including Username Token and X.509 certificates.

2. The STS provider verifies the integrity of the signed request. It then generates a security context token and delivers it to the client. The Web service itself can also act as the STS, or you can deploy the STS as a separate service. The security context token is actually returned from the STS as a so-called request security token (RST). The client can then extract the security context token from the RST. WSE 3.0 provides all of the support classes that you need to handle these tasks in code. Alternatively, you can simply reconfigure an existing turnkey security scenario to implement secure conversation with no code changes required. We will review how this is done in the next section, "How to Implement Secure Conversation Using WSE 3.0."

3. The client issues a secured Web service request using the security context token.

4. The Web service issues a secured response using the security context token. The security context token can be used like any standard security token. It inherits from the same base classes, and its usage is no different from the security tokens you learned how to work with in Chapter 6. Security context tokens may be cached in a global cache for future retrieval, for example, when the client will be issuing multiple requests over a period of time.

Programmingwise, WSE 3.0 makes it very easy to implement a service token provider because the WSE infrastructure will automatically issue security context tokens. This feature is enabled by simply adding a configuration element to the service token provider's configuration file. The STS provider can be incorporated into the client's target Web service, or the STS provider can be implemented as a dedicated Web service. There is little difference in the code between a *hosted* service token provider (that resides in the client's target Web service) and a dedicated service token provider (that resides on a separate domain). There are some significant configuration and deployment differences between the two models, but codewise they are very similar.

■**Note** The feature you know as Secure Conversation uses several WS- specifications, including WS-Trust, WS-Secure Conversation, and WS-Security. In addition, you can reduce code listings (and potential errors) by implementing policy frameworks for the participating services and clients. This chapter does not focus on when particular WS- specifications come into play. Instead, the focus is on understanding the concepts and discussing practical code samples.

How to Implement Secure Conversation Using WSE 3.0

A secure conversation is simply a session between a service and a client, where the exchanged
SOAP messages are encrypted and signed using tokens that are generated from an STS provider.
WSE 3.0 allows any Web service to act as an STS provider via simple policy configuration settings. Consider a Web service that already implements the UsernameForCertificateSecurity
turnkey security profile. It can be reconfigured to issue security context tokens (SCTs) by setting the attribute establishSecurityContext to true, as shown in Listing 7-6.

Listing 7-6. *Configuring a Web Service to Issue Security Context Tokens for Secure Conversation*

```
<UsernameForCertificateSecurity establishSecurityContext="true"
  renewExpiredSecurityContext="true"
  RequireSignatureConfirmation="false"
  MessageProtectionOrder="SignBeforeEncrypting"
  RequireDeriveKeys="true" ttlInSecconds="300">
```

The attribute renewExpiredSecurityContext causes the secure conversation to automatically renew in the event that the session times out (due to the SCT token expiring). In the
event of a time-out the STS provider will issue a replacement SCT that has a different identifier
from the original, but this fact will be transparent to the secure conversation participants.

In the event of a communication interruption between the service and client, the SCT
token may be lost from memory (at the service) and the secure conversation will not renew
unless the client has implemented a stateful session, which is simply a method of holding the
SCT token outside of memory. A stateful session is maintained from the client perspective in
that the client will store the SCT token identifier in a cookie and will retrieve it if the SCT token
is lost from memory at the service. This behavior can also be leveraged to implement secure
conversation in a Web farm, so that the client may communicate with different instances of
the same Web service across multiple servers in a Web farm.

Finally, secure conversation sessions may be explicitly canceled by the Web service following the successful completion of the secure conversation. The purpose of canceling a
session is to allow the Web service to clean up its cache of SCT tokens and to thereby conserve
resources. A Web service can cancel a secure conversation session by retrieving an instance of
the SCT from the client's Web service proxy and then calling a cancel method on the SCT
instance. For more information on secure conversation, including session management, consult both the WSE 3.0 documentation as well as the selected references that are listed in the
appendix under the WS-Secure Conversation section.

Final Thoughts on Secure Conversation

The WS-Secure Conversation specification provides a token-based, session-oriented, on-
demand, secure channel for communication between a Web service and client. WS-Secure
Conversation is analogous to the SSL protocol that secures communication over HTTP.

WSE 3.0 provides support for implementing secure conversation in the following ways:

- It provides a prebuilt assembly for the STS provider.

- It provides a UsernameTokenManager class for processing a signed request from the client to initiate the secure conversation.

- It provides a specialized proxy class for the client to request a security context token from a provider.

- It provides a dedicated global cache for storing security context tokens.

Summary

In this chapter we discussed the concepts of direct and brokered authentication. You learned about the advantages and disadvantages as well as the main implementation options provided by WSE 3.0. We provided an overview of how brokered authentication works when you use X.509 certificates or the Kerberos protocol. The samples included in this chapter guide you through the implementation of the mutual certificates and the Kerberos security assertions.

We also reviewed how to prevent replay attacks, which are a specific form of denial-of-service attack that can be avoided by having the Web service analyze simple SOAP header settings before responding to an incoming request.

Finally we reviewed how to implement secure conversation, which has been greatly simplified in WSE 3.0 to basic configuration settings that can be easily applied to existing Web services projects.

In Chapter 8, we will shift the focus to SOAP messaging and the collection of support specifications that includes WS-Addressing and WS-Referral. The discussion on WSE 3.0 support for SOAP messaging will bring you back full circle to where the book began, with the discussion on the importance of messages in service-oriented applications.

CHAPTER 8

■■■

SOAP Messages: Addressing, Messaging, and Routing

Traditional Web services are built on the HTTP request/response model. This is fine for some applications, but is limiting for others. The WSE 3.0 messaging framework is designed to give you more control over the transport and processing of SOAP messages. There are three transport channel protocols that are supported by the WSE 3.0 messaging framework out of the box: HTTP, TCP, and an optimized mode called In-Process for Web services and clients that reside within the same process. In addition, WSE 3.0 provides framework support for implementing your own custom transport protocols. For example, a number of developers are experimenting with integrating SOAP with Microsoft Message Queuing (MSMQ). Note that when using non-HTTP protocols, interoperability with other platforms is contingent upon their support for non-HTTP protocols. For example, Apache Axis 1.2 does not natively provide support for the soap.tcp protocol that is currently supported by WSE 3.0.

Of course, WSE 3.0 does not force you to leverage any of its messaging capabilities. You can continue to write traditional HTTP-based Web services if you prefer. But this design pattern is only suitable if you need to implement a request/response communication design, and if you want to host your service within a virtual directory.

This chapter will focus on working with the WSE 3.0 implementation of the WS-Addressing specification and with messaging and routing. Together these specifications and features provide support for

- Several transport protocols—HTTP, TCP, and In-Process for clients and services that reside on the same application domain

- True asynchronous communication using TCP

- SOAP messages that contain their own addressing headers and endpoint reference information

- Automatic routing and referral for SOAP messages

- Custom SOAP routers

Communication Models for Web Services

Before starting a discussion on WS-Addressing and messaging, we need to step back and take the big-picture view, starting with a review of how Web services communicate with clients. Traditional Web services communicate over the HTTP protocol and use a traditional request/response communication pattern, in which a client request results in a synchronous, direct service response. Unfortunately, this model is very limiting because it does not accommodate long-running service calls that may take minutes, hours, or days to complete. A typical synchronous Web service call will time out long before the response is ever delivered.

There are five generally accepted communication design patterns, or models, that govern the exchange of SOAP messages between a service and its client (or between two services):

1. *Request/response (classic)*: The service endpoint receives a message and sends back a correlated response message immediately, or within a very timely fashion.

2. *Request/response with polling*: The client sends a request message to a service endpoint and immediately returns a correlation message ID to uniquely identify the request. The service takes a "significant" amount of time to process the request, meaning more than you would expect if you were receiving a timely response message. Knowing this, the client must periodically poll the service using the correlation ID to ask if a response is ready. The service treats this query as a standard request/response, and replies in the negative or in the affirmative (with the actual response message). So this model involves two pairs of correlated request/response messages.

3. *Request/response with notification*: The client sends a request message to a service, and the service takes a "significant" amount of time to process the request, meaning more than you would expect if you were receiving a timely response message. The service does not reply back to the client until the processing of the request is complete. The client is responsible for waiting for the response. This model describes classic asynchronous communication.

4. *One-way, or notification*: The service endpoint receives a request message, but does not generate a response message. This model is not widely used.

5. *Solicit/response*: The reverse of request/response, whereby the service endpoint sends the client a solicitation request and receives a response. This model is not widely used.

Standard ASP.NET Web services, which you build by default in Visual Studio .NET, give you the illusion that they support an asynchronous communication pattern. The Web service's WSDL document contains asynchronous versions for each operation, and the autogenerated proxy class also dutifully provides asynchronous method calls. Listing 8-1 shows a comparison between synchronous and asynchronous versions of the same Web method as they appear in an autogenerated WSE 3.0 proxy class.

Listing 8-1. *The WSE 3.0 Proxy Class for a Traditional XML Web Service*

```
public partial class StockTraderServiceWse : ➡
    Microsoft.Web.Services3.WebServicesClientProtocol
{
    public Quote RequestQuote([System.Xml.Serialization.XmlElementAttribute(
        Namespace="http://www.asptechnology.net/schemas/StockTrader/")]
        string Symbol)
    {
        object[] results = this.Invoke("RequestQuote", new object[] {Symbol});
        return ((Quote)(results[0]));
    }
}

    public void RequestQuoteAsync(string Symbol, object userState)
    {
        if ((this.StockQuoteRequestOperationCompleted == null)) { ➡
            this.StockQuoteRequestOperationCompleted = new ➡
                System.Threading.SendOrPostCallback( ➡
                this.OnStockQuoteRequestOperationCompleted);
        }
        this.InvokeAsync("StockQuoteRequest", new object[] {symbols}, ➡
            this.StockQuoteRequestOperationCompleted, userState);
    }

    public Quote OnStockQuoteRequestOperationCompleted ( ➡
        object arg)
    {
        if ((this.StockQuoteRequestCompleted != null)) { ➡
            System.Web.Services.Protocols.InvokeCompletedEventArgs ➡
                invokeArgs = ➡

((System.Web.Services.Protocols.InvokeCompletedEventArgs)(arg)); ➡

            this.StockQuoteRequestCompleted(this, new ➡
                StockQuoteRequestCompletedEventArgs( ➡
invokeArgs.Results, invokeArgs.Error, ➡

                invokeArgs.Cancelled, invokeArgs.UserState));
        }
    }
}
```

The callback functions RequestQuoteAsync and OnStockQuoteRequestCompleted give you the illusion of asynchronous communication, but you cannot truly disconnect the calling thread once the request message has been sent out. The burden falls on the client to manage the wait time for a response, but this is handled for you by the autogenerated proxy classes in Visual Studio.

A true asynchronous method call completely releases the thread that is used for the request, and then later creates a new thread to receive the response. The limitation here is not with .NET per se, it is with the HTTP-based response/request model, since the HTTP response is delivered over the same underlying connection that sent the request. Simply spacing out the request and the response does not equate to an asynchronous call. One solution available to you is to drop HTTP and to use a different protocol such as TCP. The consequence of this approach is that the architecture of your solution will also need to change. How you do so is a central focus of this chapter.

■**Note** If you implement hardware-based load balancing, you may experience issues using the TCP proto-col, because the pooling of TCP connections by the load balancer may lead to an uneven availability of connections between services, which could interrupt messages. You should consider software load balanc-ing for your Web services solutions or, better yet, avoid load balancers and implement a routing-based manager to direct service calls for you. Routing and referral is discussed in detail in this chapter in the section titled "Overview of Routing and Referral."

Overview of WS-Addressing

The WS-Addressing specification enables messages to store their own addressing information, so that the source, destination, and reply URI locations are self-contained within the message. This allows a message to hop across multiple endpoints without losing information about the source of the original request. And it allows intermediate services to route and refer the mes-sage across multiple endpoints until eventually a response is sent back to the specified reply location.

If you are writing a very basic Web service that uses the HTTP transport protocol, you are implementing a classic request/response model in which the client issues a request and the service is expected to issue a direct response. In this scenario, it is unnecessary for the mes-sage to contain its own addressing information. But the need changes in other scenarios, such as a message that hops across multiple endpoints over the TCP transport protocol.

WS-Addressing is not interesting in and of itself. It is a support specification for other important specifications such as WS-Reliable Messaging. Still, it is important to understand the WS-Addressing constructs and how they are written to a SOAP message. Without WS-Addressing, it would not be possible for messages to travel anywhere other than within the well-established HTTP-based request/response model. Nor would it be impossible to write truly asynchronous Web service calls.

Overview of the WS-Addressing Constructs

The WS-Addressing specification supports two types of constructs:

1. Message information headers

2. Endpoint references

These constructs are closely tied to elements that you find in a WSDL document, such as operations, ports, and bindings. The WS-Addressing constructs are a complement to the WSDL document, not a replacement; although it is likely that future versions of the WSDL specification will evolve in conjunction with the WS-Addressing specification. Let's consider each of the constructs in turn.

Message Information Headers

These are the most intuitive addressing headers because they work in a similar fashion to e-mail message addresses, which provide a set of headers including From, To, and ReplyTo. Of course, SOAP message information headers include additional entries that are SOAP-specific and have no relation to e-mail. For example, the Action header stores the XML qualified name of the operation that the SOAP message is intended for.

Table 8-1 provides a summary of the available message headers, including their XML representations.

Table 8-1. *XML Elements for Message Information Headers*

Header	Type	Description
To	URI	The destination URI for the message (required).
Action	URI	The SOAP action for the message (required). The action identifies the specific endpoint operation that the message is intended for.
From	Endpoint Ref	The source of the message (optional). At a minimum, the From header must provide a URI, if it is specified. But you can also add more complex endpoint reference information (optional).
ReplyTo	Endpoint Ref	The reply-to destination for the message response. This may be different from the source address (optional).
Recipient	Endpoint Ref	The complete endpoint reference for the message recipient (optional).
FaultTo	Endpoint Ref	The endpoint that will receive SOAP fault messages (optional). If the FaultTo endpoint is absent, then the SOAP fault will default to the ReplyTo endpoint.
MessageID	Endpoint Ref	The message ID property (optional). The ID may be a GUID identifier, or it may be a qualified reference, for example, a UDDI reference.

The only required message headers are To and Action; although, if you expect a response, you will also need to set the From or ReplyTo headers. Table 8-1 shows you the type that the header supports. Notice that the majority of the headers require endpoint references.

Listing 8-2 shows you how message information headers appear within a SOAP message.

Listing 8-2. *A SOAP Message with Message Information Headers*

```
<S:Envelope xmlns:S="http://www.w3.org/2002/12/soap-envelope"
    xmlns:wsa="http://schemas.xmlsoap.org/ws/2003/03/addressing"
    xmlns:st="http://www.bluestonepartners.com/schemas/StockTrader">
  <S:Header>
      <wsa:MessageID>uuid:7ae86g-95d...</wsa:MessageID>
      <wsa:ReplyTo>
          <wsa:Address>http://investor123.com/client</wsa:Address>
      </wsa:ReplyTo>
      <wsa:FaultTo>
          <wsa:Address>http://investor123.com/faults</wsa:Address>
      </wsa:FaultTo>
      <wsa:To S:mustUnderstand="1">http://stocktrader.com/StockTrader</wsa:To>
      <wsa:Action>http://stocktrader.com/StockTrader#RequestQuote</wsa:Action>
  </S:Header>
  <S:Body>
      <st:RequestQuote>
          <Symbol>MSFT</Symbol>
      </st:RequestQuote>
  </S:Body>
</S:Envelope>
```

Listing 8-2 is a SOAP message that is being sent from a client at investor123.com to a stock trading service at stocktrader.com. The client is requesting a stock quote, using the RequestQuote operation. This operation is described in the StockTrader schema, as referenced in the envelope header. Note that the StockTrader schema is qualified using the XSD namespace reference `http://www.bluestonepartners.com/schemas/StockTrader`.

This simple code listing displays the best aspect of SOAP messages: they are fully qualified and self-describing. Every element in this SOAP message is qualified by a specific XML namespace. And the addressing information for the message is self-contained. Nothing that is included in a SOAP message is allowed to exist in a vacuum.

Endpoint References

Endpoint references are a little less intuitive than addressing headers, and they are more akin to the WSDL <service> tag. Think of endpoint references as complex XML data types that provide a collection of child elements to describe the various facets of the type. Endpoint references provide both addressing and SOAP binding information.

Recall from Chapter 2 that the <service> element provides port information and binding information combined. The <service> element describes the operations that are available at a service endpoint, and also provides you with a message protocol–specific binding address. The only message protocol we are really focused on here is SOAP. So, to be more specific, an endpoint reference tells you what operations are supported at a given port and also how you should address SOAP messages to that port.

Listing 8-3 shows an example of an endpoint reference as it is included within a SOAP message. Compare this with Listing 8-2, which uses message information headers. Notice that the endpoint reference stores the addressing destination information in a different tag, and that it also contains dynamic reference information (such as AccountID) that is specific to the endpoint reference.

Listing 8-3. *Endpoint Reference XML*

```
<wsa:EndpointReference>
    <wsa:Address>soap.tcp://stocktrader.com/StockTrader</wsa:Address>
    <wsa:ReferenceProperties>
        <st:AccountID>123A</st:AccountID>
    </wsa:ReferenceProperties>
    <wsa:PortType>st:StockTraderSoap</wsa:PortType>
    <wsp:Policy />
</wsa:EndpointReference>
```

Endpoint references do not replace message information headers because they are focused on describing binding information for the endpoint, not specific operation information. You do not get to choose between using message information headers vs. endpoint references. Message information addressing headers may include endpoint references for the destination elements in the message. But from a conceptual perspective, you can draw a distinction between the two constructs. Message information headers are a general construct for storing addressing information, for both the sender and the receiver. Endpoint references are more complex and dynamic and include SOAP binding information to the specific endpoint that the SOAP message is intended for. Luckily, WSE 3.0 sets up the classes so that the constructs can be kept distinct from a programming perspective.

As with all the WS- specifications, you can drill down as far as you want to go and dive into increasing complexity. Inevitably, if you drill down far enough, you will discover a rich interaction between the specification elements, and the overall conceptual picture will begin to blur. Our goal here is to keep the conceptual discussion clear and to provide you with a solid grounding so that you can continue to explore on your own.

WSE 3.0 Implementation for WS-Addressing

WSE 3.0 implements the full WS-Addressing specification in a dedicated namespace called Microsoft.Web.Services3.Addressing. Table 8-2 summarizes some of the important WS-Addressing classes (each of which corresponds to an XML element in the WS-Addressing specification).

Table 8-2. *Classes in the WSE 3.0 Addressing Namespace*

Class	Description
Action	Specifies the XML qualified name of the operation that the SOAP message is intended for.
Address	Stores a binding-specific address and may be assigned to other classes, including To, From, and ReplyTo. The properties of the Address class correspond to classes that are based on endpoint references. For example, the Address.To property corresponds to the WS-Addressing To class, which is an endpoint reference.
AddressingHeaders	Indicates the collection of properties that address a message, including To, From, ReplyTo, and MessageID.
AddressingFault	Occurs when there is an invalid header in the message or when an exception occurs along the message path.
EndPointReference	Stores endpoint reference information, which is binding information for a service.
ReferenceProperties	Indicates the collection of properties that add additional description elements for an endpoint.
To	Stores the source address as an endpoint reference.
From	Stores the destination address as an endpoint reference.
ReplyTo	Stores the reply-to address for the response as an endpoint reference.

There are three interesting things to note about the Addressing classes:

1. Most of the Addressing classes derive from XML and SOAP base classes, which reflect their obvious close ties to these specifications. (In fact, the majority of WSE 3.0 specification classes have similarly close ties to XML and SOAP base classes.)

2. You will not often need to instance these classes directly. Instead, it is more likely that you will access them via properties on other classes. For example, the SoapEnvelope class (in Microsoft.Web.Services3) provides a Context.Addressing property that exposes the AddressingHeaders class. Here, you can directly set message addressing information, such as From, To, ReplyTo, and Action properties.

3. The Addressing classes are independent of the underlying transport protocol. It does not matter if the addressed SOAP message is transported over HTTP, TCP, or SMTP. The addressing headers and references will apply, regardless of how the message is transported.

The two more important classes in the Addressing namespace are the AddressingHeaders class and the EndpointReference class. These correspond to the two main constructs in the WS-Addressing specification: message information headers and endpoint references. Your SOAP messages may use one or the other, depending on how you prefer to set addressing to service endpoints. In the future it is likely that most addressing will be done in terms of endpoint references, particularly as the WSDL specification evolves and as the WS-Addressing specification becomes more established and refined.

> ■**Note** Do not confuse the message protocol with the transport protocol. SOAP is a message protocol (based on XML) that provides a specification for constructing messages. TCP is a transport protocol. HTTP and SMTP are application protocols, which themselves utilize TCP, but which effectively function as transport protocols in that they may be used to transport SOAP messages.

Security Considerations for WS-Addressing

Addressing information can be sensitive, especially when it contains port numbers and references to qualified endpoints. We are used to thinking of this information as being public because Web services are often publicly accessible. But with WS-Addressing, this information is attached to the SOAP message header directly. You typically do not want the body of the SOAP message to be tampered with or viewed by unauthorized parties. In the same way, you should feel equally protective about the SOAP message headers.

Another sensitive case is when messages are routed between multiple endpoints, each of which writes additional WS-Addressing information to the message header. The additional endpoints may not be designed to handle direct service requests from outside clients. Their addressing information needs to be kept protected.

There are three recommended options for securing the contents of a message that contains addressing headers:

1. Digitally sign the message, including the body and header information.

2. Encrypt the message headers.

3. Add a message ID.

Digital signing allows you to detect whether a message has been tampered with or compromised. Digital signing alone will not encrypt or hide the contents of the message, but it will ensure that a tampered message will be automatically rejected by the receiving Web service.

Encrypting the message headers will clearly protect its contents, but this approach works best if the message is not being routed or referred to another Web service endpoint. Intermediary Web services will need access to the addressing header information, so there is an additional burden on the developer to ensure that the intermediaries can encrypt the message header contents. This leads to key management issues and also performance issues if each endpoint is required to decrypt and encrypt message headers.

The message ID (<wsa:MessageID>) is important because it allows you to design against replay attacks, whereby a client repeatedly resends the same message to a Web service endpoint in order to overwhelm the service and to bring down its host server. The receiving Web service simply needs to cache this message ID and then ignore additional requests that come in. Refer to Chapter 7 for a detailed discussion on replay attacks and how to prevent them.

There is no right way to implement security to protect addressing headers. Each of these options are recommended rather than required. You need to make an individual determination as to whether security measures are required for your service-oriented application.

At this point, you should be more comfortable with the concepts behind WS-Addressing, but you are probably still wondering exactly how to put these concepts, and the code, into action. Remember that WS-Addressing is a support specification that is built for messaging. The next section on messaging will provide you with the context for addressing by showing you the important role that addressing plays for messaging.

Overview of Messaging

WSE 3.0 includes support for messaging, which provides developers with a new range of features for transporting and processing SOAP messages. Traditional XML Web services support the HTTP transport protocol only, which limits the client and server to communicating with a synchronous request/response design pattern.

WSE 3.0 messaging continues to support the HTTP protocol, but it also supports two additional transport protocols:

- *TCP*: This is a low-level protocol that communicates across processes and domain boundaries. TCP is the underlying protocol in most Internet communications.

- *In-Process*: This protocol is designed for communication between components within the same application domain. It is an optimized, low-level protocol that provides the flexibility of TCP but is optimized for communication within the same application domain.

In addition, WSE 3.0 provides classes that allow you to custom implement additional transport protocols, such as SMTP and MSMQ.

Comparing Messaging with the HTTP and TCP Protocols

Services that communicate over HTTP must reside on a Web server in order for their endpoints to be accessible. However, services that communicate over TCP are accessible over a direct port without requiring a virtual directory. Here is an example of an HTTP endpoint:

```
http://www.bluestonepartners.com/StockTrader.asmx
```

And here is an example of the equivalent TCP endpoint:

```
soap.tcp://216.70.214.118/StockTrader
```

The HTTP and TCP protocols have one thing in common: they both enable messaging between remote components that are running on separate processes and on separate domains. TCP is a lower-level protocol that operates on a port rather than a virtual directory, which is a higher-level abstraction of a port.

HTTP is designed for request/response messaging patterns, meaning that a request generates a direct response. TCP is designed for decoupled messaging patterns, whereby a sender and a receiver communicate but not necessarily as a two-way conversation. TCP enables asynchronous messaging, whereby the sender releases its calling thread as soon as the message has been delivered to the receiver. By extension, TCP also enables one-way messaging, because once a sender mails out a message its resources are released and the sender suffers no resource or scalability problems waiting for a response that will never come. This is the beauty of the decoupled TCP protocol: You can implement a request/response messaging pattern if you want to but, unlike HTTP, you do not have to.

■Note Technically the HTTP protocol does support one-way messaging. The response will generate an HTTP 202 status code (meaning "request accepted"), and no SOAP message will be returned.

Representing SOAP Messages in the WSE 3.0 Messaging Framework

The Microsoft.Web.Services3 namespace provides a class called SoapEnvelope, which you use for generating SOAP messages in code. The SoapEnvelope class derives from the System.Xml.XmlDocument class, not surprisingly, and so it supports XML document loading so that you can load preformatted SOAP messages into a SoapEnvelope object. Alternatively, you can construct the SOAP message from scratch by setting properties on the SoapEnvelope object.

Table 8-3 highlights important members of the SoapEnvelope class. Listing 8-4 shows you how to construct a SOAP message in code for requesting a stock quote from the RequestQuote operation.

Table 8-3. *The SoapEnvelope Class*

Property	Type	Description
Envelope	XmlElement	The envelope is the root element of the message XML. It contains the message body and message header elements.
Body	XmlElement	The body element is required for all SOAP messages. It contains qualified XML for the request and response messages.
Header	XmlElement	The header contains optional extended information for the SOAP message. The WS- specification settings are stored in the header.
Fault	Exception	The SOAP fault information, if present, is retrieved from the envelope and returned by the Fault property as an Exception class.
Context	SoapContext	The Context property enables you to modify the SOAP message contents within a custom WSE filter or to process the SOAP message contents within a SoapReceiver processing class.

Listing 8-4. *Constructing a SOAP Message in Code for the RequestQuote Operation*

```
public SoapEnvelope CreateSoapMessage()
{
    SoapEnvelope message = new SoapEnvelope();

    RequestQuote q = new RequestQuote();
    RequestQuote.Symbol = "MSFT";

    message.SetBodyObject(q);

    // Assign the addressing SOAP message headers
    message.Context.Addressing.Action = new Action( ➥
        "http://www.bluestonepartners.com/schemas/StockTrader/RequestQuote");
    message.Context.Addressing.From = new From(fromUri);
    message.Context.Addressing.ReplyTo = new ReplyTo(fromUri);

    return message;
}
```

Listing 8-4 illustrates several important points:

- SOAP messages cannot be empty because their purpose is to communicate requests or responses. Here the SOAP message is designed to transmit a stock quote request. It uses the RequestQuote class to generate a correctly formatted request. Recall that RequestQuote is defined in an IDC file that provides class representations for all of the StockTrader custom data types.

- The SoapEnvelope's SetBodyObject method automatically generates the SOAP message body for the RequestQuote object.

- The SOAP message headers store addressing information directly, using the WSE 3.0 addressing classes. The Action property is required and must reflect the operation that the sender is calling. If it calls a Web service that supports multiple operations, the Action property enables the service to differentiate incoming requests and to process them correctly.

■**Note** Refer back to Chapter 3 for a detailed discussion on the StockTrader XML schema. This chapter shows you how to build the StockTrader XML schema from scratch, and also shows you how to generate an IDC file of classes based on the schema.

SOAP Senders and SOAP Receivers

We are all familiar with two common messaging modes: peer-to-peer (e.g., chat applications) and request/response (e.g., Internet browsing). With SOAP messaging, the concept of clients and services does not really apply, because this implies a fixed communication pattern (meaning that the client always initiates the request and then the service responds). With SOAP messaging, it is more accurate to refer to senders and receivers, which implies roles rather than functions. A given service may function as a message receiver in some cases and as a message sender in others.

The WSE 3.0 messaging framework provides dedicated classes for the sender and receiver roles. The SoapSender class sends a message out to a specified endpoint (URI). The class is straightforward to use, as shown in Listing 8-5.

Listing 8-5. *The SoapSender Class*

```
SoapSender soapSender = new SoapSender(toUri);
soapSender.Send(message);
```

The SoapReceiver class is abstract and must be implemented in a custom class that is assigned to receive the corresponding response for a message request. In a sense, this custom SOAP receiver class acts like a callback function, in that it is called when a response is ready. But unlike a traditional callback function, the custom SOAP receiver class is decoupled from the request.

There are three steps to implementing a custom SOAP receiver class:

1. Create a custom class that implements the SoapReceiver abstract class.

2. Override the Receive method with a custom implementation for processing the incoming response message.

3. Register the custom receiver class so that the messaging framework knows it is the handler for the incoming response message.

Listing 8-6 shows you these three steps in code.

Listing 8-6. *Implementing a SOAP Message Receiver*

```
class StockTrader
{
    public void SendSoapMessage(SoapEnvelope message)
    {
        // Register the response receiver
            SoapReceivers.Add(fromUri, typeof(StockTraderResponseReceiver));

        // Send the SOAP request message
        SoapSender soapSender = new SoapSender(toUri);
        soapSender.Send(message);
    }
}
```

```
public class StockTraderResponseReceiver : SoapReceiver
{
    protected override void Receive( SoapEnvelope message )
    {
        // Process the incoming message...
    }
}
```

The code in Listing 8-6 is implemented in the sender component to process incoming response messages. It turns out that the receiver component implements very similar code but, this time, to process incoming request messages. This is the important point: the SoapReceiver class does not care whether it is implemented in a sender or a receiver component. It is agnostic in this regard. Its purpose is to support the processing of incoming SOAP messages, regardless of whether they originate from a sender or a receiver component.

Listing 8-7 shows you how to process an incoming message. This listing is taken from the receiver component, which processes the RequestQuote SOAP request message. The receiver needs to do the following:

1. Deserialize the SOAP message body.

2. Examine the SOAP message Action to determine how to process the incoming SOAP message. The SoapReceiver must be able to correlate the incoming message body to a qualified data type, in this case, the StockTrader Quote type.

3. Process the RequestQuote operation.

4. Generate a response message based on the Quote type, which is the output type from the StockTrader's RequestQuote operation. Inherent in this step is the fact that the SoapReceiver must correlate this outgoing response message with the incoming SOAP request message.

5. Send the response message back to the sender.

Listing 8-7. *Generating a SOAP Message Response*

```
public class StockTraderRequestReceiver : SoapReceiver
{
    protected override void Receive(SoapEnvelope message)
    {
        if(message.Context.Addressing.Action.Value.EndsWith("RequestQuote"))
        {
            // Retrieve the body of the SOAP request message
            // Since we have screened the Action, we know what class to look for
            RequestQuote request = ➥
                (RequestQuote)message.GetBodyObject(typeof(RequestQuote));
            string symbol = request.Symbol;
```

```
        // Call the RequestQuote() method: delegate the call
        // to a business assembly
        Quote q = RequestQuote(symbol);

        // Transform the result into a SOAP response message
        SoapEnvelope response = new SoapEnvelope();
        response.SetBodyObject(q);

        // Create the URI address objects for send and receive
        // Note, instead of hardcoding the URIs, we will pull them from
        // the original request message
        // Send response to the request message's ReplyTo address
        Uri toUri = (Uri)message.Context.Addressing.ReplyTo;
        // Return response from the request message's To address
        Uri fromUri = (Uri)message.Context.Addressing.To;

        // Assign the addressing SOAP message headers
        response.Context.Addressing.Action = new Action( ➥
    "http://www.bluestonepartners.com/schemas/StockTrader/RequestQuote#Quote");
        response.Context.Addressing.From = new From(fromUri);
        SoapSender soapSender = new SoapSender(toUri);

        // Send the SOAP request message
        soapSender.Send(response);
    }
}

// Implementation for RequestQuote()
private Quote RequestQuote(string Symbol)
{
    // Create a new Quote object
    Quote q = new Quote();

    // Retrieve the stock quote (code not shown)

    // Return the Quote
    return q;
}

}
```

Listing 8-7 highlights the following important points:

- This code is contained in a separate component from the sender, running on a separate process. However, both the sender and the receiver components must have the same understanding of the StockTrader custom types, including RequestQuote and Quote. They can accomplish this in two ways: they can generate an IDC file of classes directly from the XSD schema, or they can each implement a reference assembly of types, similar to the StockTraderTypes assembly that is used throughout the sample solutions.

- The receiver component implements business processing logic for the RequestQuote method. The sender component simply knows how to construct a qualified RequestQuote message. However, the receiver component must know how to process the operation. (Alternatively, the receiver component could call a dedicated business assembly, which centralizes all of the StockTrader processing. This approach is presented in Chapter 4.)

- The receiver component constructs a new response message with its own addressing headers in order to return the stock quote result to the sender. The receiver component uses the same SoapSender class to actually send the message out to the specified endpoint.

Note The StockTraderTypes IDC file used here is based on the StockTraderWithOperations.xsd schema file from Chapter 3, which includes complex elements to represent each of the four supported Web service operations. Please refer to Chapter 3 if you require more information.

Implement a Windows Forms–Based Receiver

The receiver component must be up and running to respond to incoming request messages. To illustrate this, the sample solutions include a stand-alone Windows Forms–based receiver called StockTraderSoapReceiver. Figure 8-1 shows the Solution Explorer for this solution.

The receiver references the Microsoft.Web.Services3 and System.Web assemblies. The startup code for the form registers the custom SoapReceiver class that will handle the incoming request message, as shown in Listing 8-8.

Figure 8-1. *Solution Explorer for the StockTraderSoapReceiver solution*

Listing 8-8. *Registering a Custom SoapReceiver Class*

```
public class StockTrader : System.Windows.Forms.Form
{
    class StockTrader()
    {
        // Use TCP
        receiverUri = new Uri(String.Format( ➥
          "soap.tcp://{0}/StockTraderSoapReceiver", System.Net.Dns.GetHostName()));

        // Register the SOAP receiver objects
        StockTraderRequestReceiver request = new StockTraderRequestReceiver();
        SoapReceivers.Add(receiverUri, request);
    }
}
```

Listing 8-7 provides the code for the custom SoapReceiver class called StockTrader-RequestReceiver.

The StockTraderSoapReceiver project acts as a listener when it is compiled and run. Figure 8-2 shows the form interface when the project is running.

Figure 8-2. *The TCP-based receiver component*

This approach is a good shortcut for ensuring that the receiver component stays up and running. In a production setting you should implement the listening receiver component as a Windows Service component.

The IDC File and WSDL

The StockTraderTypes.cs class file in the sample receiver project provides the IDC file that provides class representations of the StockTrader custom data types. This type information must be available to both the sender and the receiver, so it is best to compile a dedicated StockTraderTypes assembly and to reference it from both the sender and the receiver solutions. The IDC file is included as a class file in the sample so that you can more easily inspect its contents. Listing 8-9 shows an excerpt from the StockTraderTypes.cs file.

Listing 8-9. *The StockTraderTypes IDC File*

```
using System;
using System.Xml.Serialization;

namespace StockTraderTypes
{
    [System.Xml.Serialization.XmlTypeAttribute(Namespace=
        "http://www.bluestonepartners.com/schemas/StockTrader/")]
    public class RequestQuote
    {
        public String Symbol;
    }

    [System.Xml.Serialization.XmlTypeAttribute(Namespace=
        "http://www.bluestonepartners.com/schemas/StockTrader/")]
    public class Quote
    {
        public string Symbol;
        public string Company;
        public string DateTime;
```

```
        // Additional properties are not shown (e.g, Open, Last, etc.)
    }
}
```

Since you are no longer working with the XML Web service project type, you have lost your shortcut for generating a WSDL document directly from an .asmx service file. The StockTraderTypes.cs file can in fact be generated directly from the StockTrader.xsd schema file, which you are guaranteed to have; so technically you can do without a WSDL file when building a decoupled, TCP-based sender-receiver solution. But a WSDL file contains essential metadata information that is stored according to an established specification. You cannot build a WS-I–compliant service without including a WSDL file.

So by no means are we advocating that you build services without WSDL files. You cannot, because the service must be compliant with established specifications. If it is not compliant, then it is effectively unusable, because the WSDL file stores essential metadata information on the service that is required for widespread use by different clients. However, we are pointing out that if you bypass building a traditional .asmx Web service, you will be forced to manually generate the WSDL file. We expect that future releases of the .NET Framework will include alternate utilities for generating WSDL files. These will have to be made available once non-HTTP-based Web services become as common a service type as XML Web services are today.

Traditional XML Web Services vs. SOAP Messaging over HTTP

Traditional XML Web services are conveniently implemented using the HTTP protocol, and as a developer you never need to interact with the SOAP messages directly. In fact, prior to WSE 3.0, if you needed to interact with the SOAP message directly during processing, you had to write a custom HTTP handler to intercept the messages. You also needed to manually implement most of the plumbing for parsing, modifying, and generally interacting with the SOAP message.

WSE 3.0 does not require you to use its messaging framework if you are transporting SOAP messages over HTTP. But you will want to if you need to perform custom processing on these SOAP messages. With WSE 3.0 you do not have to write an HTTP handler yourself, because one is already provided for you. All you have to do is implement the processing code for the message itself. All of the plumbing code has already been taken care of for you.

Let's assume that the sender, or client, is a Windows Forms–based application and that the receiver, or service, is enabled for HTTP. There are three steps for implementing the service as an HTTP-enabled SOAP receiver:

1. Create a custom SoapReceiver class in the receiver component.

2. Register the custom SoapReceiver class as an HTTP handler in the web.config file (see Listing 8-10).

3. Create a virtual directory to host the service (e.g., HttpMessagingService).

Listing 8-10 shows how you register a custom SoapReceiver class in the web.config file, so that it is automatically enabled for the HTTP protocol. Listing 8-7 provides an example of a custom SoapReceiver class. Although Listing 8-7 was developed for the TCP protocol, all you need to do to enable it for HTTP is to modify the URI of the SoapReceiver response endpoint, from soap.tcp://{endpoint} to http://{virtual directory}.

Listing 8-10. *Registering a SoapReceiver Class Using the HTTP Protocol*

```
<configuration>
    <system.web>
        <httpHandlers>
            <add verb="*" path="receiver.ashx" type="MyNamespace.MyReceiver,
                MyAssemblyName" />
        </httpHandlers>
    <system.web>
<configuration>
```

Based on the earlier Listing 8-7, the type name of the HTTP handler would be

```
type="StockTrader.StockTraderRequestReceiver, StockTraderSoapReceiver"
```

Note that the <add /> section must be formatted as a single line in the web.config file or it will generate parsing errors at runtime.

The client application calls the HTTP-enabled service using a standard HTTP link, which includes the name of the virtual directory that hosts the service and the name of the standard HTTP handler. For this example, the link is

```
http://localhost/HttpMessagingService/receiver.ashx
```

The WSE 3.0 messaging framework makes it easy for you to continue working with the HTTP protocol, while at the same time making it much easier for you to manually process SOAP request and response messages.

Properties of Message-Enabled Web Services

Traditional XML Web services are very limiting compared to the new capabilities provided by WSE 3.0 messaging. As you explore WSE 3.0 in general, and the new messaging capabilities in particular, you should clearly notice that

> Web services are about both SOAP and XML. SOAP messages are the key technology in an SOA. XML is essential because the SOAP and WSDL specifications are XML-based, but without SOAP there would be no messages, and therefore no purpose for Web services.

> SOAP messages are advanced communication instruments. Previously, SOAP messages were limited to relatively simple constructs and could not be secured. But the WS- specifications now enable SOAP messages to record their own addressing information and be digitally signed and encrypted (both in the header and the body). SOAP messages have become advanced instruments for communication.

> SOAP messages are composable and have unlimited extensibility. Technically, a Web service is what is composable, not a SOAP message. But it is the message itself that must store and carry the required WS- specification elements (specifically, the SOAP header block). When you apply a communications trace, you are doing so on the exchanged SOAP messages, not on the endpoints themselves. SOAP messages are tailored to reflect the policies of their endpoints and must correctly incorporate the cumulative set of required custom elements. SOAP messages are composable and have unlimited extensibility.

SOAP senders and receivers replace traditional clients and services. With SOAP messaging, it is more accurate to refer to senders and receivers, which implies roles rather than functions. A given service may function as a message receiver in some cases, and as a message sender in others.

Overview of Routing and Referral

SOAP message routing is a topic that follows very naturally from the discussions presented so far in this chapter. Routing allows you to set up a virtual network for processing incoming SOAP messages by enabling the flexible redirection of SOAP messages to alternate servers that are not directly accessible by the original sender. We use the term *virtual network* because the routing may only take place on a subset of the actual physical network.

There are three main virtual network design models for routing:

Load balancing: This model routes SOAP messages from a logical endpoint on to one server within a cluster of back-end servers that are running the same services. This routing pattern overlaps what is provided by established network load balancing (NLB) solutions, including Cisco LocalDirector and Microsoft Network Load Balancing Services.

Chain: This model routes SOAP messages through a chain of so-called SOAP intermediaries, which are intermediate services that process a SOAP message on the way to its ultimate receiving endpoint.

Content-based: This model routes SOAP messages based on header-specific content.

Figure 8-3 provides schematic views of each of these patterns. Notice that each of them defines a common entity called the *SOAP router*. This is the immediate destination endpoint for an incoming SOAP request message. In the load balancing model, the SOAP router does no direct message processing; its sole purpose is to redirect the message to alternate servers for processing. However, in the other models the SOAP router may process the SOAP message in addition to routing it.

WSE 3.0 provides an elegant implementation of routing and WS-Referral for the load balancing model that does not require you to write any code in the SOAP router. Everything is driven by configuration file settings that reflect the routing model that you want to put in place. WSE 3.0 is generally good about saving you from writing code. With routing, this is even truer since you do not need to modify the core business logic in the receiving services. However, if you are implementing the chain routing model or the content-based routing model, the intermediary services will need to update addressing headers on the message to reflect the next destination in the chain.

WSE 3.0 provides out-of-the-box support for routing and WS-Referral using the HTTP protocol only. In theory, the specifications can apply to other transport protocols as well, such as TCP and SMTP. However, the WS-Addressing specification provides a more efficient routing and referral implementation for these protocols. In addition, WS-Addressing may be more efficient for implementing the chain routing model. For more on this, refer to the section "Routing vs. WS-Addressing" later in this chapter.

Now let's look at an example of how to build a SOAP router that implements a combination of the chain and load balancing routing models.

Chain Routing

Load Balancing and Content Routing

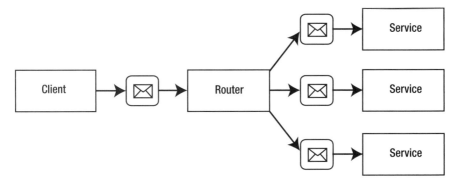

Figure 8-3. *Network design patterns for SOAP message routing*

Build a SOAP Router for the Load Balancing Routing Model

This example SOAP routing solution is included in the sample files as SOAPRouter.sln. It consists of three projects, as shown in Figure 8-4.

The three projects are as follows:

1. *SOAPSender*: A console-based client application

2. *SOAPService*: A Web service application that processes stock quotes and trades

3. *SOAPRouter*: A Web service–based SOAP router application

These projects continue to use the StockTrader application that you have seen developed throughout the book. We renamed the projects using clear names so that there is no ambiguity about the purpose of each project. Technically, this solution is a combination of the chain and load balancing routing models because it contains only one referral Web service.

Let's discuss each of the solution projects in turn.

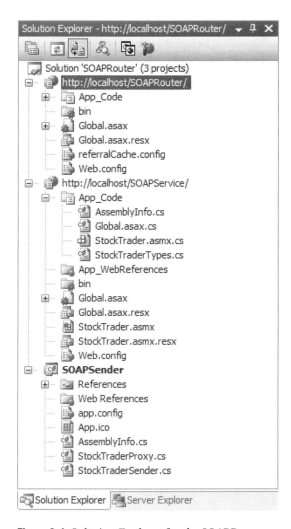

Figure 8-4. *Solution Explorer for the SOAPRouter sample solution*

Overview of the SOAPSender

The SOAPSender application requests stock quotes from the SOAP service using two possible internal method calls:

- *SendUnsignedRequest*: Sends an unsigned stock quote request to the SOAPService RequestQuote operation.

- *SignRequestUsingX509Certificate*: Sends a digitally signed stock quote request to the SOAPService RequestQuote operation. The digital signature is based on an X.509 certificate.

Each of these method calls invokes the same proxy class. The difference between the two methods is simply whether the request message will be sent out as signed or not.

The Web service proxy class provides two possible URIs for requesting a stock quote, as shown in Listing 8-11. One URI requests the quote directly from the Web service, while the other URI requests the quote via the SOAP router, which provides an .asmx file of the same name, although the virtual directory name is different.

Listing 8-11. *Service Endpoints for the SOAPSender Application*

```
public StockTraderServiceWse()
{
    // Note to user: toggle between each of these URLs
    // 1. SOAPService goes directly to the service
    //this.Url = "http://localhost/SOAPService/StockTrader.asmx";
    // 2. SOAPRouter goes to the service via a router
    this.Url = "http://localhost/SOAPRouter/StockTrader.asmx";
}
```

Of course, in a production setting, the SOAPService would not be directly accessible from outside clients. Instead, they would be forced to route their request through the SOAPRouter.

Overview of the SOAPService

The implementation code for the SOAPService RequestQuote method is shown in Listing 8-12. The most important aspect of this code listing is the SoapActor attribute, which decorates the Web service class (shown in bold). This attribute designates the specific recipient of the message response, in this case the SOAP router, which will in turn pass the response back to the original sender. If the SoapActor attribute is not provided, the Web service request will generate an addressing error upon receipt, because the most recent sender of the request (the SOAP router) will not match the first sender and ultimate recipient of the response (the SOAP sender). The SoapActor attribute allows for messages to be accepted by services after passing through intermediaries.

If you ever need to drop the SOAPRouter, and wish instead to call the StockTrader Web service directly, make sure to change the SoapActor attribute value to the URL of the Web service itself, in this case: http://localhost/SOAPService/StockTrader.asmx.

Listing 8-12. *The SOAPService RequestQuote Method*

```
using Microsoft.Web.Services3;
using Microsoft.Web.Services3.Messaging;

[SoapActor("http://localhost/SOAPRouter/StockTrader.asmx")]
public class StockTraderService : Microsoft.Web.Services3.WebService
{
    public Quote RequestQuote(string Symbol)
    {
        // Step 1: Instance a new Quote object
        Quote q = new Quote();
```

```
    // Step 2: Code to retrieve stock quote data
    // Code goes here (not shown)

    // Step 3: Return a populated Quote object
    return q; // Return a populated Quote object
    }
}
```

The rest of the SOAPService Web service is standard, as was presented in Chapter 3, with the StockTrader Web service example. The only significant difference is this addition of the SoapActor attribute to the Web service methods.

Overview of the SOAPRouter

The SOAPRouter implements a configuration file called the *referral cache*, which stores destination endpoints for the message to be routed to. Listing 8-13 provides an example of a referral cache for a chain SOAP router that forwards incoming messages on to a single back-end service.

Listing 8-13. *The Referral Cache Configuration File*

```xml
<?xml version="1.0" ?>
<r:referrals xmlns:r="http://schemas.xmlsoap.org/ws/2001/10/referral">
    <r:ref>
        <r:for>
            <r:exact>http://localhost/SOAPRouter/StockTrader.asmx</r:exact>
        </r:for>
        <r:if />
        <r:go>
            <r:via>http://localhost/SOAPService/StockTrader.asmx</r:via>
        </r:go>
        <r:refId>uuid:fa469956-0057-4e77-962a-81c5e292f2ae</r:refId>
    </r:ref>
</r:referrals>
```

This configuration file is stored as a separate configuration file within the SOAPRouter project. In order to find it, you also need to update the project's web.config or app.config files to point to the location of the referral cache file. Listing 8-14 provides an example of how to update the web.config file. You do not need to do most of this work manually. Instead you can use the WSE 3.0 Settings Tool to implement most of these tags. Note that the Settings Tool has a limitation when it comes to specifying the <httpHandler>, in that it does not allow you to type a custom path, in this case StockTrader.asmx. So you will need to accept the default path of *.ashx, and then update the actual path once you have applied the settings to the web.config file.

Listing 8-14. *The SOAPRouter web.config File, Including Location of Referral Cache File*

```
<configuration>

    <configSections>
        <section name="microsoft.web.Services3"
            type="Microsoft.Web.Services3.Configuration.WebServicesConfiguration,
            Microsoft.Web.Services3, Version=3.0.0.0, Culture=neutral,
            PublicKeyToken=31bf3856ad364e35" />
    </configSections>

    <system.web>
        <webServices>
            <soapExtensionImporterTypes>
                <add type= ➡
"Microsoft.Web.Services3.Description.WseExtensionImporter,
                    Microsoft.Web.Services3, Version=3.0.0.0, Culture=neutral,
                    PublicKeyToken=31bf3856ad364e35" />
            </soapExtensionImporterTypes>
        </webServices>
        <httpHandlers>
            <add type="Microsoft.Web.Services3.Messaging.SoapHttpRouter,
                Microsoft.Web.Services3, Version=3.0.0.0, Culture=neutral, ➡
                PublicKeyToken=31bf3856ad364e35" ➡
verb="*" path="StockService.asmx" />
        </httpHandlers>
    </system.web>
<microsoft.web.Services3>
    <referral>
        <cache name="referralCache.config" />
    </referral>
</microsoft.web.Services3>
</configuration>
```

Note that referral cache files are cached in memory, just as web.config files are. The referral cache file will refresh in the cache whenever it gets updated.

■**Caution** You *must* give the ASP.NET worker process read-write access permissions to the referral cache configuration file. Browse to the file location using Windows Explorer, right-click the file properties, and switch to the Security tab. In Windows XP and Windows 2000 add the ASP.NET worker process account (by default, [MachineName]\ASPNET), and set read-write permissions. In Windows 2003 and/or IIS 6, add the default Network Service account, or the user account that is currently running the application pool. If you do not take this step, you will get an exceedingly ugly SOAP exception call stack.

Send a Stock Quote Request Using the SOAPSender

Now all that is left is to execute the project. First verify that the SOAP sender proxy class is pointing to the SOAP router URI. Then start the SOAPSender project and test out each of the two possible request calls:

- SendUnsignedRequest

- SignRequestUsingX509Certificate

Each method call returns a successful stock quote result. This result is so uneventful that you would be forgiven for wondering whether the SOAP router actually does anything. You can quickly put these doubts to rest by renaming the referral cache configuration file, so that it cannot be loaded at runtime. This will generate a SOAP exception back to the client indicating that the configuration file could not be loaded.

What is remarkable about this code example is that the destination Web service, SOAPService, does not complain when it receives a digitally signed SOAP message from the SOAPRouter, rather than from the SOAPSender, which originally signed and sent the request. The routing and WS-Referral infrastructure automatically handles this contingency and prevents you from receiving exceptions about an invalid digital signature.

In summary, chain SOAP routers give service providers flexibility to implement an optimum service processing solution for incoming SOAP messages. Load balancing SOAP routers help network administrators maintain service networks. As servers are taken offline for maintenance, the information in the referral cache can be updated to remove the server from the list of available referral servers. Finally, content-based SOAP routers make strategic routing decisions based on the contents of the SOAP message headers.

Note The sample project SOAPSender.csproj (contained within the solution SOAPRouter.sln) allows you to toggle between a direct Web service call and an indirect one via a SOAP router (see StockTraderProxy.cs, Line 38). If you modify the URL for the Web service request, you must also modify the SoapActor attribute on the target Web service method to reflect the same target URL (see StockTrader.asmx, Line 33, in the SOAPService project). If you do not, you will receive addressing errors because the <to> header on the request must match the Actor attribute on the receiver. The sample projects contain clear notes describing how to toggle the SoapActor attribute in response to a different target URL from the sender.

Routing vs. WS-Referral

As we talk about routing, we are actually talking about both routing and referral. The term *routing* refers to the infrastructure that enables SOAP messages to be forwarded on to other destination endpoints. The term *referral* describes the physical act of forwarding a message on. It is common practice to use the term *routing* to describe the combined process of routing and referral.

Routing and Security

Remember that all Web service specifications are composable. Routing does not implement any kind of security for referred messages. However, you can use WS-Security in conjunction with routing to provide a security solution for the referred messages. For example, you can digitally sign or encrypt incoming messages, as you saw in the SOAPSender solution. Note that encrypted messages can pass through intermediary routers even if those routers do not know how to decrypt the message. Routing configuration is separate from the message contents. The intermediary only needs to decrypt the message if this is required in order to make a specialized routing decision. But in most cases this will not be necessary. If the routers do need to decrypt the message and you use X.509 certificates for encryption, you must ensure that each of the intermediary services has access to the necessary keys. In fact, this applies whenever you use an X.509 certificate, whether for digital signatures or encryption.

In a chain routing model, it is likely that intermediary services will modify the contents of an incoming SOAP request message. If the incoming SOAP message is digitally signed, the intermediary service will need to re-sign the message before forwarding it on to the next service. However, as the SOAPSender solution shows you, digital signature validation will not fail if the SOAP router simply passes on the SOAP message to a destination endpoint without altering the message contents.

There is no question that routing solutions add an administrative and development burden to implementing an SOA. And when you add security policies into the mix, the burden will become even greater. It is likely that future releases of WSE will include provisions to address this issue. To this date, subsequent releases of WSE have always managed to reduce complexity compared to earlier releases of the same features.

Routing vs. WS-Addressing

Our first thought when we saw the WSE 3.0 WS-Addressing implementation was whether it overlaps with the pre-WSE 3.0 releases for routing and WS-Referral. There is no definitive answer to this question, but it seems very likely that the WS-Addressing specification does indeed supersede the WS-Routing and WS-Referral specifications for all SOAP routing models other than perhaps the load balancing model (which is not used often in Web services solutions due to the complexities that load balancing introduces for these types of solutions).

The reason is that WSE 3.0 currently implements routing for the HTTP transport protocol only. This model requires the service endpoints to be .asmx service files or custom SOAP handlers. Either way, you need to configure a virtual directory to host the service. This can be a significant administrative burden if your virtual network infrastructure includes multiple chained services. By comparison, the WS-Addressing specification is implemented for non-HTTP protocols, such as TCP, which do not require you to configure a virtual directory.

Perhaps the clearest indication for potential overlap between routing and WS-Addressing is the fact that WSE 3.0 continues to implement routing only for the HTTP transport protocol. We believe this was a purposeful decision to avoid implementing overlapping specifications that accomplish the same thing. In this scenario, one specification will always be more efficient than the other.

■**Note** WSE 3.0 supports routing only for HTTP due to a technical issue with the request/response model and TCP. With the TCP protocol, the intermediary does not know whether to hold a thread open to wait for a response. With HTTP, the intermediary either receives a response or receives an HTTP 202 error. TCP-compliant intermediaries must be custom written.

You can further enhance your productivity with WS-Addressing by using classes called SoapClient and SoapService, which are higher-level classes than their counterparts SoapSender and SoapReceiver. The SoapClient and SoapService classes automatically handle much of the plumbing code that SoapSender and SoapReceiver require you to write for processing SOAP messages. We will not be discussing these higher-level classes here, because they shield details that are important to understanding how SOAP messaging actually works. In addition, these classes are very easy to understand once you are comfortable with the lower-level SoapSender and SoapReceiver classes. But once you find yourself writing the same kind of messaging code over again, by all means use these classes and avoid some manual coding.

■**Note** WSE 3.0 provides support for routing but does not implement the WS-Routing specification. This is because the WS-Addressing specification supersedes the WS-Routing specification. (The WS-Referral specification is orthogonal to the WS-Routing specification.)

Integrate Web Services and MSMQ

This chapter ends with a bonus section that shows you one possible approach for integrating Web services and message queuing (with MSMQ). We should quickly point out that we are not going to show you how to create an MSMQ custom transport channel. Instead, we are going to discuss how to configure a message queue and then access it from a Web service using the System.Messaging namespace.

WSE 3.0 does not implement reliable messaging, nor does it provide any kind of support for managing message delivery. If you want to implement this capability today, you will need to custom build the support infrastructure using MSMQ (or another middleware product such as MQSeries).

Use MSMQ for Reliable Messaging

Consider the following application design for a StockTrader application for mutual fund trades, which cannot be executed until after the stock exchange closes for the day. Clients can send trade requests to their broker, but they will be stored and processed later, once the stock exchange is closed. Here is the workflow between the client and service:

1. A client decides that they want to place a mutual fund trade.

2. The client formats an XML message with the details of the trade and sends it to the StockTrader Web service.

3. The StockTrader Web service receives the message but does not process the trade immediately. Instead, the Web service drops the message into a queue for later processing.

4. The StockTrader Web service formats an acknowledgment response message to the client to let them know that the trade request has been received and that it will be processed shortly.

5. The client receives the response message.

Let's implement this workflow using a TCP-based StockTrader Web service that integrates with a message queue on its host server.

Create a Message Queue Trigger

Our first step is to create the message queue using MSMQ and then create a message queue trigger, which will respond to incoming messages. MSMQ is available with the Windows 2000 operating system and higher. If you do not have MSMQ installed you can add it using the Control Panel ➤ Add or Remove Programs option (select Add/Remove Windows Components from the selection screen).

MSMQ is included under the Computer Management MMC snap-in, as shown in Figure 8-5.

Figure 8-5. *The Computer Management MMC snap-in, including MSMQ*

To create a new private queue, expand the Message Queuing node and right-click the Private Queues subfolder. Expand and select the New ➤ Private Queue menu option. Enter a name for the queue (we used wsmessaging) and click OK. You will see the new queue listed under the Private Queues subfolder.

Next, expand the wsmessaging node, right-click the Triggers node, and select the New ➤ Trigger menu option. You will see a property page, shown in Figure 8-6. Enter the configuration information as shown, selecting the Retrieval processing type.

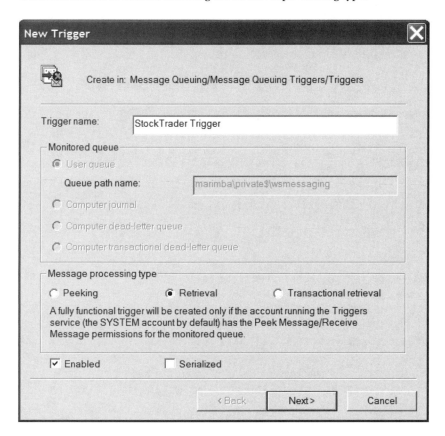

Figure 8-6. *Creating a new MSMQ message trigger*

Note that you are not creating a fully functional trigger that will fire off a process when a message is received. Instead, you will allow the message to sit in the queue so that you can examine its contents manually.

Create a Web Service That Uses MSMQ

The Web service is written as a TCP-enabled service and is included in a sample solution called StockTraderMSMQReceiver.sln. The solution includes a reference to the System. Messaging assembly, which is not included with WSE 3.0 but is instead a separate assembly within the .NET Framework.

The Web service provides a Receive method that examines incoming SOAP request messages. All messages with an action value of PlaceTrader are dropped into the message queue. Listing 8-15 provides the code listing for the Receive method and a helper method called AddSoapMessageToQueue.

Listing 8-15. *A Web Service That Uses MSMQ*

```
// This class represents the Request Receiver (i.e., the service)
public class StockTraderRequestReceiver : SoapReceiver
{
    protected override void Receive(SoapEnvelope message)
    {
        if(message.Context.Addressing.Action.Value.EndsWith("PlaceTrade"))
        {
            bool status = false;

            // Drop the incoming SOAP message to a queue, for later processing
            status = AddSoapMessageToQueue(message);

            // Generate a return status message
            AcknowledgeMessage a = new AcknowledgeMessage();
            a.AcceptedToQueue = status;

            // Transform the result into a SOAP response message
            SoapEnvelope response = new SoapEnvelope();
            response.SetBodyObject(a);

            // Create the URI address objects for send and receive
            // Do not hardcode the URIs, pull them from original request message

            // Send response to the request message's ReplyTo address
            Uri toUri = (Uri)message.Context.Addressing.ReplyTo;

            // Return response from the request message's To address
            Uri fromUri = (Uri)message.Context.Addressing.To;

            // Assign the addressing SOAP message headers
            response.Context.Addressing.Action = new Action( ➦
    "http://www.bluestonepartners.com/schemas/StockTrader/RequestQuote#PlaceTrade");
            response.Context.Addressing.From = new From(fromUri);
            SoapSender soapSender = new SoapSender(toUri);

            // Send the SOAP request message
            soapSender.Send(response);
        }
    }
```

```
private bool AddSoapMessageToQueue(SoapEnvelope message)
{
    bool status = true;
    MessageQueue mq;

    // Verify that the Queue exists
    if (MessageQueue.Exists(@".\private$\wsmessaging"))
    {
        // Assign a reference to the queue
        mq = new MessageQueue(@".\private$\wsmessaging");

        // Drop the incoming message to the queue
        mq.Send((SoapEnvelope)message, ➡
            message.Context.Addressing.MessageID.Value.ToString());
    }
    else
    {
        // Error condition if queue does not exist
        status = false;
    }
    return status;
}

}
```

Notice that the Receive method formats an acknowledgment message that corresponds to a custom data type called AcknowledgeMessage, which is included in both the Web service XML schema file and client proxy class file, and is also shown in Listing 8-16.

Listing 8-16. *The AcknowledgeMessage Custom Data Type*

```
[System.Xml.Serialization.XmlTypeAttribute(Namespace=
    "http://www.bluestonepartners.com/schemas/StockTrader/")]
public class AcknowledgeMessage
{
    public bool AcceptedToQueue;
}
```

The sample project does not include code for processing the message because this is beyond what we are trying to show. If you open the message queue in the MMC console, you will see a new message in the queue. Figure 8-7 shows an example of what the message body looks like. The property page displays both the byte array and the readable message body. Notice the SOAP contents on the right side of the figure.

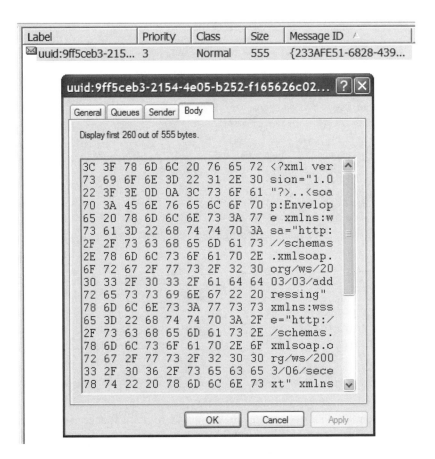

Figure 8-7. *The body contents for an MSMQ message*

Implement the Web Service Client

The Web service client is written as a TCP-enabled console application and is included in a sample solution called StockTraderMSMQClient.sln.

The Web service client sends out a trade request and provides a Receive method that examines incoming SOAP response messages. All messages with an action value of Place-Trader are dropped into the message queue. Listing 8-17 provides the code listing for the Receive method, showing how the client processes the acknowledgment message.

Listing 8-17. *A Web Service Client That Processes an Acknowledgment Message*

```
// This class represents the Response Receiver (i.e., the client)
public class StockTraderResponseReceiver : SoapReceiver
{
    protected override void Receive( SoapEnvelope message )
    {
        if (message.Fault != null)
```

```
        {
            Console.WriteLine(message.Fault.ToString());
        }
        else
        {
            if (message.Context.Addressing.Action.Value.EndsWith( ➥
                "RequestQuote#PlaceTrade"))
            {
                // Deserialize the message body into an AcknowledgeMessage object
                // Since we have screened the Action, we know
                // what class to look for
                AcknowledgeMessage a = ➥
                  (AcknowledgeMessage)message.GetBodyObject( ➥
                     typeof(AcknowledgeMessage));
                if (a.AcceptedToQueue)
                {
                Console.WriteLine("Your trade will be processed at 4PM EST today.");
                }
                else
                {
                    Console.WriteLine("Your trade can't be processed at this time.");
                }
            }
        }
    }
}
```

This concludes the discussion on the WSE 3.0 messaging framework, and the discussion of one approach for integrating MSMQ with Web services.

Summary

The most challenging aspect of understanding the WSE 3.0 messaging framework is in the concepts, not in the code. The code is straightforward, but the concepts are difficult if you are used to working with the familiar HTTP request/response model. The key to understanding messaging is to stop thinking in terms of fixed clients and services and to instead think in terms of flexible sender and receiver roles.

We began this chapter by reviewing several communication models for Web services beyond classic request/response. We then discussed the WS-Addressing specification, which provides important support functionality for Web services that communicate over alternate transport channels, such as TCP.

Next we discussed the messaging and showed you how to implement truly asynchronous client-service communication using SOAP over TCP and the WSE 3.0 messaging framework classes. WSE 3.0 provides both lower-level and higher-level classes that provide a consistent messaging framework independent of the transport channel. The framework classes shield developers from the underlying complexities of the transport layer, which increases productivity and makes it relatively easy to implement a wider range of service-oriented solutions.

Next, you saw the routing and WS-Referral specifications, which provide support for messages that are referred between multiple endpoints. We noted that there is some overlap between the routing and addressing specifications.

Finally, we provided one example of how to integrate message queuing with Web services. This approach does not implement MSMQ as an alternative transport channel, but it is a good first step toward implementing reliable messaging.

The central focus of this book is to make you rethink what Web services are all about, and nowhere is this more apparent than with the WSE 3.0 messaging framework. This chapter marks the end of the discussion on WSE 3.0. SOA is constantly evolving, so in the next chapter we will focus beyond WSE 3.0 and show you what specifications and technologies are in store for the near future.

CHAPTER 9

■■■

Beyond WSE 3.0: Looking Ahead to Windows Communication Foundation (WCF)

Today, WSE 3.0 is the easiest way to implement selected WS- specifications in your .NET Web services and service-oriented applications. WSE 3.0 provides developer support for building service-oriented applications and infrastructure support for running them. Web services and service-oriented applications require a lot of support to build and run. Developers require classes that make it easier to work with messages without having to interact with the raw SOAP. In addition, they require infrastructure support to make it easier to run service-oriented applications. WSE 3.0 provides all of these levels of support:

- A rich class framework for implementing important WS- specifications such as WS-Security and WS-Addressing.

- Infrastructure support in the form of the WSE pipeline, which automatically intercepts and processes incoming and outgoing SOAP messages.

- Infrastructure support for common service requirements, such as policy verification (using WS-Policy). For example, WSE 3.0 automatically processes XML-based policy framework files, which saves you from needing to write additional processing code in both the service and the client.

WSE is very good at implementing discrete WS- specifications such as WS-Security and WS-Policy, which can be boiled down to a set of specific operations. But where WSE falls short is in being able to provide the infrastructure support for broad-based WS- specifications, such as WS-Reliable Messaging, which provide service guarantees for message delivery.

This is where Windows Communication Foundation (WCF), formerly code-named *Indigo*, and Microsoft Windows Vista (the next version of the Microsoft Windows operating system, formerly code-named *Longhorn*) come into play. WCF refers to a new unified programming and infrastructure support model for service-oriented applications. It provides built-in support for message-oriented and service-oriented architectures, built of course on the managed .NET Framework. WCF will greatly enhance developer productivity in these application areas.

Overview of WCF

There are many reasons why you should start learning about WCF today. The most important reason in our opinion is that you need to know how relevant your existing service-oriented applications will be with a new support infrastructure such as WCF. The questions you should be asking yourself are

- How will I build service-oriented applications in the future using WCF?

- How do I preserve the existing investment that I have made in my XML Web services and .NET Remoting development?

- What current technologies are going to be phased out in WCF?

- Should I be using WSE 3.0 today?

The purpose of this chapter is to give you a preview of WCF from the perspective of where we are today with WSE 3.0. As you will see, every hour spent learning and working with WSE is a worthwhile investment that is directly applicable to Web service development with WCF. This should be of no surprise because WCF is still based on the standards and specifications that we are comfortable with today. WCF does not reinvent the WS- specifications or use exotic transport channels that we have never seen before. Instead, it provides a better support infrastructure for building service-oriented applications that implement today's important standards and specifications, including the WS- specifications. And best of all, WCF is strongly oriented toward services and messages.

Note WCF will be in beta development through 2006 and the implementation and functionality may change before the production release. You can read more about WCF at `http://msdn.microsoft.com/webservices/indigo/default.aspx`. In addition, you can read about how to implement WCF in beta with a Go-Live license at `http://msdn.microsoft.com/winfx/downloads/products/golive/`.

WCF is an exciting technology because it unifies all of the concepts that have been presented throughout this book. Developers today must contend with a variety of different technology choices for building distributed applications, including

- XML Web services (.asmx)

- Web Services Enhancements (WSE)

- .NET Remoting

- MSMQ (provided by the .NET Framework System.Messaging namespace)

- Enterprise Services (the .NET Framework namespace for COM+)

These various technologies overlap and complement each other in different ways. In many cases an application requirement can be fulfilled with two or more of these technologies. Perhaps the clearest example of a potential overlap is with XML Web services and .NET Remoting. Both technologies operate on the same principle, namely that they facilitate remote service invocation over a defined transport channel. Furthermore, .NET Remoting operates over both the TCP and the HTTP protocols, which means that the key difference with XML Web services is its use of a binary message format rather than SOAP. .NET Remoting solutions are generally more focused on object invocation using remote procedure calls (RPCs). On the other hand, XML Web service solutions tend to be more focused on invoking services by passing message-based requests, including between diverse platforms. But these differences are simply a function of what the technologies are best at today. With today's technology you do have flexibility and a choice on whether to deploy .NET Remoting vs. XML Web services for the same application solution. And where you do not, it is fair to ask why the technologies should have different capabilities. After all, they are based on the same concept: allowing remote service calls over a defined transport channel.

See Figure 1 in the January 2004 MSDN Magazine article "A Guide to Developing and Running Connected Systems with Indigo" at `http://msdn.microsoft.com/msdnmag/issues/04/01/Indigo/` for a diagram that illustrates the high-level architecture for WCF. (See the Appendix of this book for detailed reference information.)

There are five major areas within the WCF architecture:

1. *The WCF service model*: Provides general support for services and messages. The service model provides programming and infrastructure support for implementing and managing code as a message-oriented service.

2. *The WCF connector*: Provides communications support for services and messages, including multiple transport channels, ports, and built-in support for reliable message delivery. The connector provides the infrastructure that allows your service to exchange messages with the outside world in a secure, reliable fashion.

3. *Hosting environments*: Provides support for several different hosting environments for message-oriented services, including traditional IIS-based ASP.NET hosting.

4. *Messaging services*: Provides support for managing messages, including message queuing and routing. Messaging services provides the functionality that we currently associate with MSMQ.

5. *System services*: Provides support for transactions and other low-level system support infrastructure that is complex and that needs to be managed by the framework on behalf of the service.

Let's review each of these areas in more detail.

The WCF Service Model

The WCF service model provides a wide range of support for service-oriented Web services, including

- Associating Web methods with incoming service messages

- Session management for Web services

- Transaction management for Web services

- Support for security and policy

- Support for reliable message exchange

WCF contains built-in support for many of the tasks that are currently handled by WSE 3.0. In a sense, WSE 3.0 is a prerelease of the WCF service model. Of course, WSE 3.0 is not completely built out, and certain tasks still require you to write manual code. WCF will integrate the WSE 3.0 functionality in a much tighter way. But there is no better preparation for WCF than to start working with WSE 3.0 and all of the subsequent releases leading up to the release of WCF (as part of the Windows Vista operating system, and as an add-on to the Windows 2003 and XP operating systems).

WCF associates Web methods with incoming service messages using a set of declarative attributes. The service model operates in a similar way to .asmx files, which allow you to declaratively mark up methods and to associate them with incoming Web requests. Today, .asmx files provide a [WebMethod] attribute for marking methods. Tomorrow, WCF will provide a [ServiceMethod] attribute for marking up methods.

The qualified data types that are used by Web services can be represented as typed objects and manipulated directly in code without having to process the raw SOAP and XML directly. Listings 9-1 and 9-2 illustrate this point with a custom data type called Trade. Listing 9-1 displays the qualified XML for the data type, while Listing 9-2 displays its object representation.

Listing 9-1. *XML for the Trade Custom Data Type*

```
<?xml version="1.0" encoding="utf-8" ?>
<xs:schema id="StockTrader"
    targetNamespace="http://www.bluestonepartners.com/Schemas/StockTrader/"
    elementFormDefault="qualified"
    xmlns="http://www.bluestonepartners.com/Schemas/StockTrader/"
    xmlns:mstns="http://www.bluestonepartners.com/Schemas/StockTrader/"
    xmlns:xs="http://www.w3.org/2001/XMLSchema" version="1.0">
    <xs:complexType name="Trade">
      <xs:sequence>
          <xs:element name="TradeID" type="xs:string" />
          <xs:element name="Symbol" type="xs:string" />
          <xs:element name="Price" type="xs:double" />
          <xs:element name="Shares" type="xs:int" />
          <xs:element name="tradeType" type="TradeType" />
          <xs:element name="tradeStatus" type="TradeStatus" />
          <xs:element name="OrderDateTime" type="xs:string" />
          <xs:element name="LastActivityDateTime" type="xs:string" />
      </xs:sequence>
    </xs:complexType>
</xs:schema>
```

Listing 9-2. *Object Representation for the Trade Custom Data Type*

```
[System.Xml.Serialization.XmlTypeAttribute( ➥
    Namespace="http://www.bluestonepartners.com/schemas/StockTrader/")]
public class Trade {
    public string TradeID;
    public string Symbol;
    public System.Double Price;
    public int Shares;
    public TradeType tradeType;
    public TradeStatus tradeStatus;
    public string OrderDateTime;
    public string LastActivityDateTime;
}
```

Today, ASP.NET gives you the flexibility to work with raw SOAP and XML directly, or to interact with object representations instead. WCF will continue to support this approach, allowing you to work with either. Not only are typed objects easier to work with, but they are also managed custom .NET class framework types, which means that you get all the support of the managed .NET runtime, including type safety and just-in-time compilation. If you interact with the raw XML directly, you lose this automatic verification that you are using the custom data type correctly.

In SOA, Web services provide WSDL-based interfaces, and all of the nonstandard data types are represented by qualified XML schemas. Even the interface methods themselves can be described using XML and can be included in a reference schema file for the Web service. We focus on this in great detail in Chapters 3 and 4.

To use SOA terminology, service-oriented components support and conform to contracts. The term *contract* implies a formal, established agreement between two or more parties. WCF formalizes data constructs and message constructs as contracts and defines them as follows:

Data contracts: These are analogous to XML schema files and they document the data types that a Web service supports and exchanges.

Service contracts: These are analogous to WSDL document definitions, specifically the <portType> and <message> sections of the WSDL document. Service contracts document the messages that a Web service supports, both for request and response messages.

Listing 9-3 illustrates a portion of the StockTrader Web service WSDL file, showing the <portType> and <message> definitions related to the PlaceTrade Web method.

Listing 9-3. *Excerpt from the StockTrader Web Service WSDL File Showing the <portType> and <message> Definitions*

```
<portType name="StockTraderServiceSoap">
    <operation name="PlaceTrade">
        <input message="tns:PlaceTradeSoapIn" />
        <output message="tns:PlaceTradeSoapOut" />
    </operation>
</portType>
```

```
<message name="PlaceTradeSoapIn">
    <part name="Account" element="s0:Account" />
    <part name="Symbol" element="s0:Symbol" />
    <part name="Shares" element="s0:Shares" />
    <part name="Price" element="s0:Price" />
    <part name="tradeType" element="s0:tradeType" />
</message>

<message name="PlaceTradeSoapOut">
    <part name="PlaceTradeResult" element="s0:Trade" />
</message>
```

Listing 9-4 illustrates a sample of data contract attributes on an excerpt of the Trade type code implementation.

Listing 9-4. *Excerpt of the Trade Type Code Implementation Showing Data Contract Attributes*

```
[DataContract]
    public class Trade
    {
        [DataMember(IsOptional=true)]
        public string TradeID;
        [DataMember]
        public string Symbol;
    }
```

Listing 9-5 illustrates a sample of service contract attributes on an excerpt of the Stock-TraderService code implementation.

Listing 9-5. *Excerpt of the StockTraderService Code Implementation Showing Service Contract Attributes*

```
[ServiceContract]
    public class StockTraderService
    {
        [OperationContract]
        public PlaceTradeResult ➥
        PlaceTrade(string account, int amount)
        public string Symbol;
    }
```

The purpose of Listings 9-1 through 9-5 is ultimately to show you that the service-oriented concepts you have learned in this book apply to WCF, and that WCF implements very familiar service-oriented concepts despite supporting a very different class framework than the current ASP.NET class framework.

The WCF service model will end up being where you as a developer spend much of your time working because it provides the programmatic classes and the declarative attributes for your service-oriented applications.

The WCF Connector

The WCF connector provides transport-independent support for message-based, service-oriented applications. In Chapter 2 we discuss WSDL elements such as ports and bindings. These elements play an important role in the WCF connector because they govern how services provide endpoints for message requests.

The three most important WCF connector elements are

- *Ports*: These provide URI-accessible endpoints for delivering messages to a service.

- *Transport channels*: These provide a way to deliver messages, and they are based on established protocols, including HTTP, TCP, and IPC.

- *Message channels*: These channels operate in conjunction with the transport channels and provide additional message delivery support, including reliable message delivery.

Security support for message-oriented communication is provided throughout the WCF framework, including within the WCF connector, and will be fully integrated, as opposed to WSE 3.0, where the security support is more limited. WCF provides three types of security support for messages:

1. Session-based security: *Session-based security support uses an on-demand session key to provide encryption and digital signatures. This mode closely follows the approach taken by the WS-Secure Conversation specification, which is discussed in detail in Chapter 7.*

2. Message-based security: *This provides for reliable messaging scenarios where the receiver may not be online at the time that the message is received. Message-based security ensures that message integrity and security are provided during asynchronous communication between a sender and a receiver.*

3. Transport-level security: *This uses a direct security protocol such as Secure Sockets Layer (SSL) that automatically provides message encryption and signatures based on digital certificates.*

As with the WCF service model, WSE 3.0 and today's ASP.NET Web services clearly prepare you for working with the future WCF connector. Make sure that you understand the concepts that are presented in Chapter 2 on the WSDL document. The WCF connector rolls up all of these concepts and more, including transport and communication channels and message security.

Hosting Environments

ASP.NET Web services must be hosted within a virtual directory managed by IIS, and they will only communicate over HTTP. With WSE 3.0 you have additional messaging capabilities, so you can build TCP-based services in addition to HTTP-enabled services. TCP-enabled services do not have to be hosted by IIS, although they must be running at all times and listening on a defined port. WSE 3.0 also provides the interprocess communication (IPC) transport protocol, which is a good alternative to .NET Remoting in that it allows you to leverage the benefits of SOA and SOAP-based messaging in an interprocess environment.

WCF expands the number of available hosting options for services, and also introduces on-demand services. These are activated by the WCF framework when it identifies a targeted incoming service request message that is intended for a specific service. The other available hosting options in WCF are not necessarily new, but the difference is that WCF provides a good level of automated support for different hosting environments, which makes it easier for you to deploy your services. Here are some examples of hosting environments that WCF supports:

- *ASP.NET*: A traditional IIS-based, HTTP-enabled hosting environment

- *Windows Service*: A hosting environment for TCP-enabled services

- *DLLHost*: A hosting environment for IPC-enabled services

This list is not comprehensive; it represents just some of the available hosting environments and just some of the possibilities for using them.

It is important to note that the hosting environment is independent of a Web service's data and service contracts. As a developer, you can create your Web services and service components independently of the intended hosting environment. WCF will relay messages to your services equally well in all of the supported environments.

Messaging Services

Today, MSMQ-based applications support message queues for reliable message delivery, and they also support a trigger-based event model that fires up the application code when an incoming message is received. Today, messaging applications that are built around MSMQ are almost considered to be a nonstandard type of application. If they were standard, then all of us would be incorporating message queues into every application that we build. Of course this is not the case, largely because it creates a level of overhead that is considered unnecessary for many applications.

But in service-oriented applications, reliable message delivery is not an abstract concept; instead, it represents a quality of service expectation on the part of your clients. Message delivery and the potential for message loss are critically important to service-oriented applications. WCF provides built-in messaging support, including message queues and events, and makes it easier for you to implement reliable messaging in your service applications. WCF will provide a set of classes for interfacing with the messaging infrastructure.

Today's WSE 3.0 does not natively integrate with MSMQ, which is essentially just an alternate transport channel for messages. With some effort, you could custom integrate MSMQ with WSE today as a transport channel, although this is an advanced programming task. Alternatively, you could take a simpler approach and have your service simply interact with an MSMQ queue that you configure separately. The .NET Framework provides a namespace called System.Messaging, which allows you to interact with an MSMQ queue.

System Services

This category represents a catch-all of features, many of which provide infrastructure-level support that may be fully out of direct sight but is working on your behalf nonetheless. System services include infrastructure-level support for transactions (via a distributed transaction coordinator) and security. The security portion of the system services is expected to support the WS-Federation specification, which allows you to set up and manage trusted communications across application and domain boundaries. This is not the same thing as the WS-Secure Conversation specification, which we discuss in Chapter 7. However, there are shared concepts between the two specifications.

Understanding WCF Web Services

One of our first thoughts when we heard about WCF was whether WCF Web services would be different compared to ASP.NET Web services. And if so, how would they differ? The good news is that while WCF Web services are different, they still retain the core characteristics of a traditional ASP.NET Web service, but with even more functionality and flexibility. WCF Web services support the standard WSDL and SOAP specifications, in addition to the extended WS- specifications.

What Is a WCF Web Service?

Traditional .asmx pages can still be used within WCF, which will interoperate with them in addition to supporting a newer form of Web service. ASP.NET-style Web services will continue to be limited within WCF to simple HTTP-based request/response message patterns. However, WCF Web services will provide all of the extended communication capabilities that WSE 3.0 provides (and more) including alternate transport protocols and true asynchronous and one-way communications.

The characteristics of a WCF Web service are documented in the Windows Vista SDK as follows:

- Provides secure communication across any number of intermediaries, including firewalls

- Participates in widely distributed transactions

- Encapsulates two-way conversations that allow clients and servers to send messages in both directions

- Provides guarantees about the reliability of message delivery

- Supports situations requiring scalability, such as Web service farms

- Supports advanced features even with participants that are not built on Microsoft platforms

- Enables developers familiar with the .NET Framework to build messaging applications without knowing anything about XML or SOAP

- Enables developers familiar with XML Web services to leverage their XML, WSDL, and SOAP knowledge to work with XML messages described by XSD

- Supports smooth management of deployed applications

Understanding WCF Applications and Infrastructure

WCF applications decouple the messaging and transport layer from the service layer, which allows you as the developer to focus on programming the service without having to worry about implementing the lower-level communications infrastructure. The service layer is built using the class framework that is provided by the WCF service model. It includes classes that allow you to interact programmatically with the messaging layer.

In this section, we will review five important aspects of WCF that provide support for managing and processing service-oriented applications:

- The WCF service layer
- Ports
- Typed channels
- Service managers
- Transports and formatters

The WCF Service Layer

Figure 9-1 illustrates the high-level schematic architecture for a typical message-based, service-oriented application that you might build using WCF.

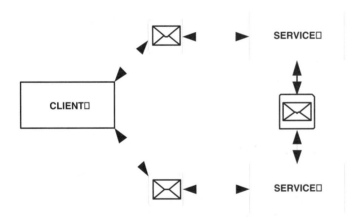

Figure 9-1. *High-level schematic architecture for a WCF application*

The application architecture uses arrows to describe the path that a message takes between service endpoints. Although they are not shown in the diagram, the service endpoints are located where the arrow head contacts the client or service. Another interesting aspect of this diagram is the chained path that the messages take. WCF supports this level of complex message pathways because of its infrastructure-level support for addressing and routing specifications. Finally, the diagram makes no mention of a specific transport channel. This implicitly emphasizes WCF's most important advantage of not having to factor in the transport and messaging infrastructure into the application design. In contrast, today's ASP.NET Web services that leverage WSE 3.0 still require the developer to write manual code that is specific to alternate transport channels, such as TCP.

In WCF, the service is the basic component of an application, and it supports a special kind of object called a *typed channel* that is equivalent to today's proxy objects for Web service clients. The typed channel provides an interface for sending and receiving messages between service components. WCF provides a utility called WSDLgen.exe, which is similar to today's wsdl.exe utility, and allows you to generate proxy class files for clients to use for accessing your service.

Typed channels are independent of the actual objects that process the service request. WCF employs Service Manager objects that are responsible for mapping typed channels to their associated business objects, including the DialogManager and ListenerManager objects.

The WCF service layer automatically handles the receiving, processing, and sending of messages, including all of the serialization work that is required to build and process a message. This is very similar to the way that the ASP.NET infrastructure processes messages that are received and sent via an .asmx Web page. WCF provides the Service object for its services, which is conceptually equivalent to the ASP.NET WebService object. The Service object provides you with programmatic access to the underlying messaging and transport infrastructure.

The WCF service layer also supports a special kind of service called RemoteObjects, which is functionally equivalent to today's .NET Remoting–enabled solutions in that it allows you to invoke remote distributed objects while preserving object type fidelity during transport. RemoteObjects uses RPC-style communications, and like .NET Remoting, it can be used for both interprocess communications and Internet communications that operate across different application domains.

Ports

Service-oriented applications send and receive messages to SOAP endpoints. In WCF, the Port object defines two things:

1. Service layer information, including the operations that the service supports

2. The supported transport mechanisms and wire formats (e.g., SOAP 1.2 encoding over HTTP)

We want to emphasize the tie-in between WCF technology and today's technology. The WCF Port object is equivalent to a WS-Addressing construct called the *endpoint reference*. In Chapter 8 we discuss endpoint references, which are equivalent to the <service> element in the WSDL document and provide both addressing and binding information for a Web service. Listing 9-6 provides an excerpt from the StockTrader WSDL document showing how the <service> and associated <binding> tags work together to document the location of a service, and the operations that it provides.

Listing 9-6. *Excerpt from the StockTrader Web Service WSDL File Showing the <service> and <binding> Definitions*

```
<service name="StockTraderService">
    <port  name="StockTraderServiceSoap" binding="tns:StockTraderServiceSoap">
        <soap:address location="http://localhost/StockTrader/StockTrader.asmx" />
    </port>
</service>

<binding name="StockTraderServiceSoap" type="tns:StockTraderServiceSoap">
    <soap:binding transport="http://schemas.xmlsoap.org/soap/http"
        style="document" />
    <operation name="RequestAllTradesSummary">
        <soap:operation
            soapAction="http://www.bluestonepartners.com/schemas/StockTrader/
            RequestAllTradesSummary" style="document" />
            <input>
                <soap:body use="literal" />
            </input>
            <output>
                <soap:body use="literal" />
            </output>
    </operation>
<!- Additional operations are not shown ->
    <operation />
</binding>
```

The WS-Addressing specification takes this concept one step further by encapsulating addressing, binding, and security policy information within a single reference, as shown in Listing 9-7.

Listing 9-7. *Endpoint Reference XML*

```
<wsa:EndpointReference>
    <wsa:Address>soap.tcp://stocktrader.com/StockTrader</wsa:Address>
    <wsa:ReferenceProperties>
        <st:AccountID>123A</st:AccountID>
    </wsa:ReferenceProperties>
    <wsa:PortType>st:StockTraderSoap</wsa:PortType>
    <wsp:Policy/>
</wsa:EndpointReference>
```

You can clearly see how the WCF Port object maps to familiar constructs such as endpoint references and the WSDL <service> and <binding> definitions.

The WCF Port object is tied into an extended processing pipeline that supports common message-processing features, including security, policy, routing, and transactions. When you write a service method, you need to add attributes for each of the specifications that you want to implement; for example, you can specify authorization access for a specific user or role.

Assuming that the incoming message includes the right specification information, it will be routed through the Port object and into an extended processing pipeline. You can programmatically control the processing further by modifying property settings on one or more dedicated manager objects. For example, security processing is handled by the Security-Manager object.

Listing 9-8 provides a very simple example of a WCF service method, showing the annotations that you require for specifying basic authorization security processing.

Listing 9-8. *A WCF Service Method Specifying Authorization Security Processing*

```
[DatagramPortType(Name="PlaceTrader", ➥
    Namespace="http://www.tempuri.org/quickstarts")]
public class Hello
{
    [ServiceSecurity(Name = "Brokerage", Role = "Traders") ]
    [ServiceMethod]
    public string PlaceTrade(string Account, string Symbol, int Shares, ➥
        System.Double Price, TradeType tradeType)
    {
        // Code to execute trade not shown
        return ("Your confirmation code is: " + TradeID);
    }
}
```

This service must still implement a policy framework file to specify authentication security, such as encryption and digital signature requirements.

Typed Channels

A typed channel is similar to a Web service proxy object, which provides a typed object representation of the Web services WSDL interface. In a similar fashion, a WCF typed channel provides a typed object reference to a messaging endpoint and its associated operations.

In order to create a typed channel, you need to first create the Web service and define its methods. This in turn defines a WSDL interface, which you can then extract automatically (for example, you can append ?WSDL to the Web service URI in order to review the WSDL document). Finally, you can use a code-generation tool to generate a proxy class based on the WSDL file. Today, we have a utility called wsdl.exe. WCF ships with an equivalent utility called WSDLgen.exe.

The output of the code-generation utility is the typed channel, which provides a proxy representation of the WSDL interface as a managed object.

Service Manager

The Service Manager objects do all of the heavy lifting in processing messages and providing the support infrastructure for managing communications. Table 9-1 summarizes the important Service Manager objects and their purpose.

Table 9-1. *The WCF Service Manager Objects*

Service Manager Objects	Description
ListenerManager	Handles listener messages and performs the appropriate actions on the router service environment. Used in a user-mode listener implementation.
PolicyManager	Provides support for consuming, applying, processing, and generating policy on a specific port.
RemotingManager	Manages the WCF remoting infrastructure.
RequestReplyManager	Creates SendRequestChannel objects through which messages can be sent and replies received.
RoutingPolicyManager	Controls the consumption and application of routing and transport policy.
RuleManager	Represents the factory for rules, and through its namespace hierarchy, the associated properties.
SecurityManager	Controls application security requirements either programmatically or by using application and machine configuration files.
ServiceManager	Manages the associations between communication channels and service instances; registers services; and produces typed channels to make requests of other services.
TransactionManager	Represents the base class for a transaction manager.
DialogManager	Manages creation and deletion of the participants in a dialog.

The Service Manager objects work with the Port object as extensions into a processing pipeline for incoming and outgoing messages. Service Managers automatically process messages as long as the associated service method has the appropriate annotations. Figure 9-2 shows the architecture of the port processing pipeline, including Service Managers.

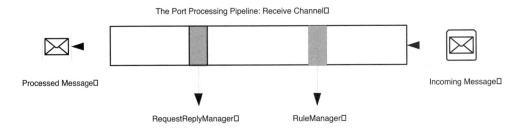

Figure 9-2. *The port processing pipeline architecture*

Transports and Formatters

The transport and formatter layer is the low-level infrastructure that sits below the activity that is occurring in the port processing pipeline. You will rarely need to interact with the transport and formatter layer directly, beyond specifying what the service will support. You can also specify directional message transport information, such as whether a service is receive-only or is enabled for both send and receive operations.

The transport and formatter layer is what enables messages to be moved across the wire. WCF supports a wide range of transport protocols, as shown in Table 9-2, which indicates the associated WCF object that abstracts the transport protocol information.

Table 9-2. *WCF-Supported Transport Protocols*

Protocol	WCF Object
HTTP	HttpTransport
POP3	Pop3Transport
SMTP	SmtpTransport
SOAP	SoapTransport
TCP	TcpTransport
InProc	InProcessTransport (on the same machine)
CrossProc	CrossProcessTransport (on the same machine)

The transport and formatter layer delegates message serialization (and deserialization) to a dedicated object called the MessageFormatter, which is responsible for translating a byte stream between a formatted message and an in-memory Message object representation of the message.

How to Get Ready for WCF

Most developers are understandably ambivalent about a major upcoming release such as WCF. On the one hand, we welcome advancements in technology and the improvements in functionality and productivity that it will hopefully bring. On the other hand, we dread having to learn a new way of doing things, and we wonder whether we will be able to migrate our existing code to the new infrastructure.

These are valid concerns, especially with WCF. But the issue is less about WCF changing things than it is about things needing to change. Developers today are faced with multiple and often competing technologies for building distributed applications, including the classic choice between XML Web services vs. .NET Remoting. Certainly, there are cases where there is no overlap and no ambivalence and where one technology is clearly the better choice than another. But these technologies share too much in common to be treated differently. They are simply variations of the same technology. In the case of XML Web services and .NET Remoting, they are both concerned with remote distributed object and service invocation over a defined transport channel.

Microsoft is starting to address developer concerns by providing guidelines for how to get ready for WCF. It is already making sure to bring this topic up at professional conferences, and it will certainly continue to do so until the release of WCF. There has simply been too much investment in existing technologies for it not to.

WCF is obviously not a replacement for the entire set of .NET Framework functionality. Instead, it is focused on supporting distributed service-oriented applications with security, transaction support, and reliable messaging. WCF primarily extends four core technologies that are available today:

- ASP.NET Web services (built with .asmx pages)

- Web Services Enhancements (WSE)

- System.Messaging

- System.EnterpriseServices

Microsoft has stated that it will make the migration to WCF from current technologies a straightforward process. Here are some guidelines on how to get ready for WCF based on professional conferences, published white papers, and conversations with members of product development teams:

- Build services using .asmx pages.

- Use WSE 3.0 for additional, extended functionality, including security, policy, and secure conversation.

- Build qualified XML schema files for all custom data types used by the service.

- Use managed framework classes for integrating your services with MSMQ message queues and with COM+ components. Use the managed System.Messaging namespace for MSMQ, and the System.EnterpriseServices namespace for COM+ components.

- Avoid using the HTTP Context object in your .asmx pages.

- Avoid using .NET Remoting sinks and channels.

Given that WSE 3.0 is such an important part of this book, let's look in more detail at how you can use the toolkit to prepare for WCF.

WSE 3.0 and WCF

WSE 3.0 allows developers to become early adopters of the next generation of service-oriented application technology. Every hour that you spend working with WSE 3.0 is an hour that you have contributed toward WCF. Applications that are built using WSE should migrate smoothly to the WCF framework, with only minor modifications required. If you choose to implement WSE today, then you should expect to accommodate changes to WSE between now and the release of WCF. It is unclear how many revisions WSE is expected to undergo prior to the release of WCF, but it is likely that we will only see service packs released, and they are not expected to negatively impact compatibility between WSE 3.0 and WCF. If anything, they should only make the compatibility tighter.

Table 9-3 compares the feature set of WSE 3.0 with WCF, based on current information provided by Microsoft.

Table 9-3. *Feature Comparison of WSE 3.0 and WCF*

Feature	WSE 3.0	WCF
Hosting	IIS/ASP.NET (.asmx) SoapReceivers	IIS/ASP.NET (.svc) ServiceHost
Programming Model	[WebService], [WebMethod], etc. (supports interfaces, generics, and the like)	[ServiceContract], [OperationContract], etc. (supports interfaces, generics, and so on)
Message Exchange Patterns (MEP)	One-way Request-response Custom (using WSE API)	One-way Request-response First/last-operation Duplex Custom
XML Serialization	System.Xml.Serialization	System.Runtime.Serialization System.Xml.Serialization (you can choose)
Encodings	XML 1.0 MTOM	MTOM
Custom	XML 1.0 MTOM	Binary
Transports	HTTP TCP Custom	HTTP TCP Named pipes MSMQ P2P Custom
Protocols	Security	Security Reliable messaging Transactions
Behaviors (enabled via attributes or configuration)	Local DTC transactions HTTP buffering HTTP caching HTTP sessions Custom (via SoapExtensions, WSE filters)	Concurrency Instancing Throttling Thread-binding Exception handling and faults Impersonation Session management Transaction behaviors Custom (via behavior types)

The main feature that is lacking in WSE 3.0 (compared to WCF) is that it does not provide wide system-level or infrastructure-level support for the enterprise aspect of service-oriented applications. Specifically, it does not provide support for transactions or reliable messaging. Certainly, WSE 3.0 provides many of the required parts, but it does not provide the whole. For example, WSE 3.0 provides support for message addressing, and it also integrates with MSMQ via the System.Messaging namespace classes. So WSE 3.0 gives you the ability today to custom build a service-oriented application that implements "reliable" messaging (via MSMQ) and which can process message addressing information and provide message correlation. But this is not the same as a built-in support infrastructure that manages these tasks for you.

These limitations are not a weakness of the WSE 3.0 technology. They simply underscore two things:

1. Infrastructure support for message-based, service-oriented architecture is most effectively handled at the operating system level.

2. WSE 3.0 allows early adopters to start designing and building their code for the future WCF infrastructure. More importantly, it gets developers thinking about application design in new ways. There is a large conceptual jump between traditional RPC-based applications and message-based, service-oriented applications.

With this being said, let's review the major feature areas of WSE 3.0 (which you should by now feel very familiar with) and explain where they fit within the WCF framework:

Security and policy specifications: The WS-Security and WS-Policy specifications are supported by the WCF connector.

Messaging specifications: WCF provides Messaging services that subsume the functionality currently provided by MSMQ. In addition, it provides support for reliable messaging. WSE does not currently provide comprehensive support for the WS-Reliable Messaging specification, but it does provide some of the component parts that you can cobble together to approximate the specification. Specifically, WSE includes support for WS-Addressing, and it integrates with MSMQ via the managed System.Messaging namespace.

Routing and referral specifications: WCF includes these within its Messaging services functionality.

Alternate transport channels: WCF provides support for several transport channels, including HTTP, TCP, and IPC. WSE 3.0 currently provides support for the same three channels, so you can begin coding with them today.

In closing, we hope that this book has ultimately convinced you of three important things:

1. Message orientation and service orientation are the way to go.

2. WCF provides a welcome level of support for this technology, which will increase developer productivity and minimize confusion by unifying today's disparate technologies.

3. WSE 3.0 is an excellent way for developers to become early adopters for WCF.

Good luck with your future adventures in service-oriented architecture!

Summary

WCF provides infrastructure and programming support for service-oriented applications. It is focused on messages and provides support for creating messages, for delivering messages, and for processing messages. With WCF, there is less ambiguity in your services: the infrastructure forces you to be message-oriented and to work with well-qualified XML-based data types.

WCF is built on five major areas:

The WCF service model: Provides support for processing incoming service request messages

The WCF connector: Provides support for communicating with services reliably and securely

Hosting environments: Provides several different hosting options for services

Messaging services: Provides reliable messaging support

System services: Provides a wide range of support infrastructure, including for transactions and trusted communications

WSE 3.0 allows early adopters to start building service-oriented applications today, using the next generation of service-oriented and message-oriented technologies. Working with WSE 3.0 provides you with excellent preparation for WCF. In addition, you should be familiar with Microsoft's guidelines for how to tailor today's development to be more compatible with WCF-based applications in the future.

References

Here is a selection of references that you will find useful for learning more about SOA, the WS-I Basic Profile, the WS- specifications, and Web Services Enhancements. The references are broken out by topic. Note that Web services standards and specifications evolve quickly, so some of the specification references that are listed here will be superseded in future months by others.

Service-Oriented Architecture (General)

"Application Architecture for .NET: Designing Applications and Services"
MSDN white paper (December 2002)
http://msdn.microsoft.com/library/default.asp?url=/library/en-us/dnbda/html/
    distapp.asp

"Building Interoperable Web Services: WS-I Basic Profile 1.0"
MSDN white paper (August 2003)
http://msdn.microsoft.com/library/default.asp?url=/library/en-us/dnsvcinter/html/
    wsi-bp_msdn_landingpage.asp

"The Evolution of Web Services—Part 2"
Adnan Masood
White paper (September 2003)
http://www.15seconds.com/issue/030917.htm

"Java Modeling: A UML Workbook, Part 4"
Granville Miller
White paper (June 2002)
http://www-106.ibm.com/developerworks/java/library/j-jmod0604/

XML Schemas and SOAP

"Understanding SOAP"
Aaron Skonnard
MSDN white paper (March 2003)
http://msdn.microsoft.com/webservices/default.aspx?pull=/library/en-us/dnsoap/html/
    understandsoap.asp

"XML Schemas and the XML Designer"
MSDN article
http://msdn.microsoft.com/library/default.asp?url=/library/en-us/vbcon/html/
    vboricreatingschemas.asp

"A Quick Guide to XML Schema"
Aaron Skonnard
MSDN Magazine (April 2002)
http://msdn.microsoft.com/msdnmag/issues/02/04/xml/default.aspx

"Place XML Message Design Ahead of Schema Planning to Improve Web Service
    Interoperability"
Yasser Shohoud
MSDN Magazine (December 2002)
http://msdn.microsoft.com/msdnmag/issues/02/12/WebServicesDesign/

"RPC/Literal and Freedom of Choice"
Yasser Shohoud
MSDN white paper (April 2003)
http://msdn.microsoft.com/library/default.asp?url=/library/en-us/dnwebsrv/html/
    rpc_literal.asp

"Web Services Encoding and More"
Aaron Skonnard
MSDN Magazine (May 2003)
http://msdn.microsoft.com/msdnmag/issues/03/05/XMLFiles/

"SOAP Is Not a Remote Procedure Call"
Ingo Rammer's Architecture Briefings (October 2003)
http://www.thinktecture.com/Resources/ArchitectureBriefings/
    SoapIsNotARemoteProcedureCall.pdf

"Increase Your App's Reach Using WSDL to Combine Multiple Web Services"
Gerrard Lindsay
MSDN Magazine (March 2005)
http://msdn.microsoft.com/msdnmag/issues/05/03/WSDL/

WS- Specifications (General)

Resources for developers and links to original standards and specifications documents
IBM developerWorks
http://www-106.ibm.com/developerworks/views/webservices/standards.jsp

"Secure, Reliable, Transacted Web Services: Architecture and Composition"
Donald F. Ferguson (IBM), Tony Storey (IBM), Brad Lovering (Microsoft),
   John Shewchuk (Microsoft)
MSDN white paper (September 2003)
http://msdn.microsoft.com/webservices/webservices/understanding/
   advancedwebservices/default.aspx?pull=/library/en-us/dnwebsrv/
   html/wsoverview.asp

"Compare Web Service Security Metrics"
Roger Jennings (OakLeaf Systems)
XML and Web Services Magazine (October 2002)
http://www.fawcette.com/xmlmag/2002_10/online/webservices_rjennings_10_16_02/
   default.aspx

"Installing Certificates for WSDK X.509 Digital Signing and Encryption"
Roger Jennings (OakLeaf Systems)
XML and Web Services Magazine (October 2002)
http://www.fawcette.com/xmlmag/2002_10/online/webservices_rjennings_10_16_02/
   sidebar1.aspx

Web Services Enhancements 2.0 and 3.0 (General)

"What's New in Web Services Enhancements 3.0"
Mark Fussell
MSDN white paper (November 2005)
http://msdn.microsoft.com/webservices/default.aspx?pull=/library/en-us/dnwse/html/
   newwse3.asp

"Programming with Web Services Enhancements 2.0"
Matt Powell
MSDN white paper (May 2004)
http://msdn.microsoft.com/library/default.asp?url=/library/en-us/dnwse/html/
   programwse2.asp

WS-Security

"WSE Security: Protect Your Web Services Through the Extensible Policy Framework in
   WSE 3.0"
Tomasz Janczuk
MSDN Magazine (February 2006)
`http://msdn.microsoft.com/msdnmag/issues/06/02/WSE30/default.aspx`

Web Services Security (WS-Security) standards documents
OASIS
`http://www.oasis-open.org/committees/tc_cat.php?cat=security`

"Web Services Security: SOAP Message Security 1.0 (WS-Security 2004)"
OASIS Standard 200401, March 2004
`http://docs.oasis-open.org/wss/2004/01/oasis-200401-wss-soap-message-` ➥
  `security-1.0.pdf`

"Understanding WS-Security"
Scott Seely
MSDN white paper (October 2002)
`http://msdn.microsoft.com/webservices/webservices/understanding/`
  `advancedwebservices/default.aspx?pull=/library/en-us/dnwssecur/`
  `html/understw.asp`

"WS-Security Drilldown in Web Services Enhancements 2.0"
Don Smith
MSDN white paper (August 2004)
`http://msdn.microsoft.com/library/default.asp?url=/library/en-us/dnwebsrv/html/`
  `wssecdrill.asp`
(Note: This reference is also listed in the "WS-Secure Conversation" section of this appendix.)

"WS-Security Authentication and Digital Signatures with Web Services Enhancements"
Matt Powell
MSDN white paper (December 2002)
`http://msdn.microsoft.com/library/default.asp?url=/library/en-us/dnwse/html/`
  `wssecauthwse.asp`

"Building Secure Web Services"
J.D. Meier, Alex Mackman, Michael Dunner, Srinath Vasireddy, Ray Escamilla, and
  Anandha Murukan
MSDN Patterns and Practices white paper, Chapter 12 (June 2003, revised January 2006)
`http://msdn.microsoft.com/library/default.asp?url=/library/en-us/dnnetsec/html/`
  `THCMCh12.asp`

"Encrypting SOAP Messages Using Web Services Enhancements"
Jeannine Hall Gailey
MSDN white paper (December 2002)
http://msdn.microsoft.com/library/default.asp?url=/library/en-us/dnwse/html/
  wseencryption.asp

"Web Services Security: Moving Up the Stack"
Maryann Hondo, David Melgar, and Anthony Nadalin
IBM developerWorks white paper (December 2002)
http://www-106.ibm.com/developerworks/library/ws-secroad/

"Web Services Security Username Token Profile"
OASIS working draft (January 2003)
http://www.oasis-open.org/committees/wss/documents/WSS-Username-11.pdf

"Web Services Security Kerberos Binding"
Giovanni Della-Libera (Microsoft), Brendan Dixon (Microsoft), Praerit Garg (Microsoft),
  Maryann Hondo (IBM), Chris Kaler (Microsoft), Hiroshi Maruyama (IBM),
  Anthony Nadalin (IBM), and Nataraj Nagaratnam (IBM)
MSDN white paper (December 2003)
http://msdn.microsoft.com/library/default.asp?url=/library/en-us/dnglobspec/html/
  ws-security-kerberos.asp

"Security Features in WSE 3.0"
Keith Brown
MSDN Magazine (November 2005)
http://msdn.microsoft.com/msdnmag/issues/05/11/SecurityBriefs/default.aspx

"Web Service Security: Scenarios, Patterns, and Implementation Guidance for Web Services
  Enhancements (WSE) 3.0"
Jason Hogg (Microsoft), Don Smith (Microsoft), Fred Chong (Microsoft), Dwayne Taylor
  (RDA Corporation), Lonnie Wall (RDA Corporation), and Paul Slater (Wadeware LLC)
MSDN Patterns and Practices guide (December 2005)
http://msdn.microsoft.com/library/default.asp?url=/library/en-us/dnpag2/html/
  wssp.asp

Web Service Security: Scenarios, Patterns, and Implementation Guidance home page
Microsoft Patterns and Practices community workspace
http://www.gotdotnet.com/codegallery/codegallery.aspx?id=
  67f659f6-9457-4860-80ff-0535dffed5e6

"Security for SOA and Web Services"
Dipak Chopra
SAP Developer Network
`https://www.sdn.sap.com/irj/servlet/prt/portal/prtroot/com.sap.km.cm.docs/library/`
`    webservices/Security%20for%20SOA%20and%20Web%20Services.article`

"Windows 2000 Kerberos Authentication"
Microsoft TechNet
`http://www.microsoft.com/technet/prodtechnol/windows2000serv/deploy/confeat/`
`    kerberos.mspx`

WS-Policy

"Web Services Policy Framework"
IBM developerWorks specification (May 2003)
`http://www-106.ibm.com/developerworks/library/ws-polfram/`

"Understanding WS-Policy"
Aaron Skonnard
MSDN white paper (August 2003)
`http://msdn.microsoft.com/library/default.asp?url=/library/en-us/dnwebsrv/html/`
`    understwspol.asp`

"Web Services Policy Assertions Language (WS-Policy Assertions)"
Don Box (Microsoft), Maryann Hondo (IBM), Chris Kaler (Microsoft), Hiroshi Maruyama
    (IBM), Anthony Nadalin (IBM), Nataraj Nagaratnam (IBM), Paul Patrick (BEA), Claus von
    Riegen (SAP), and John Shewchuk (Microsoft)
MSDN white paper (May 2003)
`http://msdn.microsoft.com/library/default.asp?url=/library/en-us/dnglobspec/html/`
`    ws-policyassertions.asp`

"Using Role-Based Security with Web Services Enhancements 2.0"
Ingo Rammer
MSDN white paper (September 2003)
`http://msdn.microsoft.com/library/default.asp?url=/library/en-us/dnwssecur/html/`
`    wserolebasedsec.asp`

WS-Secure Conversation

"Web Services Secure Conversation Language"
IBM developerWorks specification (May 2004, updated February 2005)
`http://www-128.ibm.com/developerworks/library/specification/ws-secon/`

"Web Services Trust Language"
IBM developerWorks specification (May 2004, updated February 2005)
`http://www-128.ibm.com/developerworks/library/specification/ws-trust/`

"WS-Security Drilldown in Web Services Enhancements 2.0"
Don Smith
MSDN white paper (August 2004)
`http://msdn.microsoft.com/library/default.asp?url=/library/en-us/dnwebsrv/html/`
   `wssecdrill.asp`
(Note: This reference is also listed in the "WS-Security" section of this appendix.)

"Managing Security Context Tokens in a Web Farm"
Chris Keyser
MSDN white paper (November 2004)
`http://msdn.microsoft.com/library/default.asp?url=/library/en-us/dnwebsrv/html/`
   `sctinfarm.asp`

WS-Addressing

"Web Services Addressing"
IBM developerWorks specification (March 2004, updated August 2004)
`http://www-106.ibm.com/developerworks/webservices/library/ws-add/`

WS-Messaging

"Asynchronous Operations and Web Services, Part 1: A Primer on Asynchronous Transactions"
Holt Adams
IBM developerWorks white paper (April 2002)
`http://www-128.ibm.com/developerworks/library/ws-asynch1.html`
"Asynchronous Operations and Web Services, Part 2: Programming Patterns to Build
   Asynchronous Web Services"
Holt Adams
IBM developerWorks white paper (June 2002)
`http://www-106.ibm.com/developerworks/library/ws-asynch2/index.html`

"Introducing the Web Services Enhancements 2.0 Messaging API"
Aaron Skonnard
MSDN Magazine (September 2003)
`http://msdn.microsoft.com/msdnmag/issues/03/09/XMLFiles/`

WS-Routing and WS-Referral

"Routing SOAP Messages with Web Services Enhancements 1.0"
Aaron Skonnard
MSDN white paper (January 2003)
http://msdn.microsoft.com/library/default.asp?url=/library/en-us/dnwse/html/
    routsoapwse.asp

WS-Reliable Messaging

"Web Services Reliable Messaging"
IBM developerWorks specification (March 2004, updated February 2005)
http://www-106.ibm.com/developerworks/webservices/library/ws-rm/

"Reliable Message Delivery in a Web Services World: A Proposed Architecture and Roadmap"
IBM Corporation and Microsoft Corporation
MSDN white paper (March 2003)
http://msdn.microsoft.com/webservices/webservices/understanding/advancedwebservices/
    default.aspx?pull=/library/en-us/dnglobspec/html/ws-rm-exec-summary.asp

Windows Communication Foundation (Indigo)

"Introduction to Building Windows Communication Foundation Services"
Clemens Vasters
MSDN white paper (September 2005)
http://msdn.microsoft.com/webservices/indigo/default.aspx?pull=/library/en-us/
    dnlong/html/introtowcf.asp

Windows Communication Foundation articles and white papers
Resources page
http://wcf.netfx3.com/content/resources.aspx
"A Guide to Developing and Running Connected Systems with Indigo"
Don Box
MSDN Magazine (January 2004)
http://msdn.microsoft.com/msdnmag/issues/04/01/Indigo/

"Creating Indigo Applications with the PDC Release of Visual Studio .NET Whidbey"
Yasser Shohoud
MSDN white paper (January 2004)
http://msdn.microsoft.com/library/default.asp?url=/library/en-us/dnlingo/html/
    indigolingo01062004.asp

Miscellaneous

MSDN Web Services Books
List of books on building Web services using .NET in particular
`http://msdn.microsoft.com/webservices/understanding/books/default.aspx`

Discussions in .NET Framework Web Services Enhancements
MSDN Newsgroups
`http://msdn.microsoft.com/newsgroups/default.aspx?dg=microsoft.public.`
`    dotnet.framework.webservices.enhancements`

"Orchestrating XML Web Services and Using the Microsoft .NET Framework with Microsoft
    BizTalk Server"
Ulrich Roxburgh
MSDN white paper (February 2002)
`http://msdn.microsoft.com/library/default.asp?url=/library/en-us/dnbiz2k2/html/`
`    bts_wp_net.asp`

"Accessing Custom Attributes"
.NET Framework Developer's Guide
MSDN articles
`http://msdn.microsoft.com/library/default.asp?url=/library/en-us/cpguide/html/`
`    cpconaccessingcustomattributes.asp`

Index

You Need the Companion eBook

Your purchase of this book entitles you to buy the companion PDF-version eBook for only $10. Take the weightless companion with you anywhere.

We believe this Apress title will prove so indispensable that you'll want to carry it with you everywhere, which is why we are offering the companion eBook (in PDF format) for $10 to customers who purchase this book now. Convenient and fully searchable, the PDF version of any content-rich, page-heavy Apress book makes a valuable addition to your programming library. You can easily find and copy code—or perform examples by quickly toggling between instructions and the application. Even simultaneously tackling a donut, diet soda, and complex code becomes simplified with hands-free eBooks!

Once you purchase your book, getting the $10 companion eBook is simple:

1. Visit **www.apress.com/promo/tendollars/**.

2. Complete a basic registration form to receive a randomly generated question about this title.

3. Answer the question correctly in 60 seconds, and you will receive a promotional code to redeem for the $10.00 eBook.

2560 Ninth Street • Suite 219 • Berkeley, CA 94710

eBookshop

Offer valid through 3/06.